PENGUIN BOOKS

## ARGUING FOR A BETTER WORLD

Arianne Shahvisi is a Kurdish British writer and academic philosopher. Raised in Lancashire and Essex, she studied astrophysics and
philosophy at the universities of Cambridge and Oxford and now
teaches applied philosophy at the Brighton and Sussex Medical
School where her research focusses on gender, race, migration, and
health. She writes regularly for the *London Review of Books*, and her
essays have also appeared in *The Guardian*, *Prospect*, *The Independent*,
and *The Economist*.

# Arguing for a Better World

*How Philosophy Can Help Us Fight for Social Justice*

## ARIANNE SHAHVISI

PENGUIN BOOKS

PENGUIN BOOKS

An imprint of Penguin Random House LLC

penguinrandomhouse.com

First published in Great Britain by John Murray
(Publishers), a Hachette UK company, 2023
Published in Penguin Books 2023

Library of Congress Control Number Permalink: https://lccn.loc.gov/2023005100

ISBN 9780143136835 (paperback)
ISBN 9780525508335 (ebook)

Printed in the United States of America
1st Printing

Set in Bembo MT

For my parents

خۆشم دەوێن هەموو رۆژێ، یەکشەممانە دوو جار

The splinter in your eye is the best magnifying glass.

Theodor W. Adorno, *Minima Moralia* (1951)

Oppressive language does more than represent violence; it is violence; does more than represent the limits of knowledge; it limits knowledge ... [W]hether it is the malign language of law-without-ethics, or language designed for the estrangement of minorities, hiding its racist plunder in its literary cheek – it must be rejected, altered and exposed.

Toni Morrison, Nobel Lecture (1993)

# Contents

# Introduction: Show Your Work!

> The world changes according to the way people see it, and if
> you alter, even by a millimeter, the way a person looks or people
> look at reality, then you can change it.
>
> James Baldwin, *New York Times* (1979)

When I was a child, I'd spend rainy weekends working through mathematical problems for fun. Every now and then I'd try to prove famous
conjectures, the sort that had resisted the efforts of mathematicians
for hundreds of years, but most of the time I chose tamer problems
that I knew I could solve with enough scribbling. The clean thrill of
getting the right answer gave me a sense of efficacy and rootedness.
Even so, on tests at school I rarely got good grades, because I had a
terrible habit of not showing my work. I'd write down the solution
and move on, pleased at having figured it out in my head. Exasperated
teachers pleaded with me to play along, reminding me that outlining
a sensible method meant credit could be given if an error led to the
wrong answer, and was also a way of proving I hadn't cheated. It was
less important to be right, they maintained, and more important to
show that I knew what I was doing.

The exhortation has stayed with me: show your work! It's a helpful
precept in my work as a philosopher, where conclusions are less
important than reasoning, and in my role as a teacher, where it is
more effective to show than to tell.

This book is an attempt to share my work with regard to a set of
debates that have dominated the 'culture wars' in recent years. These
disputes are sometimes dismissed as distractions from more 'serious'

issues, and have undoubtedly been stirred by those who seek to siphon off the energy available for dissent, but I hope to show that they undergird the more obvious threats to our collective thriving.

In the two or three years before I sat down to write, fascist leaders held power in the United States, India, Russia, the Philippines, Poland, Brazil, Hungary, Turkey and Italy, to name just a few; the 'Black Lives Matter' and 'Me Too' movements rose up in response to unaddressed racist police brutality and gendered sexual violence; tens of thousands of migrants drowned or suffocated as they fled conflict, environmental degradation and poverty; micro-plastics were found in our bloodstreams and air pollutants in our brains; the Covid-19 pandemic and the ensuing vaccine nationalism laid bare the extent of global health inequalities; one in three people lacked access to adequate nutrition as food insecurity rose precipitously; our ailing planet was pushed through life-threatening heat records, while 88 million barrels a day of oil were dragged out of the ground.

Philosopher Mary Midgley once wrote that philosophy, 'in spite of all its tiresome features, is not a luxury but a necessity, because we always have to use it when things get difficult'.[1] This book is a response to the difficulties just mentioned. The tools of philosophy can help us to uncover and confront the ideology that underwrites and connects these issues. Doing so requires that we study the social world and examine the words and concepts that are the atoms of how we think, speak, categorise and resist.

The chapters ahead have also arisen from my disappointment in the tendency, particularly among those who practise their politics largely through social media, to focus on being 'right'. The effect of this trend has been to make conversations about social justice insular, punitive and sloppy, as people fixate on their *identity* as a person who is right, and consider mistakes – their own or those of others – to be ruinous, rather than inevitable and correctable. Where being right takes precedence, it can seem safer to adopt, wholesale, the views of others, instead of trying to work things out from scratch. To be clear, I do think that some perspectives are correct, morally speaking, but knowing and showing why is important, not least because the same tools will help us to see when and how we are wrong.

Showing your work is a way of being open with others, in the sense of being intellectually honest, which means making your assumptions and reasoning vulnerable to criticism. Being open in this way is also a challenge to another concerning trend. In online skirmishes about political issues, people sometimes respond to perfectly reasonable requests for explanation with the refrain, 'It's not my job to educate you!' or are quick to assure others that 'You don't owe anyone anything!' These proclamations are sometimes the result of an understandable frustration: marginalised people are often burdened with explaining their marginalisation and thereby expending energy that could be used for rest or resistance. It is, as feminist scholar Audre Lorde pointed out in 1984, 'an old and primary tool of all oppressors to keep the oppressed occupied with the master's concerns'.[2] So much free or cheap labour is extracted from certain groups that the uncompensated work of teaching others about oppression can seem like part of that extractive trend.

Yet explaining marginalisation need not be a distraction from resistance. It can be part of that resistance. How else are we supposed to learn? And while self-care is important, it would be less so if we cared for each other more effectively. Teaching and learning is an important part of how we care for one another and our communities. Besides, it is in fact my job, as a university lecturer, to teach. It's hard to see who the job of educating others falls to, if not to people like me, who have the privilege of being paid to learn. This book is, among other things, an attempt to discharge that duty.

There are many ways to write about the philosophy of social justice. This book focusses on some of the language and concepts that enable the subjugation and exploitation of particular people, as well as the words and ideas that might be used to construct a different way of living together. My aim is to sketch out some debates that will already be familiar to most readers, not with the aim of settling any particular issue, but instead to undertake some careful unsettling. I try to complicate topics that have been made to seem simple and bring some clarity to those that have been made to look difficult. I do not aim to be 'objective' or 'apolitical', if such a thing were even possible, but I have tried to make my reasoning clear enough that those who disagree with me will at least see where we part ways. Most obviously and importantly, I am vehemently opposed to capitalism, and some of my arguments for being so are outlined at various points in the book.

I focus on language and concepts because while we move through the material world of cars and concrete and growling stomachs, we make sense of that world through words and ideas. Language helps us to understand our observations and organise them into categories, and material realities spring up from those uses of language. Deploying the word 'terrorism' has given moral cover to mass surveillance, incarceration and murder; the term 'illegal' allows us to enjoy the same beaches on which the bodies of others wash up; the label 'criminal' means we can freely go about our lives while others are violently denied theirs. The categories of gender and race have facilitated an economy that sustains itself on the exploitation of particular groups. One of the key messages of this book is that words and concepts do things to the world, but could do other things, if we put our minds to it. As the anthropologist David Graeber wrote: 'the ultimate, hidden truth of the world is that it is something that we make, and could just as easily make differently'.[3]

Another theme that is central to this work is the idea that mistakes are unavoidable features of our moral and political lives, and should be seen as occasions for learning, rather than reasons for exclusion. I hope readers will take the errors and oversights of the text itself in this spirit. If there are more than is usual, that may be because I finished writing with a newborn baby sleeping (or often not) in my lap, or crying for me from the next room while my partner made space for me to work. This served as a reminder of the limitations on and of projects like this, and of the people whose valuable perspectives aren't heard because they are taken up with that most important and foundational element of any liberation movement: caring for others. Their voices are among the many omissions in this text. For that reason, among others, this book should be seen as a spur for discussion, rather than an exhaustive survey of how injustice works and how it can be challenged. Many of the arguments I make can be extended beyond the contexts in which I have developed them. Perhaps others will find ways to do that. I hope the chapters ahead will help readers to think about the world that makes them and imagine how they might work with others to make it differently.

# I

## Can You Be Racist to a White Person?

What woman here is so enamored of her own oppression that she cannot see her heelprint upon another woman's face? . . . I am not free while any woman is unfree, even when her shackles are very different from my own. And I am not free as long as one person of Color remains chained. Nor is anyone of you.

Audre Lorde, 'The Uses of Anger' (1981)

In 2017, former British football player Trevor Sinclair was arrested for driving under the influence of alcohol. He challenged the police officers, demanding to know whether the arrest was taking place because he was Black. It's a reasonable question: Black people in the UK are nine times more likely to be stopped and searched.[1] In the police van on the way to the station, Sinclair, drunk and aggrieved, called the arresting officer a 'white cunt'. He was eventually given a twenty-month driving ban and 150 hours of community service for driving while intoxicated, and a fine for a 'racially aggravated public order offence'.[2] He lost his position as a television sports pundit, and the anti-racism football charity *Kick It Out* stated that: 'There is too much racism across society currently, with it being even more regrettable and unacceptable when it is perpetrated by individuals who should know better.'[3]

During his trial it emerged that on the evening of his arrest, while Sinclair and his family were eating in a restaurant, a stranger approached them, patted him on the head and referred to him as a 'little chocolate man'. Sinclair explained that this humiliating incident, witnessed by those close to him, had led to his dangerous and self-destructive behaviour later that night.

This case contains two instances in which a person makes a reference to another person's race, but only one is properly described as racism. Sinclair may well have been abusive: calling someone a 'white cunt' refers to their race in a way that is intended as a slur. Nonetheless, according to any reasonable definition of the concept, Sinclair was not racist to the police officer. The woman in the restaurant, on the other hand, used no expletives, but made a comment that was unequivocally racist.

Making and maintaining the above distinction is vitally important. 'Reverse-racism' and 'reverse-sexism', which is to say, racism towards white people and sexism towards men, aren't the problems they're sometimes made out to be. That isn't to deny that there are insults and prejudices that turn on the race or gender of white people or men, but they tend to be one-off incidents, or collateral effects of privilege, and therefore belong to a separate category of wrongs to the profound and repetitious harms of racism and sexism. Keeping them apart is essential to taking seriously the role of power, which allows us to devise targeted actions to tackle racism and sexism and the system they thrive within. Engaging in productive conversations about these issues requires an understanding of the concepts of 'privilege' and 'oppression', and their role in producing and maintaining social and economic inequality.

## Becky with the Bad Grades

In 2008, a young white woman named Abigail Fisher sued the University of Texas at Austin, claiming that she had been denied a place at the prestigious institution as a result of anti-racist admissions policies, which, she contended, favoured academically weaker applicants from minority groups. In essence, she was claiming that, as a white applicant, she'd experienced 'reverse-racism'. 'Affirmative action' policies at universities in the United States take into account the context of candidates' applications: their race, ethnicity, gender and social class, for example. Their aim is to address the historic and enduring barriers to higher education for those from under-represented groups. White women (like Abigail Fisher) have in fact been some of the primary beneficiaries of these policies; affirmative action has played a significant role in improving women's access to educational and professional opportunities, and white women applicants – who tend to have more extensive social connections and material resources than women of colour – have seen the greatest advancement.[4]

Fisher lost the case and won the moniker 'Becky with the bad grades', a reference to Beyoncé's lyric 'Becky with the good hair' from the song 'Sorry' on her album *Lemonade*. 'Becky' is a slang term for a white woman who, as writer Michael Harriot puts it, 'uses her privilege as a weapon, a ladder or an excuse'.[5] Fisher's failure to secure the place she wanted came down not to her whiteness but to the fact that her grades were unimpressive compared to the field of candidates that year.

In 2020, the Becky put-down was overshadowed by the pejorative nickname for her older counterpart, 'Karen': a middle-aged, middle-class white woman who'd like to speak to your manager. Such people are sticklers for the rules because the rules serve them well. They wield their privilege without embarrassment, and have no compunction about summoning the relevant authorities when they feel wronged, especially when the perceived wrongdoer is a person of colour. Karens know how dire the consequences of disciplinary action can be for the people they target, and that's what emboldens them: they like to see results when teaching others a lesson.

One of the most infamous Karens is Amy Cooper, a white woman who in 2020 refused to put her dog on a lead when asked to do so in line with the rules in that section of Central Park. The request was made by Christian Cooper (their identical surnames are a confusing coincidence), a Black birdwatcher, whose video recording of the incident captures Amy Cooper saying, 'I'm calling the cops . . . I'm gonna tell them there's an African American man threatening my life' – a barefaced threat to exploit police racism.

Uses of 'Karen' and 'Becky' have been met with accusations of 'reverse-racism'. Since the slurs are only used against those from a particular social group, it has been argued that they therefore constitute racism towards members of that group, i.e. white women. No doubt the epithets are unfair to many real, blameless Karens and Beckys, but it's misguided to see the terms as instances of reverse-racism; rather, they refer specifically to those who harness white privilege in ways that can only be described as racist. To call someone a 'Karen' is to point out her racism. (Uses of 'Karen' have also been criticised for being sexist, which is a charge I'll rebut later in the chapter.)

In order to see that reverse-racism or reverse-sexism aren't mean-ingful concepts, it's necessary to understand what constitutes a case of racism or sexism. Racism and sexism are forms of oppression, as are homophobia, transphobia, ableism and classism, among others. Oppression is a kind of harm that merits special attention because it accounts for serious, long-term, widespread, predictable suffering, which, crucially, is preventable. Other kinds of contingent suffering – losing people, falling ill, failing to achieve our goals – may loom large in our personal lives, but are less interesting from a political perspective.* Nor are they as 'contingent' as we think; oppression tends to compound these harms, too. Cancer and road traffic acci-dents can affect any of us, but those whose risks are increased by living near polluting industries and busy roads are much more likely to be poor people of colour.[6]

In the sense in which they are used here, oppression and privilege are technical terms referring to specific forms of collective harm and advantage experienced by a set of people because of some feature of their identity that they have in common. Oppression doesn't just arise out of the chaos and complexity of the world; it's part of the design of our societies. It therefore has the distinctive feature of being largely inescapable for those it affects. It is characterised by 'double binds', which means that a person attempting to avoid one of its harms will only be harmed in another way. You're damned if you do, and damned if you don't. A family trying to flee their homeland after it was razed by an imperialist war then faces the risk of drowning in the open sea;

---

* Beyond the important question of which political system would optimise a person's ability to cope, and help others to cope, with life's irreducible, perennial miseries.

a woman who is labelled as 'bossy' and 'difficult' if she advocates for herself otherwise has her needs and preferences overlooked; a Muslim teenager quietly endures his peers' Islamophobic comments to avoid being seen as a troublemaker.

## The Economic Logic of Racism and Sexism

Privilege and oppression describe the standing of a person, or group of people, in relation to a social hierarchy. Men are privileged within the hierarchy of sex and gender; people of colour are oppressed within the hierarchy of race. The primary purpose of these hierarchies is to enable the subjugation and exploitation of particular groups. Racism and sexism therefore play an important role in facilitating the operation of an exploitative regime like capitalism. Capitalism is an economic system which centres on the accumulation of 'capital', that is, wealth that is used to produce even greater wealth through direct or indirect exploitation. Capital accumulation begins with people carving up and claiming ownership of the world's resources, appropriating goods that are essential to everyone's survival and that might otherwise be held as commons and shared according to people's requirements. These privatised resources are thereafter unavailable to others – no matter their level of need – without payment of some kind. Capitalist states endorse these ownership claims, and protect them via property laws and state violence. In this way, a small number of people are permitted to hoard almost all the world's basic goods and charge the rest of us to access them. We have no option but to sell our labour and exchange the money we earn for food, shelter and other necessities.

The amount of capital held by any person would remain static without some kind of ongoing extraction. Capital accumulation therefore depends on keeping wages much lower than the value of a person's labour (in terms of how wealthy that work makes their employer), and demanding payment for goods and services that exceeds their value (in terms of how much it costs the owner or seller to make or maintain them). For example, a garment worker in

Vietnam might earn thirty-five cents an hour, but the items she sews will be sold for thirty-five dollars, and the difference between the value of her contribution and that of her salary is claimed by the clothing company. Similarly, renting a one-bedroom flat in London costs around $26,000 per year, even though the cost to the landlord of wear and tear to the property will be a mere fraction of this, and when the tenant leaves, the landlord still owns the property and can begin the extraction anew. Capitalist states make these forms of bare-faced exploitation legal.

Accumulating capital also requires the continual growth of markets, because increased demands for goods and labour means more value can be extracted. This is not an abstract notion: growth means extracting more physical 'stuff' from the earth and using more energy, both of which degrade the environment. It also requires that we are urged to covet and buy commodities or services that we do not need, in the promise that doing so will stave off the misery of living under an exploitative regime. As philosopher Rosa Luxemburg wrote in 1913, capitalism

> ransacks the whole world, it procures its means of production from all corners of the earth, seizing them, if necessary by force, from all levels of civilisation and from all forms of society . . . It becomes necessary for capital progressively to dispose ever more fully of the whole globe.[7]

Such a patently unjust system could not persist without some degree of assent from those it harms. This compliance is secured by produc-ing and maintaining divisions between people in order to consolidate its rule. The objective of extracting as much labour as possible while paying the lowest possible wages is helped along by the entrenchment of gender categories. There are many ways to define and understand gender, but one of the most concrete characterisations follows from a simple question: which group of people performs the majority of the world's unpaid labour? (This is not just a question about historic allo-cations of work: in the UK and the US, women who also do paid work outside the home perform the equivalent of an extra work day of additional housework compared with men.[8]) Without continual housework – maintaining safe and sanitary conditions, preparing food, gestating and birthing children, cleaning clothes, caring for the young, old and ill – no one would be able to work outside the home and sustain the process of capital accumulation. In order to have a functional supply of labour, you need a *shadow* workforce that recharges the more visible workforce. If you can get away with not paying those invisible workers, all the better.

Myths are created or entrenched in order to support the devaluation of women and their roles: that housework is not really work, that it is the 'natural' duty of certain people by virtue of some biological propensity, that it is not important, that anyone could do it. (Consider the phrase 'Oh, she doesn't work', when a person means 'She doesn't work *outside the home for pay.*') And those myths, among others, reinforce the idea that some people – men – have certain roles and strengths, while others – women – have different roles and strengths. The positions and properties that are associated with men are more highly valued, and tend to be linked to greater power, prestige and pay. This is 'male privilege'. The system is more permissive to men than equivalently positioned women, even though they're also being exploited and corralled into restrictive social roles. Most notably, much less is asked of men in terms of unremunerated care and consideration for others, and their wrongdoing, especially their violence, is more readily ignored or forgiven. It is through these relative advantages that men's complicity is bought, and many defend their status by keeping women in their place and policing the norms and boundaries of heteronormativity.

This kind of analysis dates back to Black American sociologist W. E. B. Du Bois, who described the way in which 'white privilege' serves to divide Black and white workers from one another, and thereby protect the interests of powerful (white) people. In 1935, Du Bois wrote:

> the white group of laborers, while they received a low wage, were compensated in part by a sort of public and psychological wage. They were given public deference and tides of courtesy because they were white. They were admitted freely with all classes of white people to public functions, public parks, and the best schools. The police were

drawn from their ranks, and the courts, dependent upon their votes, treated them with such leniency as to encourage lawlessness.[9]

White privilege can be understood as a 'psychological wage' in the form of greater leeway (from the police, say), a sense of superiority and relative fortune, and a ready set of scapegoats on which to pile blame or take out frustration. White workers' wages were, and still are, higher than their Black counterparts', but those wages are nonetheless, in the general case, much lower than the value of that labour in terms of its social worth or how rich it makes their bosses. But there's a non-monetary top-up: the 'psychological wage' of white privilege. It comes in the form of an unspoken promise – life will be better because *you* are better – and on the strength of that promise, white people are often willing to put aside class loyalty in favour of race loyalty. This divide-and-rule system suppresses everyone's actual wages and has people fighting over crumbs.

Grasping these economic uses of privilege is essential to understanding how oppression came about, how it works, and why it persists. Under capitalism, almost everybody is exploited, but the stability and longevity of such an intuitively intolerable system requires that some groups of people are marked out to be exploited to a much greater degree. This is necessary both because capitalism subsists on exploitation, so it needs a large reserve of exploitable people, but also because a hierarchy of exploitation is a more stable arrangement since, if the balance is right, those with a modicum more power and freedom will better tolerate their own exploitation and defend a regime that favours them. Creating these hierarchies of exploitation requires division into social groups, and requires that some of those groups be subjugated relative to others or, in other words, that some groups are oppressed.

## *Oppression: A Primer*

Instances of oppression can be identified through a set of characteristic features. They involve some kind of *unjustified negative treatment* that happens to a person as a result of belonging to a particular *social group*; such treatment has *historical* precedents and is part of a pattern that emanates from the way our society is organised, rather than merely the actions of individuals, which is to say that it is *structural*.

The subjugation of women has a long and dispiritingly unvarying history. In Medieval Europe, women taking charge of their own reproductive capacity in devising and using methods of contraception and abortion, or those who were deemed to be unruly, unpleasant or insufficiently feminine, could be killed as 'witches'. Until the twentieth century, married women in the UK and the US were legally erased by 'coverture' laws, which treated them as 'covered women', i.e. subsumed by their husbands, who could make all legal decisions on their behalf. The term 'sexual harassment' didn't exist until the 1970s, which meant there was no legislation to protect women against this common form of sexist harm. A 1736 British legal treatise mandated that 'the husband of a woman cannot himself be guilty of an actual rape upon his wife, on account of the matrimonial consent which she has given, and which she cannot retract.' A woman getting married amounted to open-ended sexual consent. This remained in force until 1991, so within my lifetime, a man in the UK could rape his wife and it didn't count as rape.[10]

Contemporary incarnations of sexism bear the imprints of their progenitors. Women are no longer considered to belong to their husbands, but 90 per cent of married women in the UK adopt their husband's surnames, while just 3 per cent of US men take their wife's name on marriage.[11] And while women's bodies are now in many places ostensibly liberated from the dominion of their husbands and fathers, reproductive freedom remains in peril for those who have wombs. The right to decide when and whether to become or remain pregnant are under constant threat, and while we no longer speak of 'witches', in many jurisdictions, including various states within the US, women and the health workers who assist them can be jailed for ending an unwanted pregnancy. In the text that overturned Roe v. Wade in 2022 and thereby removed pregnant people's constitutionally protected right to abortion, US Supreme Court Justice Samuel Alito cited Matthew Hale, a seventeenth-century jurist. Hale not only penned influential writings on witchcraft, and sentenced women to death on that charge, but was also responsible for writing the marital rape exception into law.

Racism also straightforwardly meets the historical criterion. An estimated 13 million Africans were kidnapped and torn away from their land, homes and families and chained in piles below the decks of ships, rolling in their own excrement and vomit. Those who died or became diseased were thrown overboard. Those who survived were thrust into an alien world, trapped into back-breaking labour without pay, and their children sold and given away to others who would do the same. Their capture, enslavement and subjugation were facilitated by scientific views of Black people as subhuman, barbaric peoples, which set an expedient ceiling on their moral worth that enabled their exploitation with minimal guilt on their oppressors' part.

This history is often presented as though it belongs to a defunct moral regime of the distant past (though at the point of writing, slavery continued for longer than the time since its abolition, and slave labour in prisons remains constitutionally sanctioned in the United States). But just as the labour of slaves produced the wealth of European and North American nations, so too did slavery produce the moral conditions of the present day, and determine the character and persistence of anti-Black racism. Contemporary racism exists because of colonialism. Colonialism follows from the logic of capitalism. Racism was a way of justifying an economic regime that was so obviously heinous as to require the creation and insistence of differences between human groups that were bolstered by spurious scientific claims. To say colonialism is part of the past is to neglect and misunderstand the origins and purposes of race and racism. 'Freedom' in the United States eventually came in the form of a vicious apartheid state, in which the police, judiciary and prison system inherited the role of subjugating Black people. As African American studies scholar Saidiya Hartman puts it, 'I, too, live in the time of slavery, by which I mean I am living in the future created by it.'[12]

Slavery was abolished in the British Empire by the 1833 Slavery Abolition Act, not primarily for humanitarian reasons, as is often argued, but because it was becoming unprofitable and rebellions were increasingly difficult to suppress.[13] Britain rushed to compensate slave-owners for the 'property' they could no longer legally own. The cost of doing so was eye-watering, and the Treasury had to borrow the equivalent of $19 billion, a debt that was only paid off in 2015, so that most British workers have paid taxes towards the 'compensation' of slave-owners. Former slaves received no compensation for a life of unpaid labour and their descendants haven't been offered a penny in reparation. The African communities that lost family members received no recompense and continued to experience overt colonialism for over a century, and still face economic marginalisation and resource extraction today. Black people in the UK and beyond must now negotiate a world replete with anti-Black racism, which limits their health, life expectancy, and education and employment prospects.

While it is now less socially acceptable openly to suggest that there are innate differences between different races (partly because the idea of a scientific basis for race has been firmly and repeatedly debunked), myths about biological differences between white and Black people are still widespread. A 2016 study found that half of white medical students and doctors surveyed in the US held false beliefs about biologically based differences between races, including the view that Black people's nerve endings are less sensitive than white people's, that white people have larger brains and that Black people's skin is thicker.[14] The consequences of these misnomers is serious: Black patients' pain is systematically discredited and undertreated due to bias. For instance, it has been shown that Black children with appendicitis are given fewer, less effective painkillers than white children.[15]

Serious forms of unjustified harm towards people from particular social groups do not arise out of thin air, and the fact that they have a protracted history is proof of how difficult it is to shake them. Among other things, this means learning our history well enough that it becomes a tangible, significant part of the present, rather than allowing present realities to seem mysterious, unavoidable and apparently unchangeable.

History is also important because it gives additional weight to the harms of oppression. Every time a girl experiences sexual harassment or assault, she joins a procession of girls and women, stretching back millennia, who have endured some variant of the same fury, shame and violation. The length of that shadow makes the violation graver and leaves the victim feeling even more hopeless.

In some cases, historical context is a key part of what makes an incident harmful. If a white person wears an afro wig or paints their face black or brown for a costume party, the harm of this decision may not be automatically evident if the person is ignorant of history or its importance. Blackface was a form of costume used in minstrel shows in the nineteenth and twentieth centuries, in which white performers would entertain white audiences by acting out and thereby reinforcing exaggerated racist stereotypes of Black people, representing them as ugly, stupid, dishonest, frivolous, cowardly, hypersexualised and lazy. Without engaging with this history, it may be hard to see why instances of blackface are so hurtful and offensive, or to recognise the role they play in perpetuating racism. (Blackface is particularly disturbing when it occurs at parties in elite educational institutions, where the excuse of ignorance is unconvincing and where these practices look more like a shared joke which consolidates dominance.) A Black person wearing white face-paint as part of a costume (as a clown, perhaps, or in order to imitate a white person) carries no such connotations, and would instead be merely another costume. History breaks the symmetry between two otherwise comparable acts.[16]

Blackface, sexual assault and all other forms of oppression tap into deeper, longer memories of pain, humiliation and tyranny that have not yet been adequately acknowledged, let alone atoned for. This is one of the chief characteristics that sets oppression apart from other forms of harm. As sociologist Sara Ahmed writes in *Living a Feminist Life*, 'I am not willing to get over histories that are not over.'[17]

Last, but most importantly, oppression is *structural*, which is to say that it arises from causes that are deeper and more influential than the actions of any individual person. 'Structures' are the forces that regulate the distribution of value – both in terms of resources and esteem – in our societies. Just as gravitational forces arise because of objects which have a mass, but also thereby operate on all objects that have a mass, so too are structures created by our collective actions, but also constrain and determine those actions. We do not knowingly contribute to structures, rather we react to the influences we are subject to, in much the way that planets are drawn into orbits by a star's gravity, and are thereafter bound to move in predictable ways. When we say that oppression is structural, we mean that understanding how it works, and tackling its harms, requires us to study the overall system, rather than focussing on the actions of individuals or institutions.

For example, in UK hospitals, white people are over-represented in the highest-paid positions, as doctors and managers, while Black people are over-represented in the lowest-paid positions, as cleaners and porters. This might initially be attributed to racism among the individuals who are responsible for hiring staff, but it's obvious that other factors play a more important role. Clearly, disparities in access to education and training must be taken into account, but these are in turn determined by the uneven distribution of other resources: nutrition, housing, healthcare. (And then there are higher-level features that deserve scrutiny. We might reflect on disparities in the distribution of esteem, and ask whether it is fair that doctors and managers earn more than cleaners and porters, and whether there should be pay hierarchies at all.)

The structures which oppress people are the stuff of the system itself and must be continually navigated, negotiated and endured. Imagine finding your way through a city: you try to take the shortest way from one point to another, but there's a river without a bridge. You decide to take public transport, but you don't have the right change and everyone else has a bus pass. You revert to walking, but the route is not pedestrianised, and you must traipse along the side of a motorway, fearing for your life and breathing exhaust fumes. This is how oppression works. There are a great many obstacles which must be overcome, but unless a person is oppressed along that dimension, they will not experience these features as hindrances and may not notice them at all, or understand why others seem to struggle.

This metaphor is not entirely abstract. The effects of structural oppression are evident in the lengths that women go to, as a matter of course, in order to avoid street sexual harassment. We choose routes that might not be the most direct, picturesque or pedestrian friendly; wear sunglasses and headphones to shut out unwanted attention; pretend we're on the phone; choose the cuts and colours of our clothes according to how likely they are to be met with comments or violence (some women report that the colour red makes them feel too 'bright' and conspicuous); adjust our faces so that we don't look like easy targets but are careful to avoid appearing sad or angry, which could elicit the dreaded 'cheer up' or 'give us a smile' or, worse, aggression at the denial of an assumed right to feminine cheerfulness; splay our keys between our fingers, and are asked by friends and sisters for messages of confirmation that we survived the journey.[18] And still, we are not safe. For racialised women, the stakes are higher, the range of adjustments more intricate and specific, the gear-shift to violence more sudden. We learn these strategies when we are still children and deploy them throughout our lives as we use public spaces. We get so good at it that we do it automatically, while most men go about their lives with no awareness of the effort and anxiety they are spared.

Oppression being structural means that it's everywhere. The variety of scenarios in which its obstacles and humiliations might arise are potentially infinite. This is not the case for 'reverse-racism' and 'reverse-sexism'. If someone calls a white person a 'white cunt', chances are it's the first time that's happened and in all likelihood it'll never happen again. It might be unpleasant or intimidating, but managing isolated affronts is very different from weathering a succession of indignities. For people of colour, calls of 'go home' or 'go back to your country' peal through countless moments of their lives, and that's often the friendlier end of the spectrum of racist abuse. Further, these offences always contain the threat of more direct, serious violence. Reverse-racism has no fulcrum in the world through which it can automatically summon the menace of graver harms.

## Crying, Caring and Custody

One of the most common responses to the idea that men are privileged is the objection that men's lives tend to be nasty, brutish and short. Across the world, men don't live as long as women, and are more likely to be murdered and to kill themselves. They often work in dangerous, dirty, demeaning jobs and face strong social pressure to earn enough to care for dependents; they must tolerate mental and physical suffering without showing weakness; and they are more likely to be drafted into fighting in wars.

Masculinity is undoubtedly harmful to men, as well as women. But it's a bit like chemotherapy: toxic and associated with an array of grim side effects while having a good chance of being beneficial. Men are harmed by precisely the behaviours that promise them power, autonomy and social status. Feeling greater pressure to be a breadwinner is a heavy burden, but it tends to come with greater financial power and autonomy, giving a person more control over his life and the ability to leave an unhappy domestic arrangement. The benefits of meeting the ideals of masculinity generally outweigh the side effects, while women have just side effects to choose between. Succeeding at femininity means being physically attractive, amiable, gentle, empathetic and caring. It means making yourself available to meet the needs – sexual, emotional and domestic – of others, especially men. It demands self-effacement, sacrifice and the relinquishing of autonomy. Failing to meet those ideals can at times lead to invisibility and ostracism, or hostility and violence.

Keeping this difference in mind, we can tackle some specific examples which are used to argue that men are oppressed through their social roles as men in ways that are structural, group-based and historic. For example: men generally cannot cry in public, are often deemed to be unfit to work in caring professions or to provide unpaid care, are sometimes overlooked when seeking legal custody of their children.

It's true that men are judged more harshly for crying in front of others, which is one part of a broader culture of emotional suppression that damages their wellbeing and, in turn, that of those around them. But women being permitted to cry in public is comparable to the way in which babies can defecate in public without anyone batting an eyelid: we don't care what babies do because we don't think very much rests on their behaviour, and we know they can't help it. There are widespread stereotypes about women being excessively emotional by nature, which are used to argue that women don't make good decision-makers or leaders and which are, accordingly, used to withhold power from women. Being allowed to cry in public stems from the notion that women are emotionally incontinent, so it doesn't matter if they display this shortcoming openly. Men are thought to be stronger and more stable, and are therefore held to higher standards.

Besides, the requirement that men do not cry is policed primarily by men, and those men who are able to refrain from showing vulnerability thereby acquire and maintain social status. As feminist philosopher Marilyn Frye wrote in 1983:

> Can men cry? Yes, in the company of women. If a man cannot cry, it is in the company of men that he cannot cry. It is men, not women, who require this restraint; and men not only require it, they reward it . . . It is to their benefit to practice this discipline.[19]

Men are also often ridiculed for working in caring professions because this choice means they have degraded themselves by doing 'women's work'. There's a scene in *Friends* in which Rachel and Ross are interviewing nannies for their baby.[20] Several women apply for the role, but the only male candidate, played by Freddie Prinze Jr, is clearly the most qualified. Ross is uncomfortable with hiring a man to take care of their child and finds his sensitivity unsettling. He ends up firing him without good reason.[21]

Men who raise children instead of working in the paid workforce are a rarity, and are still liable to be seen as having failed to secure 'proper' work or being 'under the thumb' of a partner who 'wears the trousers'. Those who care for children who aren't their own as a paid profession are often viewed with suspicion. Similarly, men who train as nurses are often teased, assumed to be gay or else are taken to be doctors. One male nurse, writing about gender stereotypes in nursing, recalled being asked, 'Were you not clever enough to be a doctor?'[22] This last is telling. Women who are nurses are not quizzed as to whether they were clever enough to be doctors. Two questionable assumptions are at play: the idea that doctors are cleverer than nurses, which rests on a problematic division and hierarchy between 'curing' and 'caring',* and the assumption that men are better suited to 'clever' professions, while nurturing professions are more appropriate for women.

As we saw earlier, caring jobs, such as looking after the young, the old and the sick, are largely invisible where they're performed for free in the private sphere and are vastly underpaid in the public sphere. They're often considered to be 'unskilled' and unimpressive, and unsurprisingly, are generally carried out by women. Though it is not included in indices of economic activity, like gross domestic product, unpaid care work alone has been valued at $10.8 trillion a year globally, which is more than three times the size of the UK economy.[23]

Men may be ridiculed for working in these roles but, again, this is because care work is thought to be beneath them, so that the sneering is partly a response to a perceived abasement or failure. By contrast, women who end up in stereotypical 'men's' jobs such as engineering, aviation or surgery are applauded for having conquered gender stereotypes and found rewarding employment. These responses reveal the hierarchy in which we hold men and women, and the jobs we associate with them.

Last, it's often said that men are less likely to be granted legal custody of their children. In the UK this is in fact a myth – a 2015 report showed no evidence of gender bias in determining which parent a child should live with.[24] And in the US, only 4 per cent of custody cases are decided by courts, which means the overwhelming majority of decisions about custody are figured out between parents, without any legal involvement.[25] Yet there is a widespread presumption that a mother will be awarded custody of her children and that it's right that it should be so. This view is a hindrance to fathers who wish to be primary or equal caregivers to their children (as is the view, described above, that men who are primary caregivers are oddballs or failures). Yet it derives from the empirical fact that women shoulder a disproportionate share of parenting: fourteen hours a week

---

* There are also hierarchies at work between the two professions with respect to social class and educational access.

in the US compared with men's seven hours (in situations in which parents 'share' the care-giving).[26] We think of women as primary caregivers because they generally are primary caregivers. One corollary of this fact is that many people believe that the best place for children is with their mother, but another is that women tend to be burdened with significant amounts of largely invisible additional labour whether they like it or not. Fathers are afforded more choice in how much parenting labour they want to provide (note that many people describe fathers' supervision as 'babysitting' or 'daddy day-care' as though their involvement is a hobby or favour), and even minimal care-giving from men tends to be highly visible and widely praised, so that men who perform any parental labour at all are often deemed to be excellent fathers.[27]

Men's options in terms of the roles and behaviours they adopt *are* restricted, but these restrictions, and the distress they may cause to some men, are symptomatic not of oppression, but of privilege. They follow from the fact that a small number of fairly limited and low-status roles and behaviours – being vulnerable, being a caregiver – are cordoned off for women and are belittled and undervalued. Men are warned off those things, but are encouraged to think of the rest of the world as theirs for the taking. Of course, for most men, the world is manifestly *not* theirs for the taking, but being a man isn't what scuppers them.

## Avoiding the Spherical Cow: The Importance of Intersectionality

One of the chief reasons that people struggle to understand the one-way nature of oppression stems from a failure to take account of another important theoretical tool which guards against oversimplification. That tool is 'intersectionality'.

Among scientists, there's a joke about a farmer who asks a team of physicists to help her work out why milk production is low among her cattle. The physicists set to work and quickly come up with an answer, but emphasise that their solution only applies if we assume that cows are perfectly spherical and graze within a vacuum. The joke trades on the fact that physicists often do model the world in this way in order to make difficult problems more tractable. Spheres are mathematically straightforward because they have so much symmetry, and in a vacuum you don't have to worry about the effects of friction and turbulence. But cows are not spherical and would suffocate in a vacuum. It's a limited, unserviceable solution that only works well if we assume the world is much simpler than it is.

Too often our discussions of oppression take on the character of theoretically simple but practically useless spherical cows. We discuss people as though their identities were much tidier than they are, referring to 'men' or 'Black people' as though those within the category are sufficiently similar to one other as to be treated as a homogenous class. Those who fall between the clean axes we've constructed are at risk of being overlooked altogether, as our simplifying assumptions round things up or down in such a way as to erase some people entirely.

As feminist theorist Audre Lorde put it in 1982, 'There is no such thing as a single-issue struggle because we do not live single-issue lives.'[28] All of us have multiple identities, and privilege and oppression coexist along different dimensions of a person's experience. My father is a person of colour and a Muslim, but he is a heterosexual man. My mother is white, but she is a working-class woman. Both of them have forms of privilege and oppression marbled through their experiences in ways which are hard to untangle. Speaking of 'male privilege' or 'white privilege' will capture some of their experiences relative to one another, but not all, and speaking of these elements in isolation from their other identities may lead us awry.

The term for the ways in which social identities interact with one another to produce a blend of oppression and privilege is 'intersectionality'. It was named by Black feminist theorist Kimberlé Crenshaw in 1989,[29] but the concept has a much longer history in the work of activists. In 1977, the Combahee River Collective, a group of Black lesbian feminist socialists, described the aims of their organisation as 'the development of integrated analysis and practice based upon the fact that the major systems of oppression are interlocking. The synthesis of these oppressions creates the conditions of our lives.'[30]

Intersectionality warns against movements that are anchored to experiences that are shared by all and only those within a particular oppressed group, as this inevitably ends up prioritising the interests of the most privileged people within that category. As philosopher Amia Srinivasan puts it: 'A feminism that deals only with "pure" cases of patriarchal oppression – cases that are "uncomplicated" by factors of caste, race, or class – will end up serving the needs of rich white or high-caste women.'[31] Similarly with race and other axes of marginalisation. Suppose an initiative to tackle Islamophobia was to set aside considerations of class, race, gender and nationality in order to focus its resources on Muslim identities alone. In doing so, it would underserve Muslim women, as well as Muslims who are poor, Black and undocumented. There is no Muslim who is only a Muslim, and such a scheme would fail those who need it most.

Intersectionality is sometimes misunderstood as meaning that each of us has a unique fingerprint of intertwined oppressions, so that we should approach questions of social justice as individuals, without making assumptions or drawing parallels. It's a misapplication that's been welcomed in establishment circles because it individualises the burden of challenging injustice, prevents ordinary people from seeing their commonalities, and requires no systemic change. Taking intersectionality into account encourages collective organisation, but challenges us to build movements that recognise interlocking dimensions of oppression, and begin with the needs of the most marginalised. Three features of intersectionality deserve closer attention: heterogeneity, non-additivity and conflicting interests.

## Heterogeneity

Discussions of intersectionality go back at least as far as 1851. Three major social movements were simultaneously underway in the mid-nineteenth century in the United States, as activists fought for the abolition of slavery, women's suffrage and Black people's suffrage.[32] Neither the women's suffrage movement nor the Black suffrage movement took due account of other dimensions of oppression. 'Woman' meant '*middle-class white* woman' and 'Black' meant 'Black *man*'. Black and Indigenous women residing in the intersections of these identities were rendered invisible by the way others had carved up the categories.

Even so, there were vocal Black women abolitionists, suffragists and feminist activists working against this invisibilisation. Among them was Sojourner Truth, who had been born into slavery and had escaped to freedom and a life as an itinerant activist. In 1851, in a speech at a women's rights convention in Ohio, Truth reminded other campaigners that their conception of womanhood did not accommodate her experiences. She inserted herself, and other Black women, back into the picture, with the declaration: '*I* am a woman's rights.'[33] She went on to point out that the conception of womanhood that was being weaponised to deny women their rights was not inclusive of Black women.[34] The arguments that were used to justify excluding women from voting – for example, that they were too weak to bear the rigours of deliberating about who to vote for – could not be consistently applied to Black women, who were generally required to work as intensively as men and without any special concession to their supposed feminine delicacy or sensibilities. She assured the room that, thanks to a life of forced manual labour, she was as strong as any man. Truth's speech was a provocation: those speaking of 'women' should admit they meant 'white women' or else adopt a conception of womanhood that could accommodate all women.

Women's lives and needs are heterogeneous, and the most urgent harms women face (e.g. poverty, state violence) are often those that arise primarily because of their race or class, which are then exacerbated by gender (e.g. sexual harassment within an exploitative job). When comparing the feminisms of Black and white women in a 1980 paper, Audre Lorde wrote:

> Some problems we share as women, some we do not. You fear your children will grow up to join the patriarchy and testify against you, we fear our children will be dragged from a car and shot down in the street, and you will turn your backs upon the reasons they're dying.

Contemporary feminism still tends to centre on the concerns of middle-class white women, which means it is overwhelmingly focussed on the representation of women in elite positions – at the helm of companies, in politics, in broadcasting companies, on rich lists – while almost no attention is given to the needs of working-class women, many of them women of colour, for whom issues of pay, working conditions, housing and childcare are much more urgent. Almost all the clothes we wear were sewn in sweatshops in South and East Asia by women who work under dangerous conditions for minimal pay and are at risk of sexual harassment. Shouldn't this be the archetypal feminist issue?

## Non-additivity

After hearing me speak about racism at an event, my father marvelled at my willingness to be angry in public. He was proud to see it, and glad the issues were being raised in the appropriate emotional register, but mused that he had spent decades, as a Brown immigrant, making sure no one ever saw him angry. His anger is so readily interpreted as a potential threat to the safety of others (which could accordingly lead to his own safety being *actually* threatened) that he is forbidden from expressing it at all. He bites his tongue when people cut in front of him in queues, quells his rage when he hears racist comments, and is excessively polite in situations in which others are rude to him. I'm light-skinned and am often read as white, which means I'm given more leeway in expressing my rage. Angry women are not popular either, but my anger is more likely to be met with ridicule or contempt than with fear.

In the last two decades, Muslims (or those perceived to be Muslims) have experienced unprecedented levels of racism, as the attacks on the Twin Towers have been used by Western media and politicians as opportunities to incite, and profit from, fear and hate. Those wearing Islamic dress have been spat at in the street, mosques have been attacked, and the birth weights of babies born to those perceived as Arab or Muslim (the two are spun together in the Western imagination even though most Muslims are not Arabs and many Arabs are not Muslims) have fallen as the stress and anxiety of Islamophobia has damaged people's health.[35]

Yet the ways in which Muslim men and Muslim women experience racism are differentiated into 'his' and 'hers' versions, each insidi-
ous in its own way.[36] Muslim men are associated with violence,
dogmatism and anger while Muslim women are portrayed as being
passive, submissive and brainwashed by their husbands and fathers.
These stereotypes lead to gendered forms of racism. Men are more
likely to be racially profiled on the street and in airports, and to be
detained without trial; women are more likely to have their clothing
policed by those who claim to be acting in their best interests, or to
have their professional competence systematically underestimated.

Similar failures of non-additivity are seen when considering the
confluence of sexism and anti-Black racism. When Michelle Obama
became first lady of the United States, she faced a torrent of abuse
that wasn't just a predictable mix of the oppressions associated with
her two most visible identities. It didn't amount to the sexism
Hillary Clinton faces added to the racism Barack Obama faces
(though that would have been more than enough for anyone). It
was the unique, frenzied hate that is reserved for Black women,
which scholar Moya Bailey coined as 'misogynoir' – anti-Black
misogyny.[37] White women in the public sphere are unfairly criticised for their outfits and demeanour, but the blend of sexism and
anti-Black racism levelled at Michelle Obama was an order of
magnitude more vicious. She was treated with disgust and compared
to an animal, while doctored photographs of her proliferated online,
as though her mere existence in a position of power and influence
was at once preposterous and deserving of continual violent rancour.
There were also elements of classism intermingled with the misogynoir (the two often come together), relating to her upbringing in a
working-class family in Chicago: radio host Tammy Bruce said,
'That's what he's married to . . . You know what we've got? We've
got trash in the White House.'[38]

Considering non-additivity means recognising that you can't
compute the experience of a Black woman by adding the sexism
white women face to the racism Black men face. To think that the
sexism that white, middle-class women experience is the 'normal',
standard sexism, which is then tweaked in the case of other women,

is to believe that white, middle-class women are the 'normal', standard kind of woman.

## Conflicting Interests

In 1985, Alice Walker's Pulitzer Prize-winning novel *The Color Purple*
was made into a Hollywood film, directed by Steven Spielberg. The
film, like the book, featured domestic violence within a Black
community. Its protagonist, Celie, is a Black woman who has been
subject to the violence of her father and husband, and who ultimately finds solace and solidarity in her relationships with other
women. The film has its shortcomings but was generally positively
received and praised for its unflinching portrayal of Celie's struggle
and eventual triumph.[39] Yet it provoked animated debate, and in
some cases cinemas were picketed. Demonstrations attended largely
by Black men protested the film's portrayal of Black men as violent
and brutish. Many Black women responded by asking precisely
where their experiences with violent, brutish men could be
portrayed, if not in the adaptation of the literary work of a Black
woman. In the aftermath of its release, a reporter from the *New York
Times* spoke to a Black woman named Eartis Thomas who worked
at a telephone company. She recounted the violence endured by her
mother and aunts at the hands of their husbands, and described how
the film's recognition of the issue 'just lifted a burden'. She concluded
that 'Black women should not be sacrificed for black men's pride.
Let the film roll.' Black actor Danny Glover, who played the role of
Celie's violent husband, noted that 'Lots of times we sweep our own
problems under the rug under the justification of upholding black
history and the black man.'[40]

Portraying Black men as unusually violent contributes to the racist
idea, widely peddled by news media, film and television, of Black
men as monstrous, subhuman, unable to control their impulses and
therefore in need of the disciplining force of overseers, police officers
and prison wardens. Representations of Black men as inherently
aggressive tend to end up justifying the violence that is so overwhelmingly used against them. Yet *The Color Purple* never suggests that Black

men are unusually violent, but rather confronts the fact that Black men are socialised to be violent, not because they are Black, but because they are men. If we are forbidden from discussing or representing that violence in order to avoid adding to racist generalisations about Black men, then we are effectively choosing to protect Black men at the expense of Black women and children, whose experiences of violence are effectively erased and whose attempts to get help are scuppered. (I focus on Black women and children here, because when Black men harm people who are not Black - most notably, those who are white - there tends to be no hesitation in presenting them as violent and their victims as deserving of protection.)

Yet the conflicting moral pressures – on the one hand, not representing Black men in ways that further contribute to their dehumanisation and, on the other, not ignoring the fact that Black women experience violence at the hands of Black men – would not arise were it not the case that Black men were so grossly misrepresented in the first place. Black women are being sacrificed to gender-based violence in order to prevent the racism towards Black men from being made any worse. As Kimberlé Crenshaw puts it:

> Of course, it is true that representations of black violence – whether statistical or fictional – are often written into a larger script that consistently portrays black and other minority communities as pathologically violent. The problem, however, is not so much the portrayal of violence itself as it is the absence of other narratives and images portraying a fuller range of black experience.[41]

In reality there is no conflict of interests here. Black men must not be represented as unusually violent, and Black women must not be prevented from speaking about the violence they face. The clash is the product of racism – manifesting in a lack of positive or neutral representation – which sets off a cascade of harm that ends up creating this rift.

## Karen and the Boomers

Intersectionality can also help us in returning to the question of whether 'Karen' might be a sexist slur. As we saw, Karen refers to a white woman who weaponises her privilege, most notably in her interactions with people of colour. Karen cannot be a racist slur because the purpose of the label is generally to identify instances of racism and the people who enact them. Yet Karen doesn't just mean 'racist white person', it means 'racist white *woman*'. Accordingly, it has been charged with being sexist.[42] Armed with intersectionality, it's easier to see why this critique is misguided.

While a couple of names have been suggested (e.g. Ken), no slur for the male equivalent of a Karen has really caught on. This is one of the core arguments of those who insist that Karen is a sexist term – the slur is used in ways that specifically condemn the actions of women. But that's not quite true. The term targets *white* women, and not just any white woman, but a white woman confident enough of her privilege relative to certain other groups to know she can deploy it against them and come out unscathed. It's worked for her before; she knows the world is on her side. White women who are sex workers or trans or unhoused do not generally call the police on people; they know it wouldn't end well for them. When we say 'Karen' we generally mean a middle-class, cisgender, heterosexual, able-bodied white woman who hurts someone who is already worse off.

Yet there's another intersectionality-related reason as to why Karen is a legitimate insult. There is a widespread misnomer that women are less racist than men. In reality, there's no gender difference in racist attitudes.[43] (More than half of white women voted for Trump, putting their interests as white people ahead of their interests as women.) The myth that women are less racist partly stems from the fact that women's racism presents in different ways. Just as the sexism a white woman experiences differs from the sexism a woman of colour experiences, so too does the racism she doles out tend to differ from that of a white man. Intersectionality modulates our privilege as well as our oppression.

Our conceptions of what racism looks like are often based on the ways in which men typically express racism (as in all things, they set the standard). The racism of white men tends to be more direct, aggressive and outspoken. There is a long history of white men using women as a justification for their violence towards men of colour. Lynchings of Black men were often carried out under the cover of protecting white women and girls. Fourteen-year-old Emmett Till (who may or may not have whistled in the presence of a white woman) was beaten to death and thrown in a river for behaving 'offensively'. As Charles M. Blow notes in the *New York Times*, 'anti-black white terrorists used the defense of white women and white purity as a way to wrap violence in valor. Carnage became chivalry.'[44] Other women of colour are also used to justify spectacular violence; George W. Bush and Laura Bush claimed that the 'War on Terror' was 'a fight for the rights and dignity of women'.[45] (Politicians who supported the 'War on Terror' have since voted against resettling the women displaced by its violence.[46])

But the racism of white women also tends to capitalise on a femininity under threat, albeit in ways that are more gender-stereotypical. A commonly noted tactic deployed by white women accused of racism is to cry, thereby recentring themselves as victims and attempting to thwart the charges by claiming that the accuser is being aggressive or 'uncivil'. Another gender-stereotypical form of racism often used by white women is to eschew the direct violence that is more often enacted by men, and instead practise violence through the conduit of the authorities: the police, security guards, airport officials, 'the manager'. A white woman is less likely to be racist in ways that get her hands dirty, yet is liable to leave a person of colour at the mercy of someone who can more effectively enact serious, direct forms of harm.

For all these reasons, 'Karen' is not a sexist slur. It's a gender-specific accusation of racism deployed in response to gender-specific instances of racism. It's the right word for the job. But note: if she's not being racist (or transphobic, or otherwise punching down), chances are you're being sexist.

The Karen phenomenon, and the attendant backlash, proceeds along comparable lines to the 'OK boomer' controversy of 2019. 'OK boomer' is a deliberately dismissive response that's issued when an older person, typically born in the two decades after the Second World War, criticises or dismisses young people for values or practices relating to social or environmental justice, or which depart from the norms that are familiar to older people. An older person says something contemptuous, often implying that young people are idealistic, immature, spoilt 'snowflakes' and gets an 'OK boomer' in response. It is a taunt reserved for a person of a particular age and level of affluence, who derides young people's attempts to build tolerable lives and a hopeful political vision while staring down the barrel of an austere future.

Boomers do not like it. In a since-deleted melodramatic tweet, US radio show host Bob Lonsberry described the term as the 'N-word of ageism'. Ageism is a very real form of oppression: it refers to the systematic neglect of older people, who are devalued as their economic 'productivity' declines. 'OK boomer' is not ageist, but as with 'Karen', some of us need to stop being sloppy about how we use it. Age is clearly *relevant* to the phrase; the provocation is some older people's refusal to acknowledge the challenges of widening economic inequalities and the unfolding climate crisis, and the role they have played in creating those problems. Yet an older person saying something we disagree with is not, on its own, cause to pull out 'OK boomer'.

It was members of the baby-boomer generation who fought hard to bring us some of the most radical political changes of the last century, including the Civil Rights movement and improved abortion access. Even so, statistics show, time and again, that boomers are more likely to be politically conservative. Three-quarters of eighteen- to twenty-four-year-olds in the UK voted to remain in the European Union; two-thirds of those aged sixty-five to seventy-four voted to leave. (Under the circumstances, voting to leave generally indicated the endorsement of anti-immigration policies, even if that's not, strictly speaking, what was on the ballot.) Thirty-seven per cent of eighteen- to twenty-nine-year-olds voted for Trump as opposed to 53 per cent of those over the age of sixty-five. But intersectionality is important: clearly not all boomers are alike. Disaggregating this data by race tells a different story: 53 per cent of white people voted for Brexit, compared with 27 per cent of Black people. Just 8 per cent of Black people voted for Trump, compared with 58 per cent of white people. Most older people were not beneficiaries of the relative economic luck of their generation, and many have social identities (e.g. being a woman, a person of colour, trans or gay) that were much more marginal or dangerous when they were young. But the term isn't intended for them; the 'boomer' in 'OK boomer' is not merely coding for age, it's about how a person is positioned with respect to the status quo.

'Karen' refers to racist white women; 'OK boomer' is a response to conservative older people. They are ways of saying 'I see your selfishness; I see your abuses of power.' Both slurs are small acts of political resistance enacted from the margins of society, to provoke, shame and agitate, but neither comes with any capacity to cause real harm. While power and material resources continue to be distributed as they are, there can be no such thing as 'reverse-oppression'.

# 2

# Has 'Political Correctness' Gone Too Far?

> We should perhaps frankly admit that we have agreed in advance to have our community sundered, racial and sexual minorities demeaned, the dignity of trans people denied, that we are, in effect, willing to be wrecked by this principle of free speech.
>
> Judith Butler, 'Limits on Free Speech' (2017)

When moderating the first Republican presidential debate in 2015, Fox News journalist Megyn Kelly attempted to call out Donald Trump for his misogyny:

> You've called women you don't like fat pigs, dogs, slobs and disgusting animals . . . Your Twitter account has several disparaging comments about women's looks. You once told a contestant on the *Celebrity Apprentice* it would be a pretty picture to see her on her knees. Does that sound to you like the temperament of a man we should elect as president?[1]

Trump didn't miss a beat. He shot back the following, to thunderous applause:

> I think the big problem this country has is being politically correct. I've been challenged by so many people and I don't, frankly, have time for total political correctness. And to be honest with you, this country doesn't have time, either.[2]

He knew what he was doing: 80 per cent of those polled in the US believe that 'political correctness is a problem in our country'.[3] In the

UK, any suspicion that concessions have been made to the needs of marginalised groups is liable to provoke the complaint, 'It's political correctness gone mad!' When polled, two-thirds of Britons agreed with the statement that 'Too many people are too easily offended these days over the language that others use,'[4] and 'wokeism' was the third most concerning 'ism' after racism and religious fundamentalism, though 38 per cent of people admitted being unfamiliar with the term.[5]

'Woke' has its origins in early twentieth-century African American vernacular English, where it referred to a person who was especially vigilant or alert. Over time, it came to be associated specifically with an awareness of racism, and as it has entered mainstream parlance in recent years, it has come to refer to a sensitivity to all forms of injustice, and is now used synonymously with 'political correctness'.

There are many stories as to how political correctness took on the stature it has in contemporary public discourse. Once upon a time, it was a jibe reserved for sticklers who unquestioningly followed the party line on a given issue. In a 1934 article headlined 'Personal Liberty Vanishes in Reich', a *New York Times* writer warned that in Nazi Germany 'All journalists must have a permit to function and such permits are granted only to pure "Aryans" whose opinions are politically correct. Even after that they must watch their step.'[6] In the 1970s and 1980s, feminists and other left-wing political groups often used the term ironically amongst themselves. They wanted social change, but knew that 'politically correct' orthodoxies were antithetical to the kind of liberated thought and action that was necessary to bring about justice, and recognised the importance of continually challenging any prevailing norms.[7]

As anti-racist and feminist campaigns gained traction in the second half of the twentieth century, conservatives ramped up their efforts to undermine their credibility. Young people were the vanguard of these movements, and the ire of right-wing ideologues was concentrated on presenting them as dangerous, reckless and immature. Conservative philosopher Allan Bloom's 1987 book *The Closing of the American Mind* accused universities of bringing about the 'homogenization of American culture' and contended that students were no longer capable of critical thinking.* It's an eccentric book, in that it's essentially a grumpy, stuffy white man in his late fifties getting peculiarly upset that twenty-year-olds aren't sufficiently interested in the Great Books and classical music that he's into. (Nowadays he'd get an 'OK boomer', and indeed, philosopher Martha Nussbaum wrote at the time, 'How good a philosopher, then, is Allan Bloom? . . . we are given no reason to think him one at all,'[8] while Noam Chomsky called the book 'mind-bogglingly stupid'.[9]) Yet it was a bestseller, and was pivotal in cementing the view that there was a malaise in the United States that had its origins in universities and young people.

In October 1990, this variety of complaint became tied to the term 'political correctness' when journalist Richard Bernstein wrote an article for the *New York Times* entitled 'The Rising Hegemony of the Politically Correct'. He warned of 'a growing intolerance, a closing of debate, a pressure to conform'.[10] His comments were a reaction to a recent reporting trip to Berkeley in California, where he'd been covering student activism. He criticised the political climate he found there, complaining that 'a cluster of opinions about race, ecology, feminism, culture and foreign policy defines a kind of "correct" attitude toward the problems of the world, a sort of unofficial ideology of the university'.[11]

Since its co-option as a tool of the right, 'political correctness' has enjoyed a high-profile career in the UK and the US, being carted out by politicians and right-wing columnists in response to any sign that the needs or preferences of marginalised groups have been accounted for. In the nineties and noughties, political correctness started to be presented as a threat to all forms of fun: an ever-present killjoy spectre that threatened to ruin comedy, 'banter', costume parties, 'British values' and sex. In the UK, its scope ballooned, and it was used to complain about the excessive bureaucracy of an apparently escalating 'health and safety culture' or 'nanny state'. (In fact, safety regulations were so lax in this period that the hazards at Grenfell Tower were ignored, and many equally flammable buildings were given the green light.[12]) Across the anglophone world, political correctness came to

---

* Bloom refused the label 'conservative', but it's hard to think of a better word to describe his views.

refer to any kind of regulation or threat to conservative values. In 2017, ahead of a vote on same-sex marriage legislation, Australian politician and former prime minister Tony Abbott warned: 'If you're worried about religious freedom and freedom of speech, vote no, and if you don't like political correctness, vote no because voting no will help to stop political correctness in its tracks.'[13]

Universities and young people remain in the crosshairs of anti-PC conservatives. In 2020, the UK government started to refer to a new 'war on woke'.[14] Conservative MP Kemi Badenoch announced that 'we do not want to see teachers teaching their white pupils about white privilege and inherited racial guilt' and claimed that doing so could be illegal. Former UK Education Secretary Gavin Williamson announced the introduction of a 'free speech and academic freedom champion' for universities, tasked with investigating breaches of free speech and issuing fines (because this is exactly how people *opposed* to authoritarianism behave). This was a strange move, because a 2018 parliamentary committee report concluded that 'we did not find the wholesale censorship of debate in universities which media coverage has suggested'.[15] Nor was the idea that students are 'no platforming' – i.e. denying platforms to particular speakers – evidenced. A review of ten thousand student events found that only six had been cancelled (four missed deadlines for paperwork, one was a scam and the other was a Jeremy Corbyn rally arranged without sufficient notice).[16]

A similar story has unfolded in the United States, where there has been a feverish terror about the teaching of 'critical race theory' in schools. Critical race theory is a sub-discipline of jurisprudence that examines extra-legal racist structures and is usually only offered in graduate school, so it's about as likely to be taught to children as fluid dynamics or tensor calculus. What's really going on is that conservatives are referring to any teaching on social justice, and particularly racism, as 'critical race theory', and then trying to get it banned as 'anti-American'. That includes teaching accurate histories of how the modern United States came about. At the time of writing, twenty-seven US states have introduced bills or taken other measures to restrict teaching on racism and sexism.[17]

How did such an extreme situation arise? Conservatives have

undertaken deliberate and sustained efforts to manufacture outrage with the intention of bringing about an ideological shift in educational curricula. One of the architects of this effort is activist Christopher Rufo, who, in early 2021, tweeted the following to his quarter of a million followers:

> We have successfully frozen their brand – 'critical race theory' – into the public conversation and are steadily driving up negative perceptions. We will eventually turn it toxic, as we put all of the various cultural insanities under that brand category.
>
> . . .
>
> The goal is to have the public read something crazy in the newspaper and immediately think 'critical race theory.' We have decodified the term and will recodify it to annex the entire range of cultural constructions that are unpopular with Americans.[18]

What we're seeing is not a genuine issue of social concern that has arisen through the good-faith anxieties of ordinary people, but the construction and bolstering of a straw 'person' (see what I did?) by those in powerful positions, with the intention of fomenting 'moral panic'. Sociologist Stanley Cohen describes moral panics as taking the following trajectory:

a. A new or long-standing phenomenon, trend, or group of people are defined as a threat to societal values and interests. Often, the perceived threat relates to children (e.g. paedophilia), young people (e.g. political correctness), or new technologies (e.g. video games or social media).

b. The object of the panic is presented in a hyperbolic and stereotypical fashion by mass media.

c. Political, cultural, and religious figures warn of the threat and offer solutions. Politicians and media outlets encourage the panic as an easy way of generating interest, support, and chances for opportunistic intervention and the illusion of virtue.

d. Policies or guidelines are developed.

e. The panic then either fades away or becomes ever more visible and threatening.[19]

One of the most common themes of moral panics in contemporary Western contexts is Islam. There are two elements to this moral
panic. The first is that Islam is seen as a threat to 'Western culture'
(whatever that means) and the safety of Western people. The second
is the view that 'political correctness' has gone so far that it is no
longer possible to criticise or guard against the dangers of Islam openly
because to do so would be seen as racist. Rather, 'political correctness'
demands that Islam is tolerated and accommodated at the expense of
others.

In 1997, the UK city of Birmingham was rejuvenating its commercial centre. They had planned forty-one days of events across
November and December, spanning a fundraising event for a children's charity, the opening of an outdoor ice rink, the annual
Christmas lights switch-on, the festival of Divali, theatre and arts
events, and New Year's Eve celebrations. To cut costs, the council
decided to market this disparate, but roughly coincident, package of
events under a joint banner, and cast around for a name that would
cover everything. Eventually, they settled on a portmanteau of 'winter'
and 'festival': 'Winterval'.[20]

No sooner had Winterval been announced than a strange and
enduring moral panic emerged. An inaccurate report in a local newspaper became ammunition for politicians and the tabloid press. The
council was accused of 'trying to take the Christ out of Christmas'
and the bishop of Birmingham suggested that Christmas was being
'censored'. Over the intervening years, the error has been perpetuated by newspapers and has contributed to the urban myth of a 'war
on Christmas' which is reliably rekindled every winter. It is invariably
Muslims who are blamed, a fact that the Muslim Council of Britain
attempted to counter in 2013 by issuing humorous Christmas cards
using the 'Keep calm and carry on' font and the slogan 'Don't panic:
Christmas is not banned.'[21] (It's funny, but also mortifying that they
felt the need to do this.)

Similar myths have arisen elsewhere. In 2016, the Swedish Transport
Administration banned the hanging of Christmas lights from its street
poles, both to minimise electricity use and for safety reasons. The
decision was reported in the US as a 'capitulation to Islam'. Far-right

website *Breitbart*'s Milo Yiannopoulos stated that the lights were 'offending Muslim migrants – the same ones responsible for destroying local businesses'.[22]

In 2016, tabloid newspaper the *Daily Express* published a story with the headline 'New £5 notes could be BANNED by religious groups as Bank CAN'T promise they're Halal'. (This kind of frenzied capitalisation is common in British tabloid newspapers.) The article reported that religious leaders were discussing banning the new, polymer-based £5 banknotes from their places of worship, on the grounds that they contained beef tallow. It is true that Hindu leaders had expressed concerns about the use of cow products in the new note. Cows are sacred in Hinduism, but not in Islam, and no Muslim leader had so much as mentioned the tallow in the new banknotes. Yet 'halal' was included in the headline as a way of stoking rancour towards Muslims even though this particular discussion had nothing to do with them. The paper accepted that is was wrong to print such a headline, and issued a correction.[23]

There are countless other examples of newspapers offering outrageous or exaggerated incidents as evidence of 'political correctness', and subsequently having to publish corrections and pay damages. The myth of a crisis of 'political correctness' requires continual upkeep from politicians and the media. But at the root of their preposterous claims there is a kernel of truth: some of us really *are* pushing for justice-oriented language and policies.

## Sticks and Stones

Freedom of speech is of vital importance. But as with other freedoms, it is limited. For example, while I do, in principle, have the freedom to walk alone at night through any part of town, I am in practice rarely able to exercise that freedom because as a woman there is a real risk to my safety in doing so. While I am entitled to make use of public spaces, if I decided to stand in the middle of the picnic mat of a group of strangers as they ate their lunch, I would ruin their enjoyment of that public space. Similarly, freedom of speech often clashes with other rights we think are important, and some people are able to exercise their freedom of speech more effectively than others. While we are all, in principle, free to speak, for some groups the consequences of doing so are so serious as to keep them silent. Others do not have access to the platforms to be heard, so they might as well be silent. Freedoms are never unlimited and are rarely fairly distributed.

I grew up with the playground mantra: *sticks and stones may break my bones, but words can never hurt me*. It was a spoken amulet to ward off verbal abuse; you chanted it back at those who called you names, as a sort of post-exposure prophylaxis. Adults encouraged it, presumably in an attempt to harden us against the inevitable cruelties of the playground. Yet words do hurt, as anyone subject to cruel or insulting comments can attest. Brain scans suggest that social rejection, of the kind that can be effected through verbal abuse, activates the anterior cingulate cortex: the same area of the brain that lights up when we're subject to physical pain.[24] Further, sometimes words contribute to, or escalate into, sticks and stones; verbal abuse is often a gateway to physical harm. Racism, sexism, ableism, transphobia and homophobia are enacted primarily with words, and where they are manifested through acts of physical violence, these are rarely wordless. Words are not just noises, computer pixels or ink markings. They *do* things.

Many philosophers have noted that in saying something, you invariably also *do* something. If I say 'Black Lives Matter', I thereby *do* many things: express my solidarity with a political movement, criticise the way Black people are treated, and upset conservatives. The reverse is also true: when we do things, we say things. If a footballer takes the knee before a match, through that act she says 'Black Lives Matter' or something along those lines. As feminist legal scholar Catharine MacKinnon wrote 'Speech acts. Acts speak.'[25]

Philosophers refer to any instance of speech that through its utterance does something in the world as a 'speech act'. Speech acts were first formally noted and characterised in 1962 by philosopher J. L. Austin, who observed that 'to say something is to do something'.[26] When we make an utterance, we don't just produce meaningful noises, we actually do something by saying those words out loud. In practice, almost everything we utter does something in the world. An easy example is 'You're fired!' If your boss makes that utterance, the *action* of you losing your job has, by the fact of the utterance, just taken place. Or, in the context of sex, if someone says 'I want to stop' then they have effectively withdrawn their consent, so that the continuation of the sex act instantly becomes a violation, and in some legislatures, a crime. Their words transform the act, if continued, into a moral wrong or legal transgression. Words therefore quite often have the power to modify something in the world just by being voiced.

To give a more everyday example, if, in the context of a meal, I say to my sister 'Is there any chilli sauce left?' I not only ask about the state of the jar of chilli sauce, I also *request* that it be passed to me. My words therefore perform the action of making that request. By contrast, if I was to sing along to Bonnie Tyler while later washing the dishes, that utterance would perform no action in the world. (No hero would appear, even at the end of the night.)

The objection that 'words are just words!' or that 'people should be able to say whatever they like' ignores the important fact that words not only cause certain acts, they are also often themselves acts, and it is much harder to make the argument that 'people should be able to *act* however they like!'

Pornography can be understood in similar terms. In the 1980s, US feminist activists Catharine MacKinnon and Andrea Dworkin worked together to draft an anti-pornography ordinance which would allow those harmed by porn to file civil lawsuits. The judge accepted that 'depictions of subordination tend to perpetuate subordination' which in turn 'leads to affront and lower pay at work, insult and injury at home, battery and rape on the streets'.[27] Yet the ordinance was ultimately deemed to be unconstitutional, as it was argued that regulation would violate pornography producers' right to freedom of expression. This verdict missed the point. MacKinnon and Dworkin were making a much subtler argument. Yes, porn can be understood as speech that depicts women in dehumanising ways, and thereby causes harm to the women it represents. But they weren't just saying that porn *depicts* women in troubling ways, and *causes* women to be treated badly as some undesirable side effect, they were saying that porn is *itself* an act which constitutes harm. It needs therefore to be regulated as harmful action, rather than as harmful speech. Philosopher Amia Srinivasan writes that, for anti-porn feminists like Dworkin and MacKinnon, 'the whole point' of pornography is the intentional speech act of '*licensing* the subordination of women, and *conferring* on women an inferior civic status'.[28] Pornography is able to do this because it is not mere escapism, it is how many people learn to have sex and learn to think of the personhood and preferences of others. Pornography speaks, and by speaking, acts, and by acting leaves women subordinated and silenced.

One of the most famous examples of speech contributing to serious harms is the broadcasts of the Rwandan radio station Radio Télévision Libre des Mille Collines (RTLM) from July 1993 to July 1994. The station was aimed at listeners from the Hutu ethnic group (who were at that time in government), and it stoked existing hatred towards the Tutsi ethnic group, urging Hutus to 'weed out' the *inyenzi* (cockroaches) and *inzoka* (snakes). A million people were killed in the space of a hundred days, most of them Tutsis. The animosity had been encouraged and exploited by the Belgian colonial administration, but the dehumanising, rallying words of the RTLM broadcasts are widely acknowledged to have played a role in the resulting genocide. What begins with words can end with machetes.

Oppressive speech peddles damaging stereotypes, misrepresentations that limit the lives of those with marginalised identities and determine what is possible for them. Girls are told (in direct and indirect ways) that their brains are ill-suited to science and math. (This stereotype is not universal; in Iran, for example, the majority of science and engineering graduates are women.[29]) The end result is that many girls and women believe the stereotype and are discouraged, and the prophecy, the *lie*, ends up becoming true. This is called 'stereotype threat'. In a study evaluating the effects of stereotypes on women's mathematical ability, a group of women were given a 'geometry' test, while a second group were given the same test but it was instead referred to as a 'drawing test'.[30] Women's scores were higher in the second group because they didn't have to overcome a gendered preconception that they were bad at it. There isn't a single reputable scientific study which shows that a 'female brain' is less capable than a 'male brain' (or indeed, that either concept is meaningful) when it comes to mathematical problem-solving or anything else for that matter. Brains are not sexed; they are shaped by what you do with them.

Stereotypes are speech acts. Each time they're uttered, they entrench existing constraints on our behaviour in such a way that the world more closely conforms to their misrepresentations. Stereotypes make girls worse at physics and reduce boys' ability to express their emotions. 'Political correctness' tends to combat stereotypes and may thereby reduce some of the internalised barriers people face, allowing them a better chance of finding something they enjoy and doing well at it. This brings us to the first of a number of anti-PC arguments employed by those wishing to oppose political correctness: concerns about a threat to meritocracy. The idea is that, because of policies such as affirmative action, positive discrimination and 'diversity hires', political correctness places greater emphasis on identity than ability, which drives down standards. This view is typified by author Lionel Shriver's contention that a 'gay transgender Caribbean who dropped out of school at seven and powers around town on a mobility scooter' is more likely to have their writing published even if it is subpar.[31] (It's remarkable that anyone would claim that 'political correctness' has gone 'too far' when public figures casually make statements like this.)

Shriver's claim is as baseless as it is abhorrent. Seventy-six per cent of books published in 2019 in the US were written by white people, who make up 57.8 per cent of the population. Ninety-seven per cent of published authors were cisgender, 81 per cent were heterosexual and 89 per cent were not disabled.[32] The odds for a 'gay transgender Caribbean' person do not look good. And if such a person did break through, they'd likely be paid a lot less than their white counterpart; there is a significant race pay gap for book authors.[33]

Her implication that 'political correctness' pulls down the quality of artistic work is also easily refuted. First, even if prioritising the platform-ing of a broader set of voices *did* lead to a reduction in standards from time to time (and it is telling that Shriver simply assumes that it does), would that really be a problem? Should we prioritise performance above every other consideration? Even if they were mutually exclusive, an unorthodox perspective is at least as valuable as yet another sharp sentence from a Great White Man. Second, Shriver assumes that the system is meritocratic, so that initiatives to increase diversity threaten the opportunities that would previously have been won by talent alone. But success in literature, as elsewhere, is strongly determined by a person's privilege. (I read the Wikipedia entries of all the writers whose work I enjoy, and am dismayed at how many were privately educated.) This is evidenced by the fact that when meaningful action is taken to include under-represented groups, those groups tend to do better, which suggests that their marginalisation or exclusion – economic, social, or both – was previously holding them back. And while privilege tends to produce conditions under which people can thrive in their work, it can also breed underperformance through complacency. A 2017 study showed that introducing gender quotas in Sweden has tended to weed out incompetent men from politics, leading to an overall increase in competence.[34] Similarly, a 2015 report found that the most racially and ethnically diverse companies were 35 per cent more likely to exceed the sector mean for financial returns, while greater gender diversity has been shown to correlate with more radical innovations in research and development teams, and higher levels of cultural diversity have been linked to more imaginative product development.[35] A 2006 psychology study showed that an all-white jury underperformed compared with a racially diverse jury when it came to evaluating the facts correctly in a mock-trial relating to a Black defendant.[36] Not only were jurors of colour more attentive to details and more willing to correct their errors, but their presence improved the performance of their fellow white jurors. The idea of measuring 'competence' or 'performance' is questionable, but such studies give the lie to the unthinking assertion that encouraging greater diversity necessarily comes at a cost.

## The Not-So-Slippery Slope and the Sausage Tantrums

Those who rail against 'political correctness' often argue in favour of a right to offend. It is dangerous, they contend, for us to impose restrictions on expression. They are right to urge caution on this front, but restrictions on speech must be judged in their contexts. Being unable to criticise or insult political leaders without penalty is cause for serious concern. Ridiculing those who have power over us is a reminder that their authority is not absolute. Facing criticism for using a hurtful term to describe a disabled person also limits freedom of speech, but it would be hard to argue that a person needs this kind of speech to be unrestricted, and any attempt to make it so would end up curbing the lives of disabled people in other ways.

Speaking responsibly requires attention to the operation of power. As we saw in Chapter 1, calling a white person a slur that makes reference to their skin tone, like 'milk bottle', is not comparable to calling a Black person the n-word. Neither is kind, but where the first is merely offensive, the second is also a contribution to existing oppression. Anti-PC folks ignore this nuance, favouring one hard-and-fast rule that will grant them carte blanche to speak without criticism or cost. It's not 'free' speech they're after so much as for oppressive speech to be free from judgement or penalty. As Reni Eddo-Lodge writes, in *Why I'm No Longer Talking to White People About Race*, political correctness is 'the final frontier in the fight to be as openly bigoted as possible without consequences'.[37]

This is why the slippery-slope argument against 'political correctness' fails. There is no obvious link between my saying 'please don't say the n-word: it hurts people and entrenches anti-Black racism' and the contention that 'soon no one will be able to say anything'. Arguments of this kind are nonetheless regularly attempted. In response to the rise of the #MeToo movement, Douglas Murray, who writes for the right-wing magazine *The Spectator*, complained that 'The rules are being redrawn with little idea of where the boundaries of this new sexual utopia will lie and less idea still of whether any sex will be allowed in the end.'[38] Imagine hearing women speak out about sexual harassment and concluding that sex is *not possible* in such a world (and then having the white-man's confidence to say so publicly!). There is no obvious stepping-stone from criticising oppressive speech to the sort of unimaginably awful consequence that right-wing commentators gesture towards: the slope isn't very slippery at all.

Douglas Murray's 'soon there will be no sex' outburst is a classic example of the ways in which those who are opposed to 'political correctness' are quick to exaggerate and fly into a frenzy when they encounter new or unwelcome ideas. The number of examples of conservatives losing their tempers over the tiniest change to the world as they once knew it gives the lie to the idea that young, social-justice-oriented people are the ones who are hypersensitive.

While those who pursue the justice-oriented aims of political correctness seek to protect against harm, it's not entirely clear what those who are opposed to political correctness are trying to defend when they object to particular actions or behaviours. At least some of the time, they appear to be expressing a discomfort that we all experience on occasion but few of us feel entitled enough to share aloud: 'The world is changing, I feel left behind and I don't like it!' And interestingly for those whose politics is ostensibly rooted in freedom and individuality, most of these tantrums relate to insufficient respect being shown to prevailing norms and institutions: *People don't respect the flag! That politician didn't bow to the Queen! Why have they let a news-reader appear on television without a poppy? They've offered vegetarian food! Young people eat avocadoes! I heard a language I don't understand in the supermarket!*

There are countless examples that fall into this category. When UK catalogue retailer Argos ran an advert featuring a Black family in 2020, they faced complaints that it was 'completely unrepresentative of modern Britain'. One Twitter user wrote: 'So @Argos_Online isn't interested in white folks then. Fine, we'll use somebody else. See how long @Argos_Online lasts without white customers!!!'[39] (Argos had previously used an advert featuring a family of blue aliens and received no complaints about them being 'completely unrepresenta-tive'.) British television presenter Piers Morgan flew into a sulk when bakery chain Greggs launched a vegan sausage roll (their normal pork sausage rolls were still available). In 2016, American football quarter-back Colin Kaepernick began to take the knee while the US national anthem played at the start of matches, in order to protest against racism and police brutality. Other players soon followed his lead. Donald Trump responded that players taking the knee 'shouldn't be in the country' and suggested that the NFL fire them.[40] (Within a year, Kaepernick found himself frozen out of the NFL as teams blacklisted him for his political views.) A school principal shared a picture of a Nike T-shirt chopped into pieces (Kaepernick is sponsored by Nike) with the post 'When Nike signs an anti-American thug to represent their brand, I will not support, wear, purchase or endorse their product.'[41] In 2017, a Houston teenager was thrown out of her school for refusing to stand during the Pledge of Allegiance.[42] Some French schools have withdrawn all meal options which don't contain pork, to prove they aren't kowtowing to the religious requirements of Muslims.[43] In their fanaticism at making Muslims submit to laïcité (French secularism) by showing that they are grateful, assimilated, sausage-eating French citizens, these schools have also sidelined anyone who doesn't eat pork or prefers to have a choice at lunchtime (thereby encroaching on another French value: liberty). Black British newsreader Charlene White was called a 'black cunt' and was told to 'go back to where you came from' because she chose not to wear a poppy in November, and when then-leader of the Labour Party Jeremy Corbyn wore an anorak to a war remembrance service, he faced accusations of 'disrespect' for not being sufficiently smartly dressed (he was wearing a poppy). Newsreader Jon Snow has also faced criticism, and has described the conservative obsession with the lapel pin as 'poppy fascism'.[44]

One might describe these cases as instances of Conservative Correctness, as writer John Wilson did almost thirty years ago,[45] or 'patriotic correctness' as analyst Alex Nowrasteh did in 2016.[46] Young, social-justice-oriented people are often accused of being hypersensitive 'snowflakes' who are unable to deal with the challenges of real life, but their sensitivity is generally focussed on minimising harm towards marginalised groups. There's a moral sense to it. Those who oppose 'political correctness' tend to be at least as sensitive, but are usually concerned with upholding traditions that already have establishment backing. Nor does the idea that young people won't be able to weather the adversities of 'real life' hold up. What is 'real life' anyway? Those of us who ask for considerate language do so because that's one part of the world we *can* make a bit easier. We should spare one another the indignities we can control. To say that politically correct language is damaging because people must be able to deal

with cruel, inconsiderate utterances is like saying: 'I must be permitted to be racist, because otherwise people won't be able to deal with
racism.' If we can subtract some of life's eliminable harms, we'll have
greater reserves to tackle the harder problems.

## Modern Manners

In my first year of infant school, we were given lessons on manners.
Our teacher solemnly announced a series of inexplicable rules. We
were told that when we ate with our families, we must keep our
elbows down, ask 'Could you pass the salt, please?' and seek permission before leaving the table. (My family sat with our elbows on the
table for the ten minutes it took us to grab and gobble all of the food,
and then dispersed once it was gone.) She urged us to say 'Pardon?'
instead of 'What?' when we hadn't heard or couldn't understand
something. The girls were taught to curtsey, and the boys to bow. All
of it felt arbitrary to me. Even at four years old, I sensed the attempt
to discipline me without good reason, and I resented it.

The baffling demand for 'good manners' followed me to secondary
school, where a teacher told me that it was 'unladylike' for me to curl
my tongue and spit orange pips onto the school playing field. At university, I was walking down a city street with a friend when he was scolded
by a stranger because he wasn't walking on the outside of the pavement
to protect me (a woman) from oncoming traffic or splashed puddles.

Manners determine the forms of social behaviour that are acceptable within a particular culture, and while they often appear to be
arbitrary and senseless, they play an important role in maintaining
social life. They are often used to consolidate social hierarchies, but
they can also be used to encourage care and respect for others.
Politically correct norms of speech and behaviour can be thought of
as a variety of manners, and this comparison is productive in exploring the purpose and potential of encouraging some forms of speech
and condemning others.

The point of manners is to direct the ways in which we behave in
relation to one another, with the intention of bringing about a range

of different outcomes. Some manners are hygiene- and safety-oriented, such as closing the door when using the toilet, removing shoes in living spaces or using a different hand for eating and greeting people than the one used for washing after defecation. These might be thought of as practical manners. Others are primarily concerned with being considerate to the needs of other people, such as holding the door open for a person passing through just after you, or giving up a seat on public transport. Such guidelines have a moral purpose: they remind us to consider the needs of others.

A third category of manners are those symbolic actions whose purpose is to reinforce particular social norms. These sorts of manners are often linked to systems of social stratification, such as gender, race and class, and therefore tend to buttress troubling hierarchies and entrench inequality. In the UK and US, speaking politely tends to require that you say 'ladies and gentlemen' when addressing groups, and 'sir' or 'madam' or 'Mr', 'Mrs' or 'Miss' or 'Ms' when speaking to individuals, thereby emphasising the genders of those addressed. The gendering of clothing is exaggerated for formal occasions; in Western contexts, the everyday androgyny of some variation on jeans and T-shirts is replaced by suits and ties or ornate dresses. Curtseying and bowing are gendered and classed. Those working in low-paid service roles (i.e. waiting staff, retail assistants) are expected in many contexts to refer to the people they serve as 'sir' or 'madam', and to behave in ways that signal their subservience. The idea of 'good customer service' tends to involve low-paid workers being polite – often excessively so – to customers, with no expectation of any of this being reciprocated. It is often considered to be bad manners (and is sometimes contractually prohibited) to disclose your salary or ask about anyone else's, which threatens the ability of workers to identify pay disparities and check they're being fairly remunerated.

A well-mannered man or boy is called a 'gentleman' and is chivalrous with women and girls, i.e. he holds open doors for them, helps them with physically arduous or frightening errands, offers his jacket or sweater when it's cold, walks them home, pays the bill, brings flowers.[47] 'Ladies' don't drink too much, don't sleep around, wear tidy and glamorous but modest clothing, aren't too talkative or loud, don't swear, don't eat too much or do so sloppily or hurriedly. In other words, well-mannered men treat women like children or convalescents, and well-mannered women make themselves presentable, unobtrusive and 'contained, like fine ornaments. Manners help to make gender. As feminist philosopher Marilyn Frye writes:

> The door-opening pretends to be a helpful service, but the helpfulness is false. This can be seen by noting that it will be done whether or not it makes any practical sense. Infirm men and men burdened with packages will open doors for able-bodied women who are free of physical burdens. Men will impose themselves awkwardly and jostle everyone in order to get to the door first . . . There is no help with the (his) laundry; no help typing a report at 4.00 a.m.; no help in mediating disputes among relatives or children.[48]

In a recent UK survey, 72 per cent of people felt that good manners have deteriorated.[49] Respondents were most annoyed by those who fail to say 'please' and 'thank you', and many blame schools and parents.[50] There is a generational divide. Younger people admit that they regularly break with what older people often consider to be good manners: 29 per cent skip queues, 53 per cent don't say 'bless you' when somebody sneezes, and 84 per cent feel that saying 'please' and 'thank you', and holding doors open for people are old-fashioned.[51] This would seem to confirm the view, often expressed by older people, that young people are ill-mannered and inconsiderate.

But the picture isn't quite so simple. Young people have jettisoned some older forms of etiquette and invented or adopted new ones. Swearing is an interesting example. Older people generally find swearing more objectionable: 45 per cent of those over the age of fifty-five report being personally offended by the use of swear words on television, while eighteen- to thirty-four-year-olds tend to swear more and have less of a problem with it.[52] Almost half of those born after 1996 say they use strong language ('fuck', 'motherfucker', 'cunt') frequently, compared with just 12 per cent of those aged fifty-five to sixty-four.[53]

It's important to consider what it is that makes language offensive. While many of us drop 'fucks' left, right and centre, there is another f-word that would never pass our lips. 'Cunt' may no longer be the off-limits 'c-word' it once was, but the *other* c-word – the one that is used as a slur against East Asian people – is out of bounds. Likewise, the n-word has never been so unspeakable. Rather than being concerned with arbitrary questions of propriety, we're instead avoiding words that are designed to hurt people from oppressed groups. This makes sense from a moral perspective, while it's harder to understand the prohibition on generic swear words. After all, they extend our vocabularies and afford us greater emotional range, often by acting as linguistic intensifiers. 'I'm so tired' has nothing of the weariness of 'I'm so *fucking* tired.' Where these words have been used to insult people, they're non-specific: you can call anyone a 'fucking shit'. The other f-word and the n-word are, by contrast, highly *specific*, and are laced with the violence and marginalisation that gay men and Black people endure. As Roxane Gay puts it:

> Don't ever use an insult for a woman that you wouldn't use for a man. Say 'jerk' or 'shithead' or 'asshole.' Don't say 'bitch' or 'whore' or 'slut.' If you say 'asshole', you're criticizing her parking skills. If you say 'bitch,' you're criticizing her gender.[54]

The demands of 'political correctness' are not some gimmicky, pernickety set of obstacles designed to make life difficult; they are instead an expansion of that second category of manners – those that encourage us to be considerate. They are a form of social etiquette that is sensitive to the contours of injustice. Unlike the third variety of manners, that upholds hierarchies of social status (and is thankfully falling out of use), the new heuristics are primarily designed to help us live alongside one another with mutual respect. Political correctness is a set of customs developed by those who want to destabilise sites of power by changing some of the rules of how we behave towards one another.

One of the most basic tenets of the new manners is that you refer to people and groups in the ways they ask you to, and you refrain from referring to them in the ways they ask you *not* to. When dealing with an individual, you use the name and pronouns they tell you to use. It is strange and spiteful to want to do otherwise. (Worse, the urge to name and categorise others against their will is a defining feature of colonialism.) In relation to groups of people, you use the words that have been developed by people from within those groups, and avoid the words they tell you are hurtful.

This isn't always straightforward. In some cases, there's ongoing disagreement about which words are most appropriate, and every few years its fulcrum shifts. For example, there is lively debate about whether to use the term 'disabled person' or 'person with a disability', and disability activists have argued compellingly for each of these positions. The friction and dynamism around these terminologies should be embraced, because that's how we resist settling into orthodoxies and guard against authoritarianism.

## New Taboos

Last summer, a white friend was telling me how racist her secondary school had been in the 1990s. She evidenced this claim by telling me that the p-word (the racist slur derived from the word 'Pakistani') was frequently used. Rather than using the term 'p-word', she uttered the slur in full. I bristled. My family and my partner's family have been harmed by that word, and in our household we think of it as unsayable. The idea of unutterable words is an important but contentious feature of the new manners I've described.

Slurs are harmful words or expressions that serve to humiliate, insult, frighten, demean, express hate, etc.[55] They express contempt and tend to homogenise and dehumanise individuals from the groups to which they refer. They're complex linguistic entities around which a rich philosophical literature has emerged in recent years, but here we only need to consider a few of their basic properties.[56]

Within the contexts in which they're used, slurs are well-established terms, which is to say that most people have a good working understanding of both their conventional targets and the range of harmful messages they are used to convey. This means that the utterance of slurs cannot be studied in isolation, but must be understood as part of the system in which they acquire their meaning and enact their harms.

Slurs tap into and activate damaging sets of background assumptions and thereby strengthen them. Like the stereotypes that they so often draw upon, every time they are uttered, they reinforce a particular kind of world. Calling someone a 'slut' draws on the patriarchal idea that there are 'correct' and 'incorrect' forms and practices of sexuality for women. Without this ideological backdrop, the word 'slut' doesn't mean anything; with it, an utterance of the term harnesses an arsenal of harmful assumptions and restrictions, and in doing so, strengthens them. Consider philosopher Judith Butler's insight that:

> racist speech could not act as racist speech if it were not *a citation of itself*; only because we already know its force from its prior instances do we know it to be so offensive now, and we brace ourselves against its future invocations.[57]

Philosophers make a distinction between *using* and *mentioning* terms; sometimes we use a word, and sometimes we are merely talking *about* that word. If I say 'Racism is harmful' I am using the word 'racism'; if I say '"Racism" gets you ten points in Scrabble', I am mentioning the word 'racism'. It seems intuitive that *mentioning* a slur is not as harmful as *using* one. For example, saying 'Some people call women "sluts"' is much less harmful than 'Some women are sluts.'

Hearing the n-word mentioned is not as bad as hearing it used, but it is much better not to have to hear it at all. Even using the word in print raises issues. Writing the n-word in full here would mean that the audiobook narrator would have to speak it and listeners would have to hear it. Seeing the word on the page might also be harmful. Scientists have shown that when we read, even quickly and silently, we subvocalise: our vocal cords twitch slightly, as though they are uttering the words noiselessly.[58] That means that writing out a particular word forces a reader into a similar physiological state to that they'd be in had they chosen to vocalise it, which seems especially troubling if there's a well-known euphemism at hand.

Mentioning the 'n-word' instead of the slur to which it refers is not just an attempt *not* to say something that is harmful, it's also an attempt to say something. It announces the rejection of a word and the system from which it derives its meaning. It inserts a blip into the conversation, a momentary discontinuity in which the hearer registers that a particular word has been avoided, and is forced to acknowledge the refusal, and be reminded of the importance of repudiating not just that word, but the background assumptions that give it sense.

It is sometimes possible for a slur to be used in casual and harmless ways by people who belong to the affected marginalised group and have gone some way towards reclaiming the term. 'Queer' is a good example: it was once more often a slur than a term of self-identification, and is now almost always used in positive ways. Ta-Nehisi Coates points out that in these cases the identity of the person who uses the word is critical, and others should not assume that the word is thereafter available to them, too.[59] While some books, television shows and films use slurs in order to be faithful to the world they aim to represent, many commentators have noted that the n-word is over-used for its shock value in contexts in which it is possible to convey the horrors of anti-Black racism by other, more thoughtful and informative, means. As Roxane Gay points out: 'The N-word is certainly not a word that has, as many people suggest, been kept alive solely by hip-hop and rap artists. White people have been keeping the word alive and well too.'[60] She grants that its judicious use can be an effective way of conveying the force of racism, but observes that there are a staggering 110 occurrences of the word in *Django Unchained*, which runs for just under three hours. That's two n-words every three minutes in a film that isn't heavy on dialogue. Gay describes *Django Unchained* as a white man's attempt at redemption from the horrors of slavery. And maybe something similar can be said about some white people's determination to *mention* the n-word, often while telling an anecdote that is supposed to evidence their anti-racist credentials. Having such an awful word in one's mouth serves as a form of self-flagellation that is simultaneously tempered by self-congratulation at not being a person who would *use* the word. Not everyone needs to handle a slur to remember how repugnant it is.

Philosopher Renée Jorgensen Bolinger notes that *mentions* of slurs can still indicate offensive attitudes 'ranging from simple insensitivity to perverse pleasure at saying discomfiting words, and disregard for the risk of encouraging derogating uses of the slur.'[61] Regardless of a person's attitude or the context of the utterance, slurs can still be harmful. Psychologists have demonstrated that articulating a slur activates implicit biases and leads to stereotype threat among members of the slur's target group even when the slur is being mentioned.[62]

Slurs are so harmful, and so liable to cause fear and discomfort, that even words that are not being used as slurs, or words that sound like slurs, can be deployed as dog whistles (see Chapter 3) or can cause unintended harm. A friend once described using the idiom 'chink in one's armour' during a lecture (she meant a weakness, or an Achilles' heel). As she did so, she looked up at her class. The only person who made eye contact was a Chinese student, whose face registered a momentary grimace. Her use of that word was unrelated to the slur, but the two became inseparable in that moment – the student *heard* a slur – so she resolved not to use the phrase again.

Other words are similarly troubling despite not being slurs. Consider 'denigrate': a synonym for disparaging or belittling someone or something. The 'de' comes from the Latin for 'away' or 'completely' and the 'nigrate' has the same root as the n-word, both of which can be traced to the Latin word for 'black'. Taken literally, denigrate means to blacken or make something dark. In its usual usage, to denigrate is to insult, abuse or otherwise treat somebody or something negatively. When we use the word 'denigrate' to mean something negative, we reinforce a supposedly obvious relationship between something being dark or black, and something being bad. No doubt the badness of darkness comes not from race but from a sensible fear of the obscurity of night. But the word 'denigrate' and its negativity is now very close to the n-word and its negativity.

In 2017, British tabloid newspaper the *Daily Mail* ran pictures of Meghan Markle's engagement to Harry, Duke of Sussex, with the headline 'Yes, They're Joyfully in Love. So Why Do I Have a Niggling Worry About This Engagement Picture?'[63] This prompted philosopher Liam Bright to joke on Twitter that:

*Daily Mail* headline be like: My Niggling Worries about Meghan Merkel – Is She Too Hung Up on Niggardly Details? We discuss this black mark on her character over negronis while holidaying in Niger.[64]

The idea of unutterable words is not some new-fangled millennial invention. Taboo words are an important part of many cultures, and typically relate to sex (fuck), body parts (dick, cunt, bollocks) and functions (shit, piss), and the supernatural (damn, God, hell). There are also often forms of etiquette around discussing death and illness which demand euphemisms (e.g. saying someone 'passed away'). There are strict guidelines, both formal and informal, about the use and context of these words; for example, in the UK, there are rules about which words can be uttered before the nine o'clock broadcasting watershed. In a great many social contexts, it is inappropriate to swear or discuss sex, excrement or the details of death and dying.

The purpose of taboo words is thought to be the avoidance of topics that relate to activities that are sacred, repulsive or private. Upholding a prohibition on those words helps to maintain the taboo more generally, i.e. if people feel weird about saying 'shit' or 'fuck', that helps to ensure that they continue to treat defecation as a filthy activity to be executed in the correct, sanitary way, and to see sex as a private, rule-governed activity. (It is no coincidence that the prohibition on everyday utterances of the word 'fuck' has correlated with the softening of norms about how we have and talk about sex.)

Requiring that people do not say the n-word is not some petty word game; it's part of a broader set of prohibitions which aim to keep anti-Black racism in the realm of social taboo. The same is true for the p-word in its relationship to racism towards South Asians, the f-word in its relationship to homophobia, and the c-word in its relationship to anti-East Asian racism. If you can't say the word, this reminds you of the *moral* prohibition on a range of associated utterances and actions. By corollary, if a person is disoriented to find that a word is becoming less acceptable, their first response should be to try to understand the associated moral issues.

The last point is helpful in responding to the charge that political correctness amounts to mere 'virtue signalling'. Those who urge care in language are sometimes accused of being unduly concerned with curating the impression of righteousness, rather than pushing for 'real' change. But first, publicly practising virtuous behaviour isn't the manifestly terrible deed that it is made out to be. (This point deserves a chapter of its own!) It can demonstrate the possibility of transformative, solidaristic behaviours, and may lift a person's morale in ways that make for healthier movements.[65] And second, there is no 'mere' language about it. Language is vital to constructing the moral landscape in which we live, and emancipatory language and action are intertwined.

## No One Left Behind

As I write, trans people are fighting for a safe, dignified place in society. Not because they are determined to draw a line between themselves and cis people, but because cis people (among them a worrying number of 'feminists' in the UK, including some prominent public figures) are doubling down on *cis* identities in order to exclude trans people. Trans women, in particular, are being dehumanised *as trans women*. They have no choice but to therefore respond *as trans women*. Hannah Arendt once made this point in relation to Jews: 'if one is attacked as a Jew, one must defend oneself as a Jew. Not as a German, not as a world-citizen, not as an upholder of the Rights of Man.'[66]

Oppressed groups did not invent the identities in which they now live. People of colour would not think of themselves as such had white people not deemed it to be beneficial to construct and elevate the idea of whiteness. Some of those who rail against political correctness claim that they do so because 'identity politics', which focusses unduly on race, gender and other social identities, drives wedges between different groups and further divides us. But such a view gets things the wrong way around. As James Baldwin wrote:

America became white – the people who, as they claim, 'settled' the country became white – because of the necessity of denying the Black presence, and justifying the Black subjugation . . . We – who were not Black before we got here either, who were defined as Black by the slave trade – have paid for the crisis of leadership in the white community for a very long time, and have resoundingly, even when we face the worst about ourselves, survived, and triumphed over it. If we had not survived and triumphed, there would not be a Black American alive.[67]

That said, we must remain attentive to the ways in which fixating too closely on social identities in isolation can leave our movements frayed and toothless. To start with, focussing on individual dimensions of oppression fails to account for the empirical reality that people live within multiple, amalgamated identities. But also, most marginalised people have a great deal in common. Above all, they are more likely to be poor, unsafe and voiceless. Being divided from one another serves none of us well. It plays into the hands of those who are glad to see our resentment turned on each other, rather than towards the places where power resides. (Those on the right are only too glad to feed those divisions. Consider their fostering of the gerrymandered categories of '*white* working classes' or '*white* working-class *boys and men*' as marginalised identities in order to promote loyalties to whiteness and gender and prevent broader class solidarity.) We have to take care to recognise our identities as components of related injustices and not isolated interests or openings for opportunistic division.

Finally, it's important to think carefully about how we help each other to adopt these new justice-oriented manners, and how we respond when people fall short. 'Political correctness' has to be dynamic and receptive to critique. That's what protects it against dogmatism. But its openness to change also means that people can feel left behind, and it'll often be those whose time and resources are limited. This concerns me, because we need movements that are genuinely inclusive, and that make space for learning and forgiveness. Change is intimidating, and there are times when we see the benefit of it, and times when we feel lost, old, awkward, judged or suspicious. We have to guard against getting so caught up in the details that we lose sight of the people the language is supposed to serve.

# 3

## What's Wrong with Dog Whistles?

For too long we have pretended we are tolerant societies in which racism is not a system of oppression but the marginal obsession of the uncouth. In reality we have simply become more sophisticated about our prejudices. We have plenty of racism, but apparently very few racists.

Gary Younge, *Guardian* (26 January 2018)

In October 2020, Sky History advertised a new programme called *The Chop*, in which carpenters complete a series of woodworking challenges in order to demonstrate their claim to the title of 'Britain's top woodworker'. The publicity video featured a burly white man named Darren Lumsden, who calls himself 'The Woodman'. Lumsden's face, scalp and neck are tattooed, and some of those who saw the clip noticed three in particular: an '88' on his cheek in a distinctive German calligraphic font, '23/16' on his forehead, and '14' on his scalp. All are white supremacist signifiers. The 88 picks out the eighth letter of the Latin alphabet, H, denoting 'Heil Hitler'; 23/16 stands for W/P: *white power*, 14 denotes the 'fourteen words' of white supremacy, i.e. 'We must secure the existence of our people and a future for white children.'[1]

Observant viewers raised the alarm, complaining to the broadcaster. When Sky confronted Lumsden, he denied the associations, claiming that 1988 was the year his father had died. Later that week, a newspaper found his father alive and happy to talk to the press, and Sky deleted their tweets defending Lumsden and pulled the whole show.[2]

Lumsden 'The Woodman' is (or, at least, was at the time he was tattooed) a neo-Nazi whose allegiance to his racist beliefs is so strong that he wears them permanently etched into the skin of his head, for all the world to see. Unlike the swastika (which made no appearance on the visible parts of his body) the more obscure alphanumerical symbols just mentioned are not easily identified as racist slogans unless one is particularly sharp-eyed and well informed. Only a select few like-minded people are supposed to notice them.

Like harmful bacteria, racism thrives if it can find shady, unnoticed corners in which to fester. In many contexts, hate speech is regulated by law, and overt racism can also lead to social ostracism, damaging a person's reputation so that they wouldn't be deemed suitable to appear on, say, a television woodworking programme. Sworn racists need ways of communicating their racism to actual or potential allies (while also presumably being able to sometimes flaunt those symbols to intimidate the targets of their hate), without being noticed by too many others. Choosing to conceal a racist slogan in numbers allows its meaning to be denied.

Politically correct language helps to militate against oppressive speech, but most expressions of racism aren't the cartoonishly obvious words and phrases we readily condemn. Implicit forms of racist utterance are much more common. As awareness of racism has grown over time, people have found ways to express their views indirectly, making use of a variety of strategies to thinly disguise their meaning and avoid saying 'the quiet part loud'.[3] Focussing only on overt racism is like pulling up weeds by ripping off only their surface growth. Unmasking indirect racism amounts to tearing up whole clods of roots and watching them wither in the light.

## The Plausible Deniability Defence

The technical term for encoding meaning in such a way as to make it easy to deny is *plausible deniability*. It's a strategy used by those whose message is likely to be seen by others as morally repugnant. In order to protect against condemnation, the speaker builds in a get-out clause.

A common version of plausible deniability is the 'I was only joking' defence. An oppressive comment is made in the hope of garnering the approval and validation of others, but deniability is invoked if the person has misjudged their company and is accused of having said something unacceptable. In these cases, the speaker doesn't deny that the content of the comment was oppressive; they instead deny their *intention* and claim their utterance was meant in jest. This strategy has the clever effect of leaving listeners on the back foot for not having spotted the joke or for not having a sense of humour. One of my colleagues refers to people who use this manoeuvre as examples of 'Schrödinger's bigot'.[4] Alphanumerical head tattoos (unlike swastikas or confederate flags) work in the same way. No one can *prove* such symbols are racist. Their bearer can flatly deny any harmful associations, and that denial will be *plausible* because the utterance or expression was sufficiently vague as to shift some of the responsibility for interpretation on to the listener or viewer. A well-informed person will see through the denial, but it may be harder for them to convince others of the harmfulness of the symbol.

This encoding of one's beliefs or identities is not always nefarious. Marginalised groups often develop forms of identification and communication that evade the notice of potentially hostile outsiders. In 1892, for the opening night of *Lady Windermere's Fan*, Oscar Wilde asked his gay friends to attach green carnations to their lapels, which thereafter became a way of gay men identifying one another (use of a subtle form of recognition was essential: in the UK, homosexuality carried a prison sentence of up to ten years).[5] Or consider the 'handkerchief code' used primarily by gay men in the US in the 1970s, in which the colour of a handkerchief attached to one's right or left pocket indicated one's sexual preferences in a way that would only be recognised by those in the know.[6]

## On Not Saying What We Mean

In order to understand the various ways in which people express racism without committing to it directly, it's important to acknowledge just how common, useful and socially acceptable indirect speech is. Every day, we say things whose literal, face-value meaning is different from our intended connotation. For instance, saying, at the end of a date, 'Do you want to come in for coffee?' is often an expression of openness to having sex. When in an unfamiliar city, asking a stranger 'Are there any pharmacies near here?' means 'Tell me how to get to a pharmacy.' Or saying to someone in a bar 'I'm actually meeting my boyfriend later' means 'Go away, I'm not interested.'[7]

Understanding indirect speech requires acquaintance with the particular context in which the speech takes place, which is something most of us manage to clock accurately and effortlessly. Yet a person who lacks the linguistic or cultural familiarity or the conversational competence to understand how a given utterance is supposed to be taken might only hear the literal meaning of the utterance. So when you ask 'Are there any pharmacies near here?' you could be met with a response that takes the question at face value, but misses the point: 'Oh yes, there are several: this city has excellent healthcare infrastructure.' Or, if at the end of a date, someone asked 'Do you want to come in for coffee?' and their companion responded 'I don't actually like coffee', they would likely assume this was a joke or that their meaning had been misunderstood.*

There are lots of morally unproblematic reasons for indirect speech. Politeness and diplomacy are key motivations. In many cultures, people speak obliquely in order to avoid appearing vulgar or pushy. Iran, my father's homeland, is famed for its intricate etiquette, which requires excessively indirect speech, known as *taarof*. According to *taarof*, you must decline any offer of hospitality, but your host must interpret your refusal as mere politeness, and continue to insist. By

---

* Or, of course, this could be intended and received as a fairly blunt rebuff, with both parties understanding the subtext of the offer (and refusal) of coffee.

cycling through several rounds of offering and refusal, you and your host may eventually surmise the truth through the subtle particulars of your evasions. Perhaps they'd really like to feed you and will be insulted if you don't oblige them; maybe you're really hungry. In other cultures, too, indirect speech is used to avoid awkwardness or embarrassment. An invitation to have coffee is ambiguous enough for its rejection to be easier to deliver and doesn't sting in the way refusing an overt offer of sex might. Speaking indirectly can also make space for plausible deniability. Responding to the offer of coffee with 'I'm not interested in you in that way' leaves the other person the option of objecting (whether truthfully or not) 'That's not what I meant! I just want to carry on our conversation.'

Indirect speech has become progressively more important for those expressing oppressive views in the public domain because overt instances of oppression are more likely to be met with condemnation, legal challenges or reputational damage. To be accused of racism is to be socially marked, and even those who are unambiguously racist resent being labelled as such.

In the US and UK, there is now a widespread belief that racial equality has been achieved and that most people have long abandoned racist beliefs (see Chapter 5). Many people claim to be 'colour-blind', which is partly why 'all lives matter' is such a common response to the 'Black Lives Matter' movement, and the awkward challenge it poses to the notion that we have collectively overcome racism. In this new world of presumed racial equality, most people are primarily concerned with not being perceived or described as racist by others. Avoiding that badge of shame is often more important than avoiding *being* racist. The end result is that, as Gary Younge says, we live in a society full of racism but 'apparently very few racists'.[8]

One can generally avoid the charge of racism by adhering to some basic heuristics, such as: *Don't use obvious racist slurs. Don't repeat obvious racist stereotypes. Don't endorse obviously discriminatory policies. Don't claim that white people are superior to other groups. Don't signal support for historic racist policies like slavery, genocide, or segregation.*[9] Staying above this woefully low bar isn't difficult, and even as the costs of being publicly branded as racist have heightened, people have easily adapted

to the environmental change by evolving forms of linguistic camou-
flage. They have learned to be racist in ways that minimise the chance
of being branded as such. That involves choosing one's words carefully, with close attention to one's company. As Roxane Gay writes in
*Bad Feminist*:

> There is a complex matrix for when you can be racist and with whom.
> There are ways you behave in public and ways you behave in private.
> There are things you can say among friends, things you wouldn't dare
> say anywhere else, that you must keep to yourself in private . . . Most
> people are familiar with these rules.[10]

In a 2017 UK study, 74 per cent of people claimed to be 'not preju-
diced at all' towards those of other races, a percentage that has stayed
more or less constant over the last thirty-five years.[11] But the details of
this survey offer a crucial insight. Only 18 per cent of participants
answered yes to the question 'Are some races or ethnic groups born
less intelligent?' yet this percentage rose to 44 per cent when the question was recast as: 'Are some races or ethnic groups born harder
working?' There is a straightforward explanation for the discrepancy
in the responses to these closely related questions, both of which are
proxies for the racism of respondents. Intelligence has long been such
a visible, hotly contested flashpoint of racist discourse that statements
relating to the cognitive capacities of particular groups are widely
recognised as being abhorrent. Most respondents spot that this question is a measure of racist attitudes and respond according to their
self-perception as a non-racist person. Being 'harder working' has few
if any obvious associations with racism, so respondents are more
comfortable agreeing that there are differences at birth, which is to
say, *genetic* differences, in relation to this trait. Changing the language
of the question offers a glimpse of what people *think* they should
believe, compared with what they really believe.

Our tendency to speak indirectly produces opportunities to encode
messages that will be obvious to some and not others, with the
comfort of deniability, or to envelop hateful content in ways that activate biases without hearers having to admit their own prejudices.

Indirect speech grants a degree of moral leeway that is especially useful to politicians seeking to capitalise on the widespread support for racist policies that was seeded by those who came before them. Their messaging must be phrased in such a way as to broadcast the racist content without triggering the sort of overt racist associations which could lead to public opprobrium or disruptions to a voter's self-image, but which leaves the listener in no doubt as to the commitment to maintaining particular hierarchies.

## Dog Whistles

As we get older, we hear less of the world around us. Our skin loses its elasticity and slackens, our metabolisms slow, our bones weaken and fray and we gradually lose our hearing, starting in the high-frequency range. It's called 'presbycusis'. The loss sets in early: by twenty-five, most of us cannot hear sounds in the highest frequency ranges which are audible to younger people. This fact has been exploited in the dystopic installation of high frequency 'ultrasound' emitters as anti-loitering devices in places where young people are deemed to be a nuisance, which produce an irritating whine only they can hear. Teenagers have themselves made use of this technology, employing high-pitched alert tones on their phones so that they can use them in class without their teachers hearing and confiscating their devices.[12]

Dogs can hear even higher frequency sounds than young humans. That's partly why they're so perturbed by fireworks: the high frequency whirring we hear amid the bangs is a deafening riot to them. In 1876, English scientist Francis Galton invented a whistle whose central frequency was around 39kHz, which meant it was audible to dogs and cats, but couldn't be heard by humans, whose upper limit is about 17 kHz. This meant it could be used to train or discipline domestic animals without annoying people within earshot. The dog whistle (also sometimes known as 'Galton's whistle') is still a popular, inexpensive piece of kit for dog owners and shepherds.

It's fitting that Galton is associated with the dog whistle, because the term 'dog whistle' has since become synonymous with racist speech, and Francis Galton is sometimes referred to as the father of eugenics, the study of the 'improvement' of the human gene pool by the elimination of 'inferior' people. Galton believed that intelligence was entirely down to genetics, an inference he drew from studying around 600 'great men' who had written influential works in the previous 400 years and realising that many of these men were related to each other. (The more obvious explanation this sloppy scientist was missing was the fact that most 'great men' come from the same social class. The fact that he and his great-man cousin, Charles Darwin, had both been raised in wealthy, eminent families seemed not to occur to him.) Galton set about measuring people with the aim of determining who was fit to reproduce, and who ought to be prevented from doing so. His ideas were critical to the concept of racial purity which underwrote the development of Nazism in Germany and laws against interracial marriage and sexual relations in the United States.

Nowadays you can pick up a dog whistle in a pet shop, but you're much more likely to hear the term in relation to political speech. Political dog whistles are symbolic versions of Galton's invention. Like high frequency whistles, they play on the idea of selective audibility. Dog whistles sound like ordinary statements, but encode specific political signals which are heard only by those who are primed to interpret the meaning in a particular way. They're therefore a variety of indirect speech.

The concept of a dog whistle first entered political discourse in the 1980s, when the polling director at the *Washington Post* noted that, when surveying respondents to determine their voting intentions, 'Subtle changes in question-wording sometimes produce remarkably different results . . . researchers call this the "Dog Whistle Effect": Respondents hear something in the question that researchers do not.'[13] Hearing dog whistles is not something that requires any particular guile or codebook. Dog whistles activate existing associations, some of which are held explicitly and some implicitly. So while those who formulate and utter dog whistles generally know what they're doing and set out to manipulate hearers, those who hear them often have no idea that particular associations are being activated, or at other times they recognise the indirect meaning and respond to it consciously. Meanwhile, those who don't hold the association may be wholly oblivious to the hidden message.

One of the most common dog whistles in political speech is the reference to 'hardworking families'.[14] It's frequently uttered by politicians, particularly those hoping to appeal to conservative voters.[15] When a politician refers to 'hardworking families' they're communicating several messages. First, the word 'families' is doing a lot of heavy lifting in ensuring hearers realise that this politician is interested in the institution of the heteronormative family as a traditional, 'natural' social unit, which tends to appeal to socially conservative voters who may oppose same-sex marriage, abortion and the disruption of stereotypical gender roles. The term 'family values' can also be used to denote 'Christian values' without alienating non-Christians.

Second, the word 'hardworking' signals the repudiation of those in receipt of welfare. Welfare recipients are often portrayed as being feckless and work-shy. Further, there is a widespread association between welfare and people of colour: consider the idea in the United States of the 'welfare queen' who, thanks to racist stereotyping, is typically understood to be Black, or the idea in the United Kingdom that immigrants are illegitimately reliant on the state. (In both cases, there are good reasons – viz. the effects of structural racism – as to why a person of colour may be more likely to require welfare payments.) Reiterating a commitment to 'hardworking families' is a way of politicians indicating that they're going to be hard on those who receive state welfare, especially people of colour, who are deemed to be unworthy of resources that are the rightful due of white, autochthonous people. By drawing on these existing associations, a politician can project socially conservative, anti-welfare, racist and xenophobic views through a phrase that not only sounds harmless but has intuitively positive connotations.

The idea that a government should do right by 'hardworking families' is difficult to argue with, and since the intended meaning of the phrase resides below the surface, it's hard to prove what a person *really* means when they say it. It's a dog whistle: a phrase that says one thing yet, to those who are sufficiently tuned into the context to hear in another register, means something else. And the fact that the surface meaning and the real meaning differ ensures that dog whistles come with built-in plausible deniability. If someone does hear the racist undertone, you can insist that they're hearing something that isn't there: they're 'reading too much into things', 'twisting your words' or being 'paranoid'.

In 2014, Republican politician Paul Ryan discussed a new report on poverty on the *Morning in America* radio show. He proposed that introducing work requirements for those in receipt of welfare would help to tackle the 'real culture problem' which afflicts men in 'inner cities'.[16] He was (quite rightly) accused of racism. 'Inner city' is one of the oldest racist dog whistles in the book. Like its synonym 'urban' it is used to refer indirectly to poor Black people, conjuring up danger, violence and crime in ways that have been repetitively linked, in media and political representations, to Black men in particular. Likewise, Trump's contention that Joe Biden is a 'servant of the radical globalists'[17] was intended to suggest that Biden is a pawn in some global economic conspiracy, which is a common antisemitic trope.

Identifying dog whistles is important to recognising the agendas of those who utter them, and cutting short their intention of manipulating our political views and decisions. Another familiar dog whistle is to refer to Barack Obama by his full name 'Barack Hussein Obama'.[18] On the face of it, this is harmless: after all, that really is his name. Yet we don't usually use middle names unless people refer to themselves that way, and if his middle name was John or Walker, say, it's unlikely that anyone would care to state his name in full. Hussein (حُسَيْن) is most commonly used among Shia Muslims; the dog whistle is an Islamophobic one. For many Americans, the name is most strongly connected with Saddam Hussein, and this association – with a callous dictator of an 'axis of evil' country – is also activated. It's supposed to emphasise some connection between Obama (a Christian raised in a non-religious household) and Islam, and it is used by people who expect their listeners to associate Islam with racist stereotypes, invoking danger, brutality, alienation and terrorism.

Dog whistles do not *explicitly* state their coded message; the reader or listener's familiarity with the context of use completes the association. We read or hear between the lines. For example, if I claim that international banks are part of our global capitalist system, that is not an antisemitic statement. But if a political candidate whose opponent is Jewish were to say 'Do you want to be ruled by international banks or do you want a politics for ordinary people?', where the opposing candidate had no major policies relating to banking, I would assume that was an antisemitic dog whistle, alluding to racist ideas about Jewish people secretly controlling the global financial system. Similarly, 'childless' is, in almost all contexts, merely a description of a person's relationships.* Yet if a gay candidate or woman candidate is referred to as 'childless' by their opponent, I would assume that was a dog whistle intended to activate homophobia or sexism.

Dog whistles play a prominent role on social media, where they serve several functions. The first is to avoid removal of content by moderators. Using a dog whistle rather than a more obviously objectionable phrase means that users can evade the algorithms designed to find and delete patently harmful content. Second, they allow people to 'find their tribes', especially where their primary use of social media is participation in racist, sexist, transphobic or otherwise oppressive conversations with like-minded people. Users often place these dog whistles in the 'bio' section on Twitter, where they're most visible to potential followers. Those who include the term 'gender critical' in their Twitter bio generally use their accounts to produce or share transphobic content. Those whose primary fixation is with nationalist forms of racism may have a particular flag in their bio.[19] In the UK, those who include the St George's flag in their name or bio on Twitter outside the context of a live international sports tournament tend to use the platform to endorse nationalist content. (This is not true of all flags. Like words, they must be taken in their broader political context.)

Political scientist Tali Mendelberg has carried out experiments to study the effect of dog whistles on political beliefs.[20] She examined the influence of political advertisements on the racism and political inclinations of participants, and found that adverts that are explicitly racist have no impact on beliefs, because people spot the racism and

* Though some prefer the more positive 'child-free'.

distance themselves, thereby blocking its effects, while adverts that are implicitly racist tend to make participants' views more racist and drive their policy preferences further to the right. Implicit racism works by activating the existing prejudices of hearers or viewers without violating their belief that they are not racist.

This empirical result, which has been replicated by other researchers,[21] is important for those looking to disrupt the manipulative effect of political dog whistles. While such dog whistles are morally slippery because of their built-in plausible deniability, if those exposed to them can be convinced of their connection to explicit racism and their intention to influence political discourse in underhand ways, there is hope that racist dog whistles can be brought into the fully audible range and be repudiated.

## Figleaves

Indirect forms of racism can be powerful, but sometimes there is greater political currency in expressing racism more overtly. Such occasions call for another strategy which gives a free pass to barefaced racist utterances without running the risk of being called racist. This is achieved via a technique that philosopher Jennifer Saul refers to as the use of racial 'figleaves'.[22] Figleaves are utterances that are made *in addition to* an overt racist statement in an attempt to draw attention away from, or take the sting out of, its offensive content, in much the way that depictions of the Garden of Eden have Eve and Adam covering their genitals with figleaves after they have eaten the forbidden fruit. A figleaf is used to negate, soften or complicate a racist utterance, blocking the usual inference and leaving the hearer befuddled and less able to object. As with genitals, conversational figleaves don't actually provide much cover, but offer just enough concealment to be socially acceptable. And just as a figleaf over one's genitals is liable to make them even more conspicuous, so too do conversational figleaves tend to put the spotlight on the harmful statements they're supposed to conceal, which makes them surprisingly easy to spot once you know what to look for.

The act of figleafing racism is so common that there are many different sub-varieties which are deployed in everyday conversation as well as in political speech. The most basic and familiar Saul describes is the 'denial figleaf', which involves prefacing a racist remark with, 'I'm not racist but . . .' When I was a teenager, I recall a friend, in the process of complaining about her boss, saying to me: 'You know me, I'm not racist, but you just can't trust Chinese people.' I was dumbfounded, and couldn't quite see how to point out that her statement was racist in spite of her denial. The figleaf succeeded.

Another common variety of figleaf is the 'friendship assertion' figleaf, which relies on the specious idea that a person who is friends with a person of a particular race cannot possibly be racist to other people of that race. This is the trick that is deployed to discredit accusations of racism by stating: 'I have lots of Black/Muslim/Jewish friends . . .' In 2019, pictures emerged from the medical school yearbook of Ralph Northam, governor of Virginia, in blackface, standing beside a person dressed in the hood and robes of the Ku Klux Klan. A childhood friend of Northam's responded to the subsequent widespread outrage with the defence that 'He is the last person on earth that would be racist. We have just as many black friends together as we do white friends.'[23] Northam's friend used *two* kinds of figleaf: the denial figleaf, and the friendship assertion figleaf.

My father, who worked for decades as a schoolteacher, was often drawn into situations in which the friendship assertion figleaf was at work. In the staff room, his colleagues would openly make racist remarks about people of colour (using much less polite terms) and immigrants. My father would sip his tea in discomfited silence, and they'd sometimes reassure him with a cursory 'Oh, Matt,* you know we don't mean you. You're not like the others; you're all right.' The assumption seemed to be that because they felt no antipathy towards my father, they were somehow rendered immune from any accusations of racism towards 'the others'. Such routines are common, and they

---

* My father's real name is Masud, but he settled on Matt after tiring of hearing it mispronounced and having it be seen as a continual prompt for 'Where are you from?' conversations.

tend to draw the exempted person of colour into a complicity with the racism. (Sometimes that complicity is so seductive as to convince the listener that they deserve to be singled out, and others deserve the racism they face.) My father did not feel empowered to speak up for himself and others without being seen as overly sensitive or ridiculous. More than that, he felt the need to be friendly and civil to his colleagues. His job was hard enough without making trouble for himself, and it was clear in such a context that the complaints of a person of colour would not be taken seriously. Though he did not intend it that way, and had little choice in these scenarios, his silence ultimately eased along their racism. Had they been called out by others, they'd undoubtedly have said, 'Well, Matt was right there and he never had a problem with it.'

A correlate of the friendship assertion figleaf is the strategy of having institutional racism expressed by a person of colour. The British government makes liberal use of this tactic. Some of the cruellest asylum policies of recent years have been dished out by home secretaries Sajid Javid, Priti Patel and Suella Braverman, all people of colour and the children of immigrants. Speaking about those seeking asylum, Javid vowed to 'do everything we can to make sure that you are often not successful';[24] Patel spearheaded a policy to criminalise those who attempt to save asylum seekers in trouble at sea, and suggested forcing all new arrivals to wear electronic tags on their ankles; Braverman stated that asylum seekers were 'invading' the south coast of England, and described the deportation of asylum seekers to Rwanda as 'my dream, it's my obsession'.[25] In 2020, Black MP Kemi Badenoch announced in parliament that teaching white privilege in UK schools as an uncontested fact was illegal, as was supporting the Black Lives Matter movement, or discussing defunding the police.[26] The government's strategy has been to guard against accusations of racism by making people of colour the public faces of their most obviously racist policies. In these cases, the people themselves act as figleaves. This is not to suggest that they are necessarily mere mouthpieces for racism (all of the above appear to be enthusiastic architects and champions of such policies) but that they are carefully selected to promulgate views that are widespread among their white colleagues.

A third variety of figleaf relies on the *use–mention* distinction, which was outlined in Chapter 2. In most cases of racism, a person *uses* a racist statement. In a 'mention figleaf', a person says something racist by *mentioning* that utterance, rather than using it. This allows them to create some distance between their own views and the racist view they're expressing. Recall Donald Trump's tendency to attribute his racism to unspecified others, via phrases such as 'A lot of people are saying . . .', 'Everybody's talking about it.', 'I've heard that . . .', 'A lot of people tell me . . .'[27]

Mention figleaves are incredibly powerful because even though the speaker does not explicitly endorse the racism they mention, the fact that they repeat it, especially via platforms that reach large audiences, propagates the view in much the way it would if they *had* endorsed it, while allowing them deniability ('I wasn't saying *I* feel that way, I was just referring to what others have said!'). Mention figleaves are common in everyday conversation, where they often involve the speaker using something they read in a newspaper, heard on the television or radio, saw on social media, or that was uttered by a public figure, as cover for their own views. They might say: 'What do you think about all these migrants coming over in boats? Nigel Farage was on breakfast television the other day and *he* was saying they're all pretending to be in need of asylum.'

One of the reasons that figleaves work so well is because when we think about oppression we tend to focus on the *intentions* of the speaker rather than the effect of their speech on others. If we see racism as a property of a few bad people, then as long as someone can convince us that they're not a bad person or didn't *intend* any harm, it seems churlish to call them racist. Further, intentions are private. Others can make assumptions or impute intentions to me, but I always have the option of denying their charges and leaving the accuser looking like the one who has a problem. Figleaves for racism therefore introduce messiness and uncertainty. They make the listener doubt herself, and thereby pose an additional barrier to identifying an utterance as racist.

The uncertainty that figleaves produce also lets us off the hook when it comes to calling out racism. As Saul puts it, the presence of a figleaf 'removes the otherwise uncomfortably present obligation to object to racism'.[28] No one can blame you for keeping quiet when the situation was so ambiguous, so silence is more easily excused. This is the most dangerous feature of figleaves: unlike dog whistles, figleaves leave instances of racism right out there in the open, relatively immune to challenge. And once the ice is broken on the utterance of a racist statement, the public conversation shifts. If we hesitate, or fail to object, the acceptability of the statement inches forward.[29] Others are emboldened, and they may not feel the need to speak indirectly. Racism becomes incrementally more acceptable.

## What Everyone Else Is Thinking

Dog whistles and figleaves are an important part of contemporary political discourse, but overt racism is also staging a terrifying come-back, invigorated and accelerated by 'plain speaking' recent or current political leaders such as Donald Trump, Boris Johnson, Narendra Modi, Recep Tayyip Erdoğan, Rodrigo Duterte, Jair Bolsonaro, Vladimir Putin, Viktor Orbán, Norbert Hofer and Benjamin Netanyahu, among others. The two trends are connected; these figures rely on indirect racism as a gateway to the manifestly racist policies they enact once in power. Dog whistles and figleaves clear a path for unasham-edly oppressive political decisions. If we can spot and block the former, we might have a better chance of averting the latter. As legal scholar Ian Haney-López puts it: 'We have learned to see racism in the spittle-laced epithets of the angry bigot. We must also learn to see racism in the coded racial entreaties promoted by calculating demagogues.'[30]

What came first, overtly racist leaders, or the voters who feel such an affinity for their views? It's a bit of both, with the cynical finagling of the news media plaiting the two forces together. The recent shift in the acceptability of barefaced racism has reminded us that hateful views rarely go extinct on their own, but instead lie dormant, primed for the incitement of scheming politicians and unscrupulous journalists. Again and again, in the last few years, I've heard people say – of the political leaders just mentioned, but also of the likes of Jordan Peterson and Nigel Farage – *They're just saying what everyone else is thinking.*

In a world in which, despite our public disavowals, racism still thrives in the private rooms of our lives, the politician who stands up in public and says it out loud in a barefaced utterance, or tempered by a figleaf, or else coded into a dog whistle and a wink, is liable to sound like the most honest person of all. He's seen as the brave one, casting off the shackles of 'political correctness' and daring to utter what so many others would surely say if only they were courageous enough to bear the consequences. By contrast, the politician who repudiates racism in the articulate, polished terms in which most well-trained public figures speak is taken to be spinning a veneer of equality to service their own image, or, if they're a person of colour, to be 'playing the race card'.

Racist public figures tap into the racism that pervades the bedrock of our society, and is usually covered over with politer forms of speech. And in bringing more of that racism into the open, they assuage some of the shame. But they also push the boundaries of acceptability in such a way as to normalise racism, to make it legitimate, reasonable, and further entrenched.

The range of acceptable political views is sometimes referred to as the 'Overton window' or the 'window of discourse'.[31] In order to become politically viable, a position must be gradually brought within the range of the Overton window. Political commentator Joshua Treviño has theorised that the process of an idea becoming mainstream moves in several stages: what is at first unthinkable becomes radical and eventually acceptable, sensible, and sufficiently popular to be written into policy.[32] In the last decade alone, new forms of racism have moved from the unthinkable to the popular, and, under some of the aforementioned leaders, have become policy. (Trump's border wall and Muslim travel bans are obvious examples.)

How can anti-racists win against such rigged odds? We have to beat the *I'm-only-being-honest* folks at their own game by being more direct than they are. We have to get better at hearing and keeping track of the dog whistles, spotting the figleaves, and calling things out for what they are. We have to meet their 'refreshingly frank' comments with a flat-out declaration of racism, and offer plain-spoken truths in their place: about economic oppression, about divide and rule, about how the media stabilises the status quo.

As we saw earlier in this chapter, experiments have shown that when dog whistles are exposed, they're no longer so effective. The same is true of figleaves, which work best when they catch the listener on the back foot and leave them too confounded to object to an obvious instance of racism. Once you see a dog whistle or figleaf for what it is, its power to manipulate your political views is neutralised. Our job, then, is to expose instances of these strategies as vocally as possible.

# 4

## Is It Sexist to Say 'Men Are Trash'?

'Why do men feel threatened by women?' I asked a male friend
of mine . . . 'They're afraid women will laugh at them,' he said.
'Undercut their world view.' Then I asked some women
students . . . 'Why do women feel threatened by men?' 'They're
afraid of being killed,' they said.

Margaret Atwood, Second Words (2011)

In June 2019, Brazilian gaming influencer Gabriela Cattuzzo was
dropped by her sponsor after responding to sexual harassment on
Twitter with the retort, 'This is why men are trash.'[1] While many of
her followers offered support, she faced fierce criticism, including
death threats, for her choice of words. Around the same time,
Facebook regularly removed 'men are trash' posts as instances of hate
speech.[2] A few months after Cattuzzo's comment, Mark Zuckerberg
tried to explain his company's policy:

> gender is a protected category. So substitute in your mind while you're
> thinking through this, what if this were 'Muslims are trash,' right? You
> would not want that on the service . . . So then you get to this ques-
> tion on the flip side, which is, 'Alright, well maybe you want to have
> a different policy for groups that have been historically disadvantaged
> or oppressed.' Maybe you want to be able to say okay, well maybe
> people shouldn't say 'women are trash,' but maybe 'men are trash' is
> okay.
>
> We've made the policy decision that we don't think that we should
> be in the business of assessing which group has been disadvantaged or

oppressed, if for no other reason than that it can vary very differently from country to country.[3]

While no one is suggesting that Facebook should be 'in the business of assessing which group has been disadvantaged or oppressed' (God forbid), as we saw in Chapter 1, it's not difficult to establish which social identities are associated with historical oppression and which with privilege. In fact, men being trash is one of those few things that doesn't vary from country to country. It is modified through its interactions with other social identities – e.g. sexuality, class, race, nationality – so that its precise nature and degree vary, but it's always the same group resenting being laughed at while another group worries about being killed.

Even so, 'men are trash' is a generalisation, and conventional wisdom has it that generalising about people is unfair. As Zuckerberg points out 'Muslims are trash' is obviously unacceptable. So is 'women are bad drivers' or 'poor people are lazy'. Clearly, there are some generalisations any decent person would object to. But how are we to tell which are reasonable, and which not?

## The Birth of #MenAreTrash

Gabriela Cattuzzo's incendiary tweet cited a well-worn complaint. The phrase 'men are trash' had found its way into popular parlance a couple of years before, when women in South Africa took to social media to denounce the violence of men. Two cases in particular were the final straw. In April 2017, Sandile Mantsoe stabbed his ex-girlfriend Karabo Mokoena and then set fire to her body in an attempt to conceal his actions. In court, he described the murder: 'I put a tyre around her and burnt her . . . I put petrol on her and walked away.'[4] A month after Mokoena's death, toddler Courtney Pieters was poisoned, raped, and killed by a man named Mortimer Saunders.[5] The brutality of these killings caught the nation's attention, as had South African athlete Oscar Pistorius' fatal shooting of Reeva Steenkamp in Pretoria four years before. A raft of shameful statistics were ploughed into the public consciousness, among them the fact that a woman is murdered every four hours in South Africa, and in 50 per cent of cases, the killer is an intimate partner.[6]

A month after Mokoena's murder made the news, #MenAreTrash was the most popular Twitter hashtag in South Africa.[7] Before long, it had gone global, and every few minutes in the intervening years, someone has tweeted #MenAreTrash, usually appended to a post that details the inconsiderate, cruel or violent behaviour of men. The hashtag collects these incidents in a constellation of online solidarity which adds to the compelling case against normative masculinity. The phrase serves as a balm for those who have been wronged, a way of connecting with others who've had similar experiences, and as a small act of defiance. While 'men are trash' is often a glib, tongue-in-cheek middle finger, it's also a statement of moral condemnation.[*]

The hashtag has collected at least as many detractors as proponents, and the backlash is an important part of what makes it an interesting object of analysis.[8] In some quarters, resentment at its perceived divisiveness exceeds indignation at the harms that make it apt. It therefore requires careful justification. It's hard to deny that there is something wrong with men, but we must be clear about the nature of the problem.

## Evidence of Trashness

In the last thirty-eight years, there have been 117 mass shootings in the US, amounting to around three a year.[9] One hundred and thirteen of them – 97 per cent of the total – were committed by men acting alone. (Just three have involved women acting alone.) Around 86 per cent of male shooters had previously abused a partner or child, and half of the attacks specifically targeted women.[10] These are sobering numbers, but in some ways the US is a global anomaly, in that its gun laws and gun culture make mass murder a chillingly mundane affair. (Feminist scholar Uma Narayan has pointed out that while those in the US often point to dowry murders in India as an example of extreme gendered

---

[*] 'Trash' is an Americanism. Its British cognate is 'rubbish', whose adjectival form isn't sufficiently condemnatory to do the work of 'trash'.

violence, which they are liable to blame on Indian cultures, the same people rarely acknowledge that domestic violence in the US is much more lethal than dowry murders in India, and should also be seen as a form of 'death by culture'.[11]) But even in countries where guns don't outnumber people, the statistics are just as dispiriting.[12]

In the UK, half of all murdered women are killed by their partner or ex-partner (compared to 3 per cent for men), amounting to two women every week.[13] It has taken me two years to write and edit this book, and in that time more than three hundred women in the UK have been killed, 92 per cent by a man, and around half by a current or previous partner. We all have some small risk of being murdered, but statistically speaking, women ought to be most worried about men they've been romantically involved with, which forces upon us the cognitive dissonance of conceiving of lovers as potential killers. Further, those who attempt to leave abusive partners are more vulnerable to murder than at any other time in their lives.[14] Walking away is not as straightforward as it's often made out to be.

Returning to South Africa, where the hashtag began, the idea that such men are just a few 'bad apples' is insupportable: 56 per cent of the 2,600 South-African men surveyed in a 2015 study admitted to having beaten or raped a woman at least once in the previous year.[15] Studying men's attitudes gives some clue as to how these behaviours are perceived. In a recent questionnaire in Australia, a third of young men said they thought that accusations of rape amount to a woman regretting sex, one in five believed that domestic violence is a normal reaction to stress, and almost a third felt that rape occurs because men can't control their need for sex.[16]

Damaging behaviour clearly isn't limited to murder and rape. At the less extreme end of the spectrum are a variety of peculiar and limiting practices. A few years ago, my friend Matt told me about a strange custom at his Catholic school. Every morning, a teacher would deliver a sermon and lead the school in collective prayer. The teachers and the girls would bow their heads and close their eyes. For the boys, it was more complicated. They came from religious families; regular attendance at church was a prerequisite for admission to the school. But they also held the view that closing your eyes in prayer was effeminate, a sign of weakness or probable homosexuality. How to balance these competing pressures? The boys would pray with *one eye closed and the other eye open*. Every single one, every single morning. Their one-eyed prayer had the advantage of allowing them to keep an eye (literally) on each other. It's a funny image until you wonder what happened to the boys who closed both eyes.

Masculinity is characterised by displays of power and dominance, and the suppression of weakness or vulnerability. It requires its adherents to practise and exhibit courage, assertiveness, independence and physical strength, and often rewards aggression, violence and exaggerated displays of (heterosexual) sexual appetite. It is hostile to departures from cisgender, heterosexual norms, and punishes women who threaten male supremacy or refuse to prioritise the emotional or physical needs of men. Only 3 per cent of UK adults associate masculinity with kindness or care, and just 1 per cent with respectfulness, supportiveness and honesty.[17] More than half of young men feel they must not ask for emotional support even in times of need, and two-thirds feel compelled to display hyper-masculine behaviours.

The pressures to conform to the ideals of masculinity start much earlier than the one-eyed prayer. Small boys are still very likely to be told, directly or indirectly, that expressions of sadness, pain, compassion or love should be avoided. The messaging comes from all sides. In 2021, a parent posted on Twitter that: 'Yesterday a male teacher openly mocked my son for turning back at the school gate to wave goodbye to me. Today my son said he wants to stop waving from now on. This is how it starts.'[18]

Men are less likely to cry and are judged more harshly for their tears. In a recent experiment, people were asked to watch a video of an employee's response to being criticised at work, and rate the person for competence and leadership. Participants' assessments of a woman employee in tears were not affected by her crying,* but a tearful man was rated as less competent, with weaker leadership skills, than in the same actor's dry-faced

---

* Note that estimations of women's competence in the workplace tend to be unfairly low to start with (see Chapter 6) and the ability to cry without social penalty is a corollary of the fact that a more general and damning social penalty is already in place (see Chapter 1).

video.[19] Men cry less often because they're punished for their tears and learn to suppress outward displays of emotion. The fact that men now typically cry twice as much as their fathers did shows that social, rather than biological, limitations are at work; masculinity is slowly becoming more permissive of men's emotional expression.[20]

Disrupting these harmful norms can be tricky, because challenges to masculinity are themselves triggers for trashness. Studies show that if a woman begins to earn more than a man within a relationship, he's more likely to cheat on her and reduce his contribution to household chores as a way of protecting what remains of his dominant status.[21] Similarly, across every socio-economic group, a man who is unemployed is more likely to assault a female partner.[22] In another study, researchers asked participants to fill out a survey in which they read a list of adjectives (such as 'competitive' or 'kind') and were asked to select those which best described their personality. Afterwards, they received feedback on their answers. This 'feedback' was pure invention: some were chosen at random to be told they were more masculine than others on the basis of their answers, others were told they were more feminine. In follow-up surveys, men whose gender identity was threatened by the feedback they received (i.e. those who'd been told they had more feminine than masculine qualities) increased their support for war, male supremacy and homophobia.[23] Women's reported attitudes didn't change if they were told they had more masculine than feminine traits.

When men are unable to meet the demands of masculinity, the consequences can be catastrophic for all involved. Consider the case of forty-two-year-old Steven Sueppel, who in March 2008 was await-ing trial for embezzlement and money laundering, having stolen half a million dollars from the Iowa bank he worked for. He'd been fired five months before, and faced a hefty prison sentence. His wife, Sheryl, had returned to work as a teacher in order to support the couple and their four young children. Sueppel never made it to trial. At 6.31 a.m. on 23 March, he made a terse 911 call, requesting that the police go to his home immediately. Five minutes later, he floored the accelerator pedal and sped his car into a concrete pillar on the motorway near his home. It burst into flames and he burned to death. When the police arrived at the house, they found the bodies of Sheryl and the children, their heads and torsos beaten with a baseball bat.[24] In his suicide note, Sueppel described his embarrassment about the criminal charges he faced, and his worries about leaving Sheryl to provide for the children in his absence (something she'd been doing for months at this point). He wrote, 'For these reasons you can see why this is clearly the best choice for me and my family.' He expected his reader to agree that it was 'clear' that his wife and children were better off beaten and dead, and to agree that the 'choice' that they should die was his to make.

This case may seem extreme, but Sueppel belongs to a well-populated category of men who have murdered their families and then killed themselves. He is what criminologists call a 'family annihilator', his crime a 'familicide'. On average, a familicide takes place in the US once every week.[25] Annihilators are almost always middle-aged white men with successful careers who've just experienced a major stressor.[26] They are invariably unknown to mental health teams, and are often described as doting husbands and fathers.[27] (Though note that around two-thirds have a history of domestic violence.[28]) Philosopher Kate Manne describes the behaviour of family annihilators as 'entitled shame'.[29] These men have experienced adultery, bankruptcy, criminal investigation – difficult life events, by any measure – and they feel frightened and humiliated. To resolve that shame by destroying one's family is a strongly gendered exercise of entitlement. Writer Catharine Skipp describes annihilators as having a 'narcissistic sense of chivalry' – they convince themselves that they are acting benevolently, that it is an extension of their gendered role as 'provider' to annihilate those for whom they can no longer provide, and thereby preclude any further failure on their part.

If one end of masculinity's injurious spectrum is men slaughtering those dearest to them, the other is an assemblage of irrational, obstreperous, uncooperative attitudes and behaviours. Men have been found to associate recycling, carrying reusable shopping bags and other environmentally conscious behaviours with femininity and homosexuality, and are accordingly less likely to engage in them.[30] Similarly, studies have shown that men protect their masculinity by littering, driving instead of travelling by foot or public transport, and eating lots of red meat.[31] When their masculinity is threatened, men have been shown to respond by defensively ordering and consuming meat.[32] The association of men with meat holds true across cultures and languages. In Japan, men who aren't deemed to be sufficiently masculine are sometimes called *sōshoku-kei danshi*, or 'herbivore men'. A 2012 study of twenty world languages with gendered noun class systems (like Thai, French and Hindi) found that words associated with meat are significantly more likely to be 'male' words (i.e. those in French that are preceded by 'le').[33] Masculinity, which is often condemned for being 'toxic', is literally toxic to the environment.

The other pejorative adjective that typically precedes masculinity is 'fragile'. Masculinity is riddled with the insecurity, fear and vulnerability it so aggressively abjures; it has little robustness against violation or challenge, and even minor infractions can be met with hostile or violent reactions. As bell hooks wrote:

> patriarchy demands of all males that they engage in acts of psychic self-mutilation, that they kill off the emotional parts of themselves. If an individual is not successful in emotionally crippling himself, he can count on patriarchal men to enact rituals of power that will assault his self-esteem.[34]

Not only do men hurt and kill women, they also hurt and kill other men and themselves. Eighty per cent of homicide victims globally are men; 95 per cent of murderers are men;[35] men make up 75 per cent of suicides.[36] If all this pain, violence and killing isn't cause for serious moral concern, I don't know what is. We can say mass shootings are a problem, that the murder of intimate partners is a problem, that rape culture is a problem, that domestic violence is a problem, that suicide is a problem, or we can take a step back and concede that there is something seriously wrong with masculinity.

## Gender and Masculinity

One of the reasons people get so upset when they hear 'men are trash' is that they interpret 'men' to be a reference to *sex*, which they take to be fixed, leaving men forever condemned to trashness. The slogan is much more powerful if it's understood as a generalisation about gender.

Sex is a socially constructed category which refers to the range of differences in chromosomes, hormones, gonads, genitals and the secondary sexual characteristics that develop during puberty, e.g. widened hips, thick facial hair, broad shoulders and enlarged mammary glands. None of these serves as a firm basis for sex. Most of us will never have any reason to know anything about our chromosomes, let alone anyone else's. Genitals are also generally a private matter unless you know a person intimately, and they lie on a spectrum, not a binary. That leaves us to make judgements based on fat distribution, bone structures and body hair, all of which are tremendously variable and highly modifiable by diet, exercise and cosmetic alterations, which are mediated by gender. In other words, while sex is often seen as the straightforward element of the sex–gender system, it's actually quite complicated, and is often inflected with the effects of gender.

Gender refers to the division of roles, behaviours and styles of self-presentation into two categories, which are then mandated for some people and forbidden to others. Like sex, gender is a social construct, which is to say that it's collectively constructed by human beings living in a society. That doesn't mean it's not real (tenancy agreements are constructed by human beings but you're still expected to pay your rent!); it just means that it doesn't follow from the biology of our bodies or any deeper laws of nature. Gender is best understood as a lifelong performance with two sets of scripts, assigned in infanthood on the basis of genitals, and rehearsed under the direction of seasoned performers until children get the hang of it and start to follow the rules without noticing they're doing it. It's an act that is taught to each generation by those already encultured.

When we say that men are trash, we are talking about those who are *gendered* as men and, accordingly, follow the script of masculinity. This is not the same as claiming that people with particular genetics, gonads, hormones, genitals or secondary sexual characteristics are trash. That would be unfair and ridiculous, because there's no good evidence that our behaviours in relation to one another within complex societies are determined by biology, even if some of the basic functions of our bodies are.[37] Instead, we're talking about the cultures that people follow, entrench and police.

This leads to a couple of important caveats and difficulties. First, if men behave in the ways they do because they are raised into strict cultures that punish them for doing otherwise, in what sense can we blame them? Yet if the alternative is to denounce the culture and pardon the individual violence and selfishness it fosters, that seems unsatisfying and unlikely to bring about change. Sociologist of masculinity Andrea Waling has criticised the way in which 'toxic' masculinity implies a noxious force to which men are unwittingly subject, rather than a set of practices that they collectively reproduce.[38] (The same criticism could be levelled at the cognate term used in China: *zhí nán ái*, which translates as 'straight man cancer'.) Toxic masculinity also implies the existence of a 'healthy' masculinity, when such a thing seems unlikely or even contradictory. Gender is itself a system of division and hierarchy. Finding ways to make it more palatable misses the deeper moral issues. (A corollary of this is that femininity is also a damaging culture. I've devoted less attention to its harms because femininity tends to be overwhelmingly injurious only to women, while masculinity hurts all of us.)

Masculinity is both collective and individual. It cannot be correct to claim that any one man authors the harms of masculinity single-handedly. But nor can it be right to say that individual men are blameless or powerless to bring about meaningful change. It is, after all, individual men, in the privacy of their homes, who beat, bully, rape and kill their partners. It is also individual men who tell their sons that they mustn't cry, and who forgo vital opportunities to show them that comfort and tenderness can come from men as well as women. It is individual men who mock their friends for expressions of emotion or self-care. It is individual men who hold their tongues when, in the private spaces they share with other men, dehumanising comments are made about women or other marginalised groups. Every small act of resistance carries the possibility of giving another man permission to defy the harmful expectations of masculinity.

Second, men are never *just* men. There are commonalities between masculinities across cultures, but there are also contextual variations, and masculinity is mitigated by the influence of other identities, e.g. being trans, gay, racialised, disabled, poor. To take an example, the sexual violence of men is facilitated by the fact that in most societies women are systematically disbelieved and men are not challenged or held to account. But that leniency comes in degrees, and is much more readily extended to wealthy white men and boys. Racialised men and boys are liable to be suspected of violence as a matter of course, especially where white women and girls are the (real or presumed) victims.

Just as whiteness makes promises that are materially advantageous to only a small number of white people, masculinity makes grand promises to men – *You will be treated with respect and esteem, women will care for you, etc.* – which are more realisable for some men than for others. The vast majority of men are poor and powerless, their male 'privilege' a currency rendered almost worthless by other oppressed identities or by bad luck. They lead lives of thwarted promises and are ill-equipped to manage their disappointment, which can lead to shabbier displays of dominance, often directed at women. There is a broader point to be made here: gender-based privilege is not as simple as whether a person is a man or a woman, it is a question of the extent to which that person successfully conforms to the ideals of femininity or masculinity. Non-binary and gender non-conforming people, as well as gay people and many trans people, are automatically punished for falling short, but so too are cis men who are not sufficiently 'masculine', and cis women who are not sufficiently 'feminine'. These ideals often also embody racism, so that people of colour routinely face specific penalties.

## Not All *Men? Not* Only *Men?*

Of course, not *all* men are trash. Family annihilators and mass shooters constitute the tiniest of minorities. And while other harmful behaviours are more pervasive, there are men who mostly manage to resist them, whose efforts should be recognised, if only to encourage others to do the same. Further, given that 'men are trash' is a derogatory generalisation applied to a social group, surely it counts as hate speech, as many social media moderators claim?

The moral basis for outlawing hate speech is that it causes harm, but in a patriarchal system, it's hard to see how 'men are trash' could gather the power or pervasiveness to harm men. Besides, 'men are trash' intends to *combat* hate; its target is the culture of masculinity, whose harms (including those done to men themselves) are serious and structural. Publicly criticising masculinity may even contribute to its destabilisation in ways that are liberating for those men seeking to evade or resist its pressures and punishments.

Further, the conduct that 'men are trash' criticises – entitlement, forcefulness, failures of empathy – doesn't tend to hold men back, and often advances their interests. Contrast this with 'women are irrational', which feeds a baseless stereotype that limits women's lives. A recent study carried out by *Fortune* analysed hundreds of pieces of workplace feedback and found that women received more negative comments, and were frequently criticised for being 'irrational', 'bossy' and 'abrasive', words which did not appear in men's feedback.[39] (The closest adjective used to describe men was 'aggressive' but in every case the recommendation was that he be *more* so.) The stereotype that women are irrational holds them back in the workplace, and also leads them to be taken less seriously by doctors, law-enforcement officials and interlocutors in arguments. It's hard to think of a scenario in which the phrase 'men are trash' limits men's pursuit of their own interests in the same way.

'Not all men' is the most common rejoinder to the claim that men are trash, as well as to reports of sexism more generally. (People don't tend to protest that 'men *aren't* trash'. Instead, they say 'not *all* men are trash'. It is widely accepted that many men *are* trash.) Tackling the 'not all men' objection puts the spotlight on men who *aren't* a problem, rather than those who are. This has the effect of derailing the discussion and trivialising the original grievance, which is sometimes exactly the intention. One of my favourite illustrations of the uselessness of the 'not all men' response was captured in a tweet by Kate Zasowki, who writes for the feminist satire site *Reductress*: 'Last night a man got out of his car and followed me, yelling, while I walked to my apartment . . . but then I remembered Not All Men and felt peaceful n safe 😊 🙏 '[40]

On the topic of derailing, there's an important comparison to be made with domestic violence. Whenever I've attended an event about domestic violence, a man has popped up to point out that men can also be victims. He's right, and they almost certainly under-report their experiences in order to protect their masculinity, so the problem is probably worse than we think. (Regardless of gender, victims of domestic violence tend to under-report because of fear of retribution, hopelessness about the alternative options, conflicted feelings about the perpetrator, financial anxieties and worries about being disbelieved, among other reasons.) Yet even accounting for that, domestic violence is nonetheless overwhelmingly a gendered phenomenon in that women are almost always the victims, and men are almost always the perpetrators.[41] Where men and boys experience domestic violence, it's generally at the hands of a man. That doesn't mean that we shouldn't take domestic violence towards men and boys seriously. But if the only time men raise this issue is in response to discussions about violence against women and girls, that looks a lot like an attempt at distraction rather than a constructive move towards protecting other men and boys, or a way of putting the two sets of concerns together and spotting the problem in common.

We could try to acknowledge the fact that not all men are trash by instead saying something like 'some men are trash', but in practice, such a statement wouldn't do the job. First, it wouldn't preserve the meaning or intention of 'men are trash'. Of course some people, regardless of their gender, are trash. That goes without saying. The point is that there is something specific about *masculinity* that increases the probability of trashness. 'Men are trash' is specific: it picks out a particular correlation between masculinity and trashness. Second, 'men are trash' isn't just a statement about men. It's also a speech act. It expresses anger and frustration for which there are few other outlets, and its citation indicates solidarity with others who've used the term before, drawing together instances of sexism to emphasise their prevalence. Responding to cases of sexual harassment or assault with 'men are trash' can also ward off victim-blaming by unequivocally attributing the wrong to a man's actions within an enabling culture. The phrase embodies discontent, condemnation and a determination to goad men into doing better.

Any attempt to soften 'men are trash' would also be a pity because its archness is intentional. To return to the chapter's epigraph, sometimes 'men are trash' is also a way of laughing at men. Given how much power they hold, it is very important that we find ways to laugh at men. Besides, justice requires provocation; in the words of Frederick Douglass: 'Power concedes nothing without a demand. It never did and it never will . . . The limits of tyrants are prescribed by the endurance of those whom they oppress.'[42] 'Men are trash' represents the limits of the endurance of those harmed by masculinity, and it should be seen not just as an utterance, but as a demand for justice. Gabriela Cattuzzo's statement that 'men are trash' arose from her frustration and anger at the sexual harassment she faces. Those who responded by claiming her outburst was an act of hate speech, or who protested that 'not all men are trash', missed the point. When someone says 'men are trash' they connect sexual harassment to masculinity. That's not an act of hate, it's an act of illumination. (By contrast, saying 'women are trash' is necessarily an expression of hate because women are oppressed *as women*.)

In saying 'men are trash' we also have to acknowledge that the harmful expectations of masculinity are not only entrenched and policed by men, they're also supported by many women. Cultures are collectively produced, and lots of women expect men to adhere to the damaging ideals of normative masculinity, and contribute to policing their behaviour and punishing them when they fail to measure up. Such women are not rare; consider the 53 per cent of white women who cast their ballots for self-confessed 'pussy grabber' Donald Trump, voting against their best interests and those of other white women as well as people of colour.[43] The psychology of what might be seen as gender betrayal is complex. Women who cheerlead patriarchy adopt a coping mechanism that's common among marginalised people: in the face of their oppression, they adapt their preferences to align them with the demands of the system that harms them, because that's a safer and less disappointing short-term strategy. Sometimes it's easier, and can feel more consensual, to accept your relegated place and insist it's for the best. But while some women support masculinity and the system that enables it, they are still much more likely than men to be harmed by it. As philosopher Lorna Finlayson puts it: 'Both men and women are worse off under patriarchy, relative to the inhabitants of a post-patriarchal world' *but* 'women are worse off under patriarchy, relative to men'.[44] Because of that asymmetry, it seems fairer to begin by making demands of the men whose self-serving behaviours sustain patriarchy, rather than the women whose lives are so constrained that they end up abetting their own subjugation.

Yet there's another important reason why 'men are trash' is an acceptable statement, and it has to do with the way that language works. In order to understand this, we need to dig deeper into the philosophy of generalisations.

## Learning from the Philosophy of Language

Generalisations are linguistic shortcuts that are critical to human communication. A generalisation is a statement which turns individual observations about the world into more general statements that apply to many different cases. They're critical to normal conversation, and we make and use them all the time. At some point when I was a toddler, I noticed that leaves were green. In fact, I probably learned the concept of green precisely from my parents pointing to the leaves on plants or trees, and saying 'green', until my brain connected the visual cue with the auditory representation. I formed a generalisation: *All leaves are green.*

Yet I'd have quickly discovered, when autumn came, that this generalisation is false. Purple beech trees and bright red Japanese maples would have further challenged my belief that *all* leaves had to be green. But the greenness of most leaves is still an important part of what it means to be a leaf. So the greenness of plants is an important property, and a less strong generalisation is still apt: *Leaves are green.*

Both of these generalisations describe the same property of leaves, but the first is what we call a 'quantified statement', because it gives a sense of how many leaves are green, i.e. *all* of them. (Other examples of quantified statements are: '98 per cent of the leaves are green' or

'none of the leaves is green' or 'the majority of the leaves are green'.)
The second is what we call a 'generic generalisation' because it doesn't
give any idea how many leaves have to be green, it just draws our
attention to their greenness as a property we ought to take note of.

According to ordinary language use, 'men are trash' doesn't mean
'*all* men are trash'. They're different kinds of statements. The second,
'all men are trash' is a quantified statement because it gives a sense of
how many men – all the men – and if even one of those men turns
out not to be trash, then the statement is false. But in order for 'men
are trash' to be true, it's not clear how many men have to be trash: the
precise number is unspecified. This is a 'generic generalisation'. We
tend to use 'generics' to draw attention to patterns which may not
always apply, but which have particular importance for the speaker
and listener.

Generics are therefore generalisations where the number of cases
necessary for them to be true isn't stated, but the correlation they
express is important. They are often accepted as true even at low prevalence rates, especially where they describe something dangerous or
noteworthy.[45] Consider the uncontroversial statement: 'ticks carry
Lyme disease'. Most of us would agree that's true. In fact, only about
1 per cent of ticks are carriers, but we accept this generalisation because
it's helpful in reminding us to be careful of ticks. (Note how ridiculous
it sounds to object 'not all ticks'.) In this way, generics can act as *warnings*. 'Men are trash' is the warning I heed when I hurry through town
alone at night or jog in wooded areas. The thing with men, as with
ticks, is you don't know which ones to look out for. British Comedian
Joe Wells made this point succinctly and hilariously on Twitter: 'TV
Idea: #NotAllSnakes/ Men who say "Not All Men" are introduced to
a variety of snakes. Not all of them are venomous.'[46]

So, unlike universal, quantified statements that say 'all' and 'none',
the truth conditions for generics are sensitive to their context and the
message they're intended to convey. They're frequently used in
common parlance, as they offer succinct, memorable guidelines for
navigating the social world, while quantified statements can be clumsy
and require greater sophistication and more detailed knowledge of
exact numbers. Indeed, it's been shown that infants as young as two

can grasp certain generics, and they are frequently used to teach children about the world through straightforward patterns and associations ('dogs go woof', 'roads are dangerous', 'leaves are green').[47]

Generics have some strange properties which emphasise their context-dependence. Most people happily accept the statement that 'ducks lay eggs', despite acknowledging, on reflection, that male ducks obviously don't, but they won't accept the generic 'ducks are female' even though it is precisely those same female ducks that can lay eggs.[48] The first statement seems true and informative; the second is false and unhelpful. Yet both statements apply to the same 50 per cent of ducks. This reminds us of the importance of context. The first statement tells us something important about ducks *compared to many other animals*. And because we are experienced language-users, we intuitively know that this is what's being communicated. The second statement has no such broader contextual aim, and so comes across as misleading or false.

Generics are invaluable tools. They convey real patterns in the world, but they leave room for exceptions to those patterns. They allow us to say 'Black people face police violence' and 'trans women's health needs are underserved'. Not *all* Black people, or all trans women, but generics can manage that. Philosopher Katherine Ritchie has argued that this property makes generics especially suitable to describe structural features of the world:

> Racial, gender, and other social generics can be useful because they accurately describe systematic patterns of injustice. An apt description of structural oppression requires capturing that it is widespread, general, and systematic. Generics capture general structural patterns in a way that overtly quantified statements do not.[49]

'Men are trash' is a generic generalisation. It doesn't mean *all* men are trash, it means that trashness is correlated with being a man in a way that's worth noting and reflecting on. As we've seen, there's ample evidence for that correlation, which gives reason to be wary of men. The phrase also functions as a provocation and as a statement of moral condemnation and of resistance.

Generics are just linguistic tools and, like any tool, they can be misused. These misuses deserve mention because generics are more vulnerable to misapplication than other generalisations since they're hard to disprove, and their meanings can be subtle and counterintuitive (as with the ducks above). This means they can be deployed to make statements which manipulate or promote misunderstanding. Since generics can be accepted as true even when the number of cases is small (as with ticks) or unspecified (as with men), this leaves open the option of forming generics which express problematic stereotypes and which are hard to challenge, for example 'boys don't play with dolls' or 'Black men are criminals'.* While it's true that Black men in the US are six times more likely to be incarcerated than white men, and that most boys don't play with dolls, generics cannot be properly evaluated without considering the context in which they're used. Two questions must be asked: *First*, why is this generic being uttered? Or, to put it another way: what speech act is the speaker aiming for? 'Black men are criminals' feeds anti-Black racism, and saying 'boys don't play with dolls' aims to admonish and humiliate those who do. *Second*, if there is some truth to the generalisation, why does its pattern hold? Black men are disproportionately incarcerated because of systemic racism in the economic, legislative, and justice systems. Boys don't play with dolls because they're shamed for doing so. We should resist these generalisations and others like them by interrogating the frame of reference.

Interestingly, the people who get most upset by the term 'men are trash' are often those who use a similar generic generalisation – 'boys will be boys' – when a boy or a man has behaved in a way that is foolish, selfish or harmful. 'Boys will be boys' is, at face value, a circular, meaningless statement. But again, it's a speech act. It is almost always intended as an excuse, along the lines of: 'boys will be foolish, selfish or harmful and *they cannot help being those things*'. It implies that such behaviours are a biologically determined property of men and boys. It's important that we firmly reject this unscientific claim, and recognise trashness as a

---

* Another is 'women have uteruses'. While many women have uteruses, some don't. This generic is most likely to be used to exclude trans women.

product of social forces, rather than evolution. To accept that masculinity is a contingent, mutable characteristic is to realise that things can be different.

## Taking Out the Trash

A year after Zuckerberg made his statement about #MenAreTrash, Facebook had a change of heart and conceded that not all forms of offensive speech are equally bad. Accordingly, its algorithms were redesigned to account for differences in the degree of harm a contemptuous comment can cause.[50] 'Men are trash' is no longer taken as seriously as statements such as 'gay people are sickening' or 'women are sluts'. Facebook places these latter, oppressive statements, and others like them, in a category labelled the 'worst of the worst'. (They could have just said 'oppressive' but tech bros like to feel innovative.) At the other end of the spectrum are low-priority statements that are less likely to cause harm and where there's only a weak consensus that the phrase is a problem. The name of this category? The 'men are trash quadrant'. Perhaps things are moving in the right direction.

Not everyone will accept the arguments in this chapter, but to the men who claim not to be trash and resent the generalisation: what are you doing to stop the men around you from trashing your reputation? Are you raising your sons to be sensitive to the needs of others? (Are you raising your children at all?) Are you compassionate to the men in your life? Do you condemn remarks that demean women, even when everyone else laughs and chalks it up to harmless locker-room talk?

In a 1983 speech, feminist theorist and activist Andrea Dworkin lamented that men do almost nothing to confront and challenge the wrongdoing of other men. She was tired of hearing men complain that feminists were misrepresenting them:

> And I say: don't tell me. Tell the pornographers. Tell the pimps. Tell the warmakers. Tell the rape apologists and the rape celebrationists and the pro-rape ideologues . . . There's no point in telling me. I'm only a woman. There's nothing I can do about it. These men presume to

speak for you. They are in the public arena saying that they represent you. If they don't, then you had better let them know.[51]

While there are no easy answers to the harms of masculinity, the carceral 'solutions' that are so often put forward promise only to make matters worse. Hurting those who have hurt others is so obviously a way of escalating harm. It's a solution that comes straight out of the masculinity rulebook: when someone steps out of line, make them suffer until they act right. Nor do I think that it is appropriate or helpful to respond, as some people do, by suggesting that men should just 'go to therapy'. There's an online meme which presents variations on this strange put-down (e.g. 'Men will literally run for president instead of going to therapy' or 'Men will literally go sit in the bathroom for 3 hours to poop instead of going to therapy'[52]) and a raft of associated op-eds.[53] These articles and posts seem oblivious to the fact that therapy is affordable to only a tiny proportion of people, which is a much more determinative barrier than anyone's gender. Further, while therapy may help some individuals to manage personal difficulties, it leaves large-scale social problems more or less intact. But most importantly, individualising the problems of masculinity is a diversion from a more robust solution, in which men – not therapists or women – routinely provide care for each other, as well as for the other people in their lives.

I hold out hope that men's efforts can change the culture from within. And whenever men are ready, the rest of us will work with them to undo the damage. As bell hooks writes, we must 'recognize patriarchy as a system women and men support equally, even if men receive more rewards from that system. Dismantling and changing patriarchal culture is work that men and women must do together.'[54]

As we witness the rise and rise of 'strongman' leaders whose violence and grandstanding endangers all of us, 'men are trash' is a provocation that dares us to imagine something more wholesome. Trashness is not the biological destiny of men, and recognising its contingency gives reason for optimism. Boys need not be boys.

# 5

## Do All Lives Matter?

The very serious function of racism . . . is distraction. It keeps
you from doing your work. It keeps you explaining, over and
over again, your reason for being. Somebody says you have no
language and so you spend twenty years proving that you do.
Somebody says your head isn't shaped properly so you have
scientists working on the fact that it is. Somebody says that you
have no art so you dredge that up. Somebody says that you have
no kingdoms and so you dredge that up. None of that is necessary. There will always be one more thing.

Toni Morrison, 'A Humanistic View' (1975)[1]

In June 2020, a white couple cancelled their contract with wedding
photographer Shakira Rochelle after discovering that she had posted
a message of solidarity with the Black Lives Matter movement on her
social media accounts. The couple explained that:

we cannot bring ourselves to support anyone who is so outspoken on
matters that simply do not concern them as well as someone that does
not believe that ALL lives matter . . . We would be truly embarrassed
to have you at our event and feel that you aren't stable enough to
complete the job we need from you.[2]

The photographer replied to inform them that the deposit was non-
refundable, but rather than keep it, she would donate it to a Black
Lives Matter organisation: 'I wish you a lifetime of growth and I
would like to thank you for your donation to Black Lives Matter.'

Around the same time, Donald Trump described 'Black Lives Matter' as a 'symbol of hate'.[3] In the UK, Premier League football teams displayed 'Black Lives Matter' on the backs of their shirts instead of their surnames, prompting MP Ben Bradley to remark:

> whilst what they are trying to achieve is very positive and laudable, what they will actually achieve by choosing to support 'Black Lives Matter' is to increase and further entrench division. When you start to push everyone to identify themselves by the colour of their skin, that is not a good thing![4]

What exactly do we mean when we say 'Black lives matter'? Why is the rejoinder 'all lives matter' so misguided and damaging? How much of the backlash arises from ignorance, and how much stems from deliberate attempts to undermine challenges to anti-Black racism? Attempting to justify such an obvious and basic moral assertion as 'Black Lives Matter' might be seen as the kind of capitulation that Toni Morrison warns against. But there is considerable misunderstanding around this slogan and others like it, and even if a great deal of that confusion has been manufactured, the stakes are too high for the record to be left uncorrected. This chapter offers arguments that might bring some clarity to these discussions and help us to think beyond them.

## What Does BLM Mean?

The Black Lives Matter (BLM) movement grew out of the 'our lives matter' hashtag that trended in 2013 after George Zimmerman was acquitted of murder, having shot dead seventeen-year-old Trayvon Martin when he was walking back from a corner shop in Florida, sweets and drink in hand. A year later, eighteen-year-old Michael Brown was just two days off starting college when he was killed by a police officer while walking down the street. The slogan went viral again, this time as 'Black Lives Matter'. It became the signifier for a large, decentralised, non-hierarchical network of activists, founded by three Black women: Patrisse Cullors, Alicia Garza and Ayọ Tometi. Over the ensuing six years, the phrase itself caused more controversy than any of the actions carried out in its name. It looked set to remain on the margins of political respectability.

BLM entered the mainstream as a political demand in 2020, after three police officers fatally shot Breonna Taylor in her bed in Kentucky and, just two months later, police officer Derek Chauvin choked George Floyd to death by pushing a knee into his trachea in Minnesota. It was the middle of a pandemic; all our lives had been knocked off kilter. Stuck at home and glued to the news, there was a focus, simultaneity and quietude that proved to be fertile ground for the BLM movement to win the support of those who were previously hostile or indifferent. The racial disparities in infection and death due to Covid-19 had made the effects of racism on occupational exposure, housing and health impossible to ignore. That summer, as protests burst through the streets of major towns and cities, disregarding social-distancing guidelines, polls indicated that the majority of people in the United States supported the statement 'Black Lives Matter', including 86 per cent of African Americans and 60 per cent of white people.[5] 'Black Lives Matter' was suddenly everywhere, as individuals, institutions and corporations scrambled to be on the right side of history.

The amplification of the phrase set off an avalanche of misunderstanding. It's hard to tell how much of this was genuine, organic confusion, because white supremacists undertook an organised programme to discredit the movement. Stickers and social media posts were distributed, bearing the hashtag #BlackLivesMatter along with the slogan 'kill a white on sight' or 'all whites are Nazis'.[6] Right-wing figures, including Ryan Fournier, who founded 'Students for Trump', and Candace Owens, of the conservative advocacy group Turning Point USA, spread the myth that donations to the BLM campaign were directed to the Democratic Party.[7] All this obfuscation has left a cloud of suspicion hanging over BLM, in much the way that industry-funded scientists (accused of being 'merchants of doubt'[8]) have spun a web of mistrust and uncertainty in relation to global heating due to human activity, despite the existence of a firm evidence base and a consensus among (non-industry-funded) scientists. By September 2020, 87 per cent of Black adults in the US supported BLM, but white people's support had dropped below a majority, to 45 per cent.[9]

'Black Lives Matter' serves as shorthand for the conjunction of the following assertions: (a) Black lives are systematically undervalued; (b) Black lives should be valued. Assertion (a) is what philosophers call a *descriptive* statement. It *describes* the world, and its truth can be ascertained by observing the world and confirming that the statement is an accurate description. Assertion (b) is what we call a *normative* statement. It makes a value judgement, i.e. it tells us not what is the case, but what *ought* to be the case. It makes the moral proclamation that it is wrong that Black lives are undervalued. Moral statements cannot be verified by observations; they must be argued for.

It might be contended that it's confusing for the statement 'Black Lives Matter' to represent both a descriptive and a normative statement at the same time, and that the backlash stems from this misunderstanding. But that's nonsense; we use language in this way all the time. In the UK, there's a famous advertising campaign which centres on the slogan 'A dog is for life, not just for Christmas'. The phrase dates back to 1978, when the National Canine Defence League (now known as the Dogs Trust) introduced the phrase to try to stop the trend of people impulsively acquiring puppies at Christmas time and then neglecting or abandoning them once the novelty wore off.* The slogan is well-known, well-understood and totally uncontroversial. It very obviously communicates two things at once: dogs are being treated as though they are relatively disposable Christmas presents (descriptive), and dogs ought to be cared for as long-term companions (normative). Both of these have to be true for the statement to make any sense. No one responds with: 'What about cats?' or 'Don't you think our culture of disposability is a problem more generally?'

---

* More recently, several commentators noted, in response to a sudden surge in dog ownership, that the refrain might be updated to 'A dog is for life, not just for lockdown.'

What does it mean for a life to *matter*? There are many ways to answer such a question, but some basic criteria seem obvious to me. A person whose life matters should first of all be *free*. They should not be enslaved, imprisoned, frightened for their life or the lives of those they love, or be so poor or blighted by insecurity as to have no control over their fate. Second, they should have adequate and reliable access to the *basic necessities* of life: food, water, sanitation, adequate housing, healthcare, education and community. Third, they should be treated *fairly* by others: they should not be misrepresented or harmed by falsehoods, they should not be exploited, they should be treated as individuals rather than as instances of stereotypes about groups to which they belong, and they should have their interests represented within the society in which they live.

All these factors come in degrees, yet it is obvious not only that some people's lives matter more than others, but that the degree to which some people's lives are valued falls below what most of us would consider to be an acceptable threshold. This point was made very clearly by bell hooks, who observed:

> In classroom settings I have often listened to groups of students tell me that racism really no longer shapes the contours of our lives, and that there is no such thing as racial difference, that 'we are all just people'. Then a few minutes later I give them an exercise. I ask if they were about to die and could choose to come back as a white male, a white female, a black female, or a black male, which identity would they choose. Each time I do this exercise, most individuals, irrespective of gender or race invariably choose whiteness, and most often male whiteness. Black females are the least chosen. When I ask students to explain their choice they proceed to do a sophisticated analysis of privilege based on race (with perspectives that take gender and class into consideration).[10]

Being Black is a powerful and robust predictor of a person's life being undervalued. That Black lives did not matter is indisputable historical fact. Colonisation was facilitated by Europeans' conceptions of Black people as sub-human. During the so-called Age of

Enlightenment in the eighteenth century, new ideas of egalitarianism were taking hold across Europe, yet colonialism, driven by economic motives, required the subjugation of those living in regions where resources were being plundered. Viewing these people as equals made it difficult to kidnap, enslave and torture them into submission, which is what the profit motive demanded in order to ensure a supply of free labour. White Europeans therefore constructed a theory of racial hierarchy, placing themselves at the top and African peoples at the bottom, precisely so that the extraction of resources, and the kidnapping and enslavement of people would be tolerable to those who thought of themselves as morally upstanding. Race is a way of making certain people matter less. It is, as Black physicist Chanda Prescod-Weinstein writes in *The Disordered Cosmos*:

> a whole artifice invented to justify the superiority of (white) Europeans, their fear of the people who were different from them, and their fear of admitting that the deity they believed in could have a more expansive vision for the world than one ruled by ruthless melaninless men from a small Asian peninsula.[11]

In the post-Civil Rights period, racism lives on in attitudes and institutions, as well as more covertly and indirectly in racist laws and policies. In *The New Jim Crow*, Michelle Alexander shows that racism hasn't gone away, it's just expressed in different, but equally harmful, forms:

> Rather than rely on race, we use our criminal justice system to label people of color 'criminals' and then engage in all the practices we supposedly left behind. Today it is perfectly legal to discriminate against criminals in nearly all the ways that it was once legal to discriminate against African Americans. Once you're labeled a felon, the old forms of discrimination – employment discrimination, housing discrimination, denial of the right to vote, denial of educational opportunity, denial of food stamps and other public benefits, and exclusion from jury service – are suddenly legal.[12]

The social, economic and psychological effects of historic anti-Black racism are ongoing, and operate in tandem with newer variants of racism, so that it is difficult to untangle the harms of legacy oppression from those caused by contemporary forms of discrimination. Regardless, the disparities are unequivocal and damning. In the UK, Black people are four times more likely to die in childbirth than white people,[13] and Black infant mortality is twice as high.[14] The unemployment rate for Black people is twice that of white people,[15] and almost half of Black households live in poverty.[16] Black people are ten times more likely to be stopped and searched than white people,[17] and four times more likely to be arrested.[18] They constitute 3 per cent of the population, but 8 per cent of deaths in police custody.[19]

In the United States, a Black person is five times as likely as a white person to be apprehended without good reason, and Black people are incarcerated at five times the rate of white people.[20] Experiments show that both civilians and police officers are more disposed to accidentally shoot an unarmed Black person than an armed white person,[21] and data show that Black people shot by the police are twice as likely as white victims to be unarmed.[22] White officers use their guns more often than their Black colleagues, and do so more often in neighbourhoods with a higher proportion of Black residents.[23]

To appreciate the breadth and magnitude of anti-Black racism, we must also look beyond Global North contexts. Around 383 million Africans live in 'extreme poverty', which means they scrape by (or don't) on less than $1.90 per day.[24] That number is predicted to rise across sub-Saharan Africa in the coming decades.[25] Just 10 per cent of resources for health research go towards tackling preventable or treatable diseases in the Global South that account for 90 per cent of total human mortality. Most of those deaths occur in sub-Saharan Africa. These realities are the result of a long history of subjugation, in which disparities introduced under colonialism have been fossilised in a global economic system that favours the interests of Global North states and institutions at the expense of Africans and other Global South peoples.

Given these disparities, it's unsurprising that almost half of the 5,000 migrants who die every year as they attempt to escape poverty, conflict and environmental devastation are Africans.[26] Around 40 per cent of those who apply for asylum in the UK are Black people from the Global South, many of whom are eventually detained and deported.[27] Blackness is critical to the possibility of these cruel realities. Extreme poverty is racialised. It is unthinkable that 400 million white people could be hungry, for generations, in full view of the world, without any meaningful intervention.

In short, Black lives *don't* matter. They're cheap, disposable and ignorable. The suffering and deaths of Black people are seen as inevitable, if regrettable. That's why Black people are over-represented among those who are incarcerated, those who are shot dead by police, and those who lead short lives on the edge of starvation in the grip of diseases that are both preventable and treatable. Black people are more likely than any other group globally to be denied their freedom, access to basic necessities and fair treatment by others. As Judith Butler writes, 'One reason the chant "Black Lives Matter" is so important is that it states the obvious but the obvious has not yet been historically realized.'[28]

## BLM: Some Misguided Responses

'Black Lives Matter' has been met with a range of worrying responses running the gamut from muddled liberals to unabashed bigots. Some of these reactions suggest genuine misunderstanding, others wilful attempts at distraction. Those who reject the phrase object to at least one of the statements of which it is composed: (a) Black lives are systematically undervalued; (b) Black lives should be valued.

When deciding how, and indeed whether, to approach a discussion with a person who objects to the term, it is important to first establish which part they take issue with, and why. There are a few common responses, which can be broadly summarised as follows:

**The 'colour-blind' response**. We should move beyond racial categories. Racism is bad, but it's now rare; things are much better than they used to be. A less confusing slogan would help us to shift the focus away from identities that divide us.

**The 'whataboutery' response**. What about other lives? Don't the lives of white people matter, too? What about the lives of police officers?

**The 'white supremacist' response**. 'Black Lives Matter' is now everywhere, and that's a sign of a world in which whiteness is under threat.

| | A. Do Black lives matter? (*descriptive* question) | B. Should Black lives matter? (*normative* question) |
|---|---|---|
| Anti-racist | ✗ | ✓ |
| Colour-blind | ✓ | ✓ |
| Whataboutery | ? | ? |
| White supremacist | ? | ✗ |

Table 1: How do the different responses to 'Black Lives Matter' relate to the components of the statement?

Table 1 sums up how each of these positions relates to the component statements of the anti-racist slogan 'Black Lives Matter'. Those who profess 'colour blindness' agree that everyone should be treated equally, but maintain that we are close to achieving that aim. Those who engage in whataboutery raise all manner of other issues, creating a veil of ambiguity that can provide cover for a number of other views. And white supremacists don't want a world in which Black lives matter. It's important to note that any of these positions might be communicated by the retort 'all lives matter'.

## Colour Blindness

Every anti-racist hopes for the world Martin Luther King Jr described on the steps of the Lincoln Memorial in Washington, DC, in August 1963: 'I have a dream that my four little children will one day live in a nation where they will not be judged by the color of their skin but by the content of their character.'[29] As it stands, race *does* matter. It may be an outlandish, baseless system of categorisation, but it underwrites the structure of contemporary societies and the operation of the global economy. We are not yet finished with race, and its end will not be hastened by denial.

Yet many people believe that racism has *already* been overcome, and that we are now living in a 'post-racial' age. 'Colour blindness' is the idea that race is no longer a significant social category, because although racism is still a problem, it's limited to isolated incidents of intentional nastiness, and has ceased to be determinative of a person's options or experiences in life. Its proponents find it easy to accept that Donald Trump is racist, but harder to believe that their friend Karen might be. They contend that continuing to focus on race as a determinant of a person's life outcomes *perpetuates* racial division and takes us further from King's dream. Conservative US chief justice John Roberts once said, 'The way to stop discrimination on the basis of race, is to stop discriminating on the basis of race.'[30] This sounds laudable, except that treating people the same way would require a radical overhaul of the distribution of resources, and even then people of colour would start from a position of inherited historical injustice that would need to be accounted for.

Colour blindness is centred on the insistence that we stop interfering and let people succeed on their own terms, and is therefore sometimes described as 'laissez-faire racism'. The idea seems to be that if some people do better, that's down to their own gumption, and if some people fail, that's on them for being lazy and stupid. No need to play the 'race card'! And if certain social groups repeatedly outperform others, well, maybe there was something to race science and cultural hierarchies after all.

For some, the Civil Rights Act marked the 'post-racial' shift. For others, the election of the first Black president of the United States was the critical juncture. After all, how could a racist nation vote a Black person into its highest office? In the UK, there haven't been the same 'landmark' moments, but the belief that we now live in a post-racial society is no less prevalent for it. There is a widespread belief that the British variety of anti-Black racism is more benign than that in the US. When people in the UK talk about anti-Black racism, they tend to reach for examples from across the Atlantic, gesturing towards plantation slavery and Jim Crow laws, and recalling the names of those killed by US police officers – Michael Brown, Breonna Taylor, George Floyd – much more readily than those killed by British police officers – Rashan Charles, Mark Duggan, Olaseni Lewis.

While it's true that the stakes of racism in the US are ramped up by the ubiquity of firearms, the idea that Britain (and Europe more generally) is a less racist place doesn't wash. To start with, anti-Black racism was a European invention, and the fact that Britain enriched itself from outsourced plantation slavery in its colonies, rather than its metropole, does not make the moral difference some people think it does. Gary Younge has reminded British readers that 'Our civil rights movement was in Jamaica, Ghana, India and so on.'[31] Further, the fact that the Mediterranean is the world's deadliest border, and all of its victims Black or Brown, makes any claim about gentler forms of contemporary European racism absurd.

The view that we're now in a post-racial age, occasionally marred by a few bad apples, is most common among white people. While only 10 per cent of Black respondents to a 2015 poll thought that people were treated equally by the US justice system regardless of race, almost half of white respondents believed this to be the case.[32] A 2016 Pew Research Center survey found that 8 per cent of Black people and 38 per cent of white people agreed with the statement 'Our country has made the changes necessary to give blacks equal right with whites', whereas 43 per cent of Black people and 11 per cent of white people agreed with the statement 'Our country will not make the changes to give blacks equal rights with whites.'[33] In the UK, three times as many white people as Black people believe that there is 'not much' racism in the UK, or none at all,[34] and twice as many Black people as white people believe that the police are institutionally racist.[35]

Many of those who take issue with the 'Black Lives Matter' movement claim to do so because of a commitment to something like colour blindness. This criticism is sometimes recast as a concern about *strategy*, on the grounds that the movement is deemed to be violent, extreme or unwelcoming, and is therefore doing itself no favours. In fact, 93 per cent of the BLM protests in 2020 involved no harm to people or property – a striking statistic, given the number of people involved and the decentralised nature of the actions.[36] (Even so, 40,000 soldiers were deployed alongside the police to manage the US protests, which has been contrasted with the modest police presence when white supremacists stormed Capitol Hill six months later.)

I do not believe that resistance should always be nonviolent, and history teaches us that it is more likely to succeed if diverse tactics are used. Violence can, as Frantz Fanon put it, be a 'cleansing force', liberating a person from 'despair and inaction; it makes him [*sic*] fearless and restores his [*sic*] self-respect.'[37] Nor do I recognise damage to property as 'violence', or as necessarily morally wrong; in many cases, it's highly effective and symbolically powerful. As environmentalist Andreas Malm points out in *How to Blow Up a Pipeline: Learning to Fight in a World on Fire*, it's a myth that the Civil Rights movement succeeded because of its nonviolent tactics. Rather, the US government capitulated to the demands of nonviolent protestors because it feared that people would otherwise support the more radical movements that were happening concurrently.[38] Yet many people – especially those most heavily invested in the status quo – argue for minimally disruptive tactics, instead promoting the use of establishment procedures, such as lobbying and writing petitions. They prefer slogans and methods that are less hostile to the way power and material resources are currently distributed, and a group of Black people marching through the city unsettles them in much the same racist way that a Black man walking down the street is seen as an automatic threat.

Such people might not think of themselves as colour-blind, but they fall into the same broader category of people Martin Luther King Jr referred to as 'white moderates'. In 1963 he hit back at their criticisms of the methods used by Black protestors:

> I have almost reached the regrettable conclusion that the Negro's great stumbling block in his stride toward freedom is not the White Citizen's

Counciler or the Ku Klux Klanner, but the white moderate, who is more devoted to 'order' than to justice; who prefers a negative peace which is the absence of tension to a positive peace which is the presence of justice; who constantly says: 'I agree with you in the goal you seek, but I cannot agree with your methods of direct action'; who paternalistically believes he can set the timetable for another man's freedom.[39]

## Whataboutery

'Whataboutery' is a conversational manoeuvre in which a person avoids engaging with the topic under discussion, or attempting to rebut the argument that has been put forward, in favour of asking 'But what about X?', where X is some other issue that is intuitively concerning. It's an easy way of changing the subject when a person can't think of a response or counterargument, and can be deployed strategically to take the spotlight off an uncomfortable topic or accusation.

Two related forms of whataboutery are particularly common. *Inclusive* whataboutery occurs when someone bombards you with other morally repugnant issues with the aim of arguing that if you are committed to one issue, you should also include multiple others in your set of concerns. The end result is exhaustion on your part. Those who use social media will be familiar with this strategy. Someone posts, 'Wouldn't it be great if we could give nurses the pay rise they deserve?' and is inundated with responses along the lines of 'What about paramedics? Also, some teachers earn less than nurses.'

*Exclusive* whataboutery describes situations in which a person implies that if you aren't simultaneously condemning other issues, you can't reasonably condemn the one under discussion either. The implication is that doing so makes you a hypocrite. The existence of other problems which haven't been mentioned or addressed is deemed to be good reason to exclude the present one from your field of concern. This strategy seems intent on making you throw your hands up in the air and admit that the world is full of bad things, so there's no point trying to change them.

Both forms undermine attempts to work towards social justice. On the face of it, whataboutery isn't linked to any political position, but it works especially well in derailing challenges to the status quo, and can therefore be an effective way of strengthening dominant political ideologies. A person criticises one particular injustice, and is urged to instead, or in addition, consider other wrongs, or else to tolerate all of them. This leaves the initial concern unaddressed, and the system untroubled by their challenge, while their opponent might appear to be especially virtuous for having a broader view of the world's ills.

Reactions to 'Black Lives Matter' often follow the faulty logic of whataboutery. Saying 'all lives matter' is a form of inclusive whataboutery. Refusing to support BLM on the grounds that there are countless other forms of injustice in the world is an exercise of exclusive whataboutery: the subtext is 'there's no point worrying about *that* when there's so much else that's also bad'.

Whataboutery isn't actually a logical fallacy, and there is often some sense to it. For this reason, it's important to ascertain a person's intentions in bringing up other moral issues. Suppose I say that Britain's treatment of asylum seekers is appalling and should be challenged, and am met with the response that Italy and Greece are also behaving cruelly. It's crucial that I establish whether my interlocutor is trying to shut down the issue, or whether they are showing me a way of extending and strengthening my critique by (say) pointing out that Britain's inhumanity is not unique, but is part of a broader pattern of twenty-first-century European colonialism. Similarly, I would expect to be held to account if I was to support one anti-racist cause, but refuse to condemn another form of anti-racism when called upon to do so. Solidarity is very important, and we should strive to be morally consistent, but it is impractical that a person who is midway through discussing or addressing one issue should have to simultaneously turn their attention and effort to an endless list of others, especially those that they may be less qualified to comment on. That's a recipe for inaction.

When we make moral statements such as 'Black Lives Matter', we are not saying 'this is the *only* issue that matters' but rather '*this* issue is particularly morally troubling in *this context*'. It's important that we uphold some kind of context-dependent hierarchy of moral concerns, because otherwise we can't act on those concerns within relevant timeframes. If a person is drowning while I'm on the beach reading an anti-racist article, attending to their needs is the priority, even though my moral education is also important. Helping to bring the drowning person safely to shore does not reflect on my commitment to any other issue.

## White Supremacy

In the summer of 2020, just a couple of months after the murder of George Floyd, a group of British football fans paid for a banner emblazoned with the words 'White Lives Matter' to be flown over a football match in Manchester, right after the players had taken the knee in solidarity with the 'Black Lives Matter' movement.[40] Three years earlier, at the 'Unite the Right' rally in Charlottesville, Virginia, white supremacists had chanted the same slogan along with 'You will not replace us!' and 'Jews will not replace us!'

It might be inferred that if, as I've argued above, BLM doesn't mean *only* Black lives matter, then 'white lives matter' doesn't mean *only* white lives matter, and is therefore unproblematic. But the context of the statements is pivotal. We're surrounded by empirical evidence that Black lives do not matter. That's the context to which BLM refers, and from which it derives its sense. White lives, on the other hand, are *already* valued for their whiteness. White people earn more,[41] have the lowest rates of unemployment,[42] and are arrested at a rate that in the UK is six times lower than that for Black people.[43] Job applications headed with 'white British' names are significantly more likely to get a call-back by UK employers than those that bear names associated with people of colour, even where the text is identical.[44] Being white is something that works in a person's favour, even if their life might be hard for other reasons.[45]

Regardless of the evidence, many white people believe that efforts to address anti-Black racism have overshot, so that it's now white people who are discriminated against. A 2011 study conducted by US psychologists Michael Norton and Samuel Sommers revealed that white people tend to believe that the reduction in anti-Black bias has amounted to an increase in anti-white bias.[46] They found that both Black and white people think that anti-Black bias decreased between the 1950s and the 2000s, but white people think it declined to a much greater extent. And while Black people think anti-white bias is negligible and has stayed so over the last few decades, white people believe that anti-white bias has risen by almost exactly the same amount that anti-Black bias has fallen. Norton and Sommers examined the two trends and found that, statistically speaking, they were indeed negatively correlated: those who responded to their survey really did think that the decrease in anti-Black bias brought about a related increase in anti-white bias. They concluded that white people see racism as a zero-sum game.

Seeing the world through a zero-sum mentality tends to favour 'neutral', 'apolitical' approaches that prop up the current system. In the course of criticising incoming Supreme Court judge Sonia Sotomayor's support for abortion, gun control and the abolition of the death penalty, former US attorney general Jeff Sessions said: 'Empathy for one party is always prejudice against another.'[47] This reductive worldview is surprisingly common, and efforts to combat racism are often seen as attempts to take things away from white people. While this worry is overblown, it's not entirely wide of the mark: justice requires redistribution, which means taking from some piles to add to others. We have seen that white people have unearned advantages when it comes to job applications and are more likely to be appointed than candidates of colour.[48] Were we to switch to a quota system, or anonymise applications, this advantage would be reduced, as would the disadvantage people of colour face.[49] The job would be more likely to go to the most capable candidate, regardless of their race (or any other irrelevant social identity), which is good news for everyone, because we all benefit from others being competent in their roles. With these measures in place a white candidate may be slightly less likely to be hired, and that might feel like a penalty, but they'd have lost an advantage they'd done nothing to deserve and ought not to have had in the first place. Similarly, a person who has been enjoying extra big portions of chips because their friend works in the chippie is going to be disappointed when they're handed a measly 'standard' portion by another server. There's no injustice; rather, the difference in portion size underscores how much of an advantage they previously had (and may raise the question of whether others should settle for so few chips).

Quotas and affirmative action in the US often incense those who are not favoured by them, even though such policies are designed to address the empirical fact that those people are *already* unfairly advantaged. Anti-racist measures therefore *intend* to discriminate, because some forms of discrimination are morally apt. Ibram X. Kendi makes this point in *How to Be an Antiracist*:

> The defining question is whether the discrimination is creating equity or inequity. If discrimination is creating equity, then it is antiracist. If discrimination is creating inequity, then it is racist. Someone reproducing inequity through permanently assisting an overrepresented racial group into wealth and power is entirely different than someone challenging that inequity by temporarily assisting an underrepresented racial group into relative wealth and power until equity is reached.[50]

As we saw in the previous section, whataboutery can be used to stabilise dominant political positions. Those peddling white supremacist arguments make liberal use of this strategy, most often in the demand that we address the question 'What about white working-class people?' There is no good reason to add 'white' to the category 'working class' when discussing economic marginalisation. All working-class people are marginalised, and that marginalisation is worse if they're also people of colour. The prefix 'white' suggests some other agenda.

Politicians often speak of 'white working-class people' or 'white working-class men' in order to encourage such people to link their difficulties to whiteness and masculinity, rather than poverty. The aim is to funnel the discontent of white people into identities other than class and encourage them to see their whiteness as a promissory note for something better. An expedient but baseless solidarity between white men is encouraged, leaving poor white men with a sense of entitlement they can only ever possess incompletely. They can roam the streets without fear of racism or sexism – and that is no small thing – but it doesn't fill their pockets or their stomachs. They're not worse off than working-class people of colour and white women, but they were promised something better, and those dashed expectations are easily soured into resentment.

'Black Lives Matter' is encountered as a threat both to the idea that white people deserve more than others, and to the limited resources that working-class people already struggle to access. If they can be made to rage in favour of whiteness and masculinity, that can only strengthen the status quo; if they instead build their fury around class, that poses a direct threat to the system that makes them poor.

Those defending the football banner stunt described above claimed to interpret 'Black Lives Matter' to mean *only* Black lives matter. Following their logic, we have to assume they also thought 'white lives matter' meant *only* white lives. That amounts to a statement in support of white supremacy. Sending a 'White Lives Matter' banner into the sky points to something much worse than ignorance.

'White lives matter' and 'white power' are not comparable to 'Black Lives Matter' and 'Black power'. That's not a double standard, it's an acknowledgement that the contexts of these statements are wildly different. (Consider the immediate and striking difference between 'girl power' and 'male power'.) Whiteness *is* power. Power is, so often, white. 'White lives matter' is a tautology, because the word 'white' already contains the mattering.

## Why Not 'All Lives Matter'?

Many of those who endorse the rejoinder 'all lives matter' are of the view that 'Black Lives Matter' is unduly divisive, or even racist. (In this respect, not much has changed in half a century; in the 1960s and 1970s, the 'Black Power' movement faced almost identical charges.) Psychologist Keon West and colleagues have shown that those who support 'all lives matter' are generally not right wing in their political beliefs, nor do they harbour explicitly racist beliefs. Rather, they are more likely to hold implicit racist beliefs, and have a narrow conception of what counts as discrimination. That is, they are liable to agree with the following statement: 'The core of anti-Black racism is that it is malicious: if a person is not being malicious, then it can't be racism.'[51]

While 'all lives matter' is sometimes presented as a more inclusive alternative to BLM, its utterance is as vacuous as it is damaging. 'All lives matter' is false if it's taken to be a descriptive statement, and is trivial if it's taken to be a normative statement; of course all lives *should* matter. But nobody was saying 'all lives matter' before 2013. It's a response to BLM that has no sense outside that context. And if BLM is understood as a commitment to tackling the violence and brutality of anti-Black racism, then blurting out that 'all lives matter' is at best, tangential and, at worst, an intentional filibuster. It's also an example of whataboutery. 'All lives matter' dissolves the specificity of the original plea, obscuring the problem that BLM seeks to foreground, and reducing the bandwidth that is available to address the urgent problem that Black lives *don't* matter. Judith Butler puts it another way: 'If we jump too quickly to the universal formulation, "all lives matter", then we miss the fact that black people have not yet been included in the idea of "all lives".'[52]

There are good reasons to believe that at least some of this 'misunderstanding' is intentional. Philosophers of language have noted that successful conversational exchanges require that conversers are *cooperative* in recognising the aims of the conversation and contributing accordingly, but also *charitable*, which means imputing to others the most rational interpretation of their utterances. Accordingly, when someone says 'Black Lives Matter' the listener must ask herself 'What do I know about Black people in this society and the extent to which their lives are thought to matter?', 'Why might a person be inclined to refer to Black lives *specifically*?' but also 'How might it come across if I choose *this* moment to express the fact that I value all lives?' The fact that these conversational norms so often falter in relation to 'Black Lives Matter' points to a deliberate desire to be obstructive, or a widespread linguistic confusion.

Part of what goes wrong for some people is that the slogan is drawn into a false equivalence with the statement 'some other lives *don't* matter', which is then *correctly* responded to with 'all lives matter'.[53]

An alternative, or additional, way of making sense of the misunderstanding has been offered by philosopher Jessica Keiser, who argues that some of the confusion occurs in considering which *question* the statement 'Black lives matter' responds to.[54] Some philosophers have argued that every conversation is structured around a set of implicit, often unspoken goals, which can be expressed as questions.[55]

The assumed question under discussion determines how a person responds. If someone believes that the live, important question under discussion is 'Do Black lives matter?' then 'Black lives matter' will seem like a reasonable response and would not imply that the lives of those from other groups don't matter. They hear an *inclusionary* reading of BLM. Those who instead think the question under discussion is 'Which lives matter?' may be confused or discomfited by hearing 'Black lives matter' chanted in the streets, because 'all lives matter' seems like a more reasonable response. They hear BLM as an *exclusionary* statement that elevates Black lives above other lives. Those who misunderstand BLM in this way tend to assume an initial situation of racial justice, so that the utterance 'Black Lives Matter' unnecessarily disrupts a system that works, while carrying some risk of making matters worse rather than better.

The assumption that BLM is exclusionary can also stem from a concern that, since time and resources are scarce, other serious issues, like poverty and inadequate housing, should be prioritised. This might be an inordinately charitable reading, but it's certainly the case that many people see interrelated aspects of injustices as being disparate and mutually exclusive, and that is a serious problem. Combatting anti-Black racism necessarily means tackling deprivation, carcerality, borders, health inequality and a host of other issues. These injustices affect Black people and other racialised groups most acutely, but they are wide-ranging, entangled problems, and the extent and importance of their connections needs to be communicated much more effectively, not least to combat the messaging of those who benefit from the fragmentation.

Finally, it's worth considering one way in which 'all lives matter' might be subverted. When a person objects to 'Black Lives Matter' with the retort 'all lives matter', on the grounds that it is more inclusive, they should be pressed as to *which* other lives they're so keen to acknowledge. Ask them whether they mean that undocumented migrants' lives matter, and the lives of incarcerated people matter, and the lives of unhoused people matter. Corner them into admitting what they really mean. (We'll return to this strategy in Chapter 7.)

## Why So Much 'Misunderstanding'?

A person who interprets 'Black Lives Matter' as '*only* Black lives matter' thereby betrays the assumptions they hold in relation to movements against anti-Black racism. As philosopher Ashley Atkins puts it:

> The truth is that people already sense in 'Black lives matter' a threat of violence. They already feel that it is divisive, that it stirs racial antagonisms, even before having a clear understanding of what it articulates and without having to have an understanding of what it articulates since what it means or can mean is constrained, for them, by anxious presentiment.[56]

Anti-racist movements are not generally vindictive: they seek justice, not retaliation. But white people are apt to fear violence because they are aware, on some level, that their privilege is built on violence. One of the effects of socialisation in racist societies is that we are unable to imagine ways of living together that do not involve one group living with fear, deprivation and invisibility. White people are therefore liable to assume that any disruption to the present system would result in them being treated as badly as Black people have been. Guilt and paranoia are the psychological levy a person pays for having more than their share and for that surfeit being the result of repugnant acts of wrongdoing (in much the way that a person who is keeping quiet about being overpaid at work always fears the day their employer demands repayment). It is perhaps this suppressed uneasiness that makes people see BLM as a violent movement despite evidence to the contrary: efforts towards addressing anti-Black racism are seen as *necessarily* violent. As James Baldwin wrote in 1961:

No matter how Southerners, and whites in the rest of the nation, too, deny it, or what kind of rationalizations they cover it up with, they know the crimes they have committed against black people. And they are terrified that these crimes will be committed against them . . . It isn't hatred that drives those people in the streets. It's pure terror.[57]

It is this fear that prevents people from hearing the 'all lives should matter' that is necessarily embedded within 'Black Lives Matter'. The phrase only becomes complicated where a person's relationship to justice for Black people is complicated. In 1966, Civil Rights activist Stokely Carmichael made this point in the *New York Review of Books* when discussing the ways in which white people feared and complicated the slogan 'Black power':

Black power can be clearly defined for those who do not attach the fears of white America to their questions about it. We should begin with the basic fact that black Americans have two problems: they are poor and they are black.[58]

White people are correct in their suspicion that, in some senses, BLM *is* about them, because racism has always been about them. For Black lives to matter, the structures that have been erected and maintained to prevent them from mattering must be dismantled. That is a job for white people, who will need to undo their work or watch it be undone. Carmichael expresses this vividly:

I maintain that every civil rights bill in this country was passed for white people, not for black people. For example, I am black. I know that. I also know that while I am black I am a human being. Therefore I have the right to go into any public place. White people didn't know that. Every time I tried to go into a public place they stopped me. So some boys had to write a bill to tell that white man, 'He's a human being; don't stop him.' That bill was for the white man, not for me.[59]

'Black Lives Matter' is therefore a threat, not to the safety of people but to the stability of the system that favours them. Black people and other people of colour cannot be included within *this* system in a dignified way. Reducing police violence and getting more Black children into elite universities and positions of power is not enough. We need to cast off a regime that is premised on constructing certain groups as exploitable.

## Beyond BLM

'Black Lives Matter' must have a global vision if it is to pose a robust challenge to racism and colonialism. That means centring the voices of Global South peoples, including those who migrate away from poverty, instability and environmental destruction. Racism is not some unfortunate, freestanding mode of marginalisation that can be tackled in isolation through affirmative action, implicit bias training and good intentions. Racism fortifies the foundations of capitalism. The two are not independent evils, they're old bedfellows. In 1983, Black philosopher Cedric Robinson described the system in which we live as one of 'racial capitalism'.[60]

'Black Lives Matter' has to be a challenge to racial capitalism and the power structures that produce and protect it: global financial institutions, governments, the media, the military, the police (including border police) and the justice system, among others. Black lives can't matter in such a world, because even if dedicated interventions might improve the lives of some Black citizens of wealthy nations, those measures will do nothing for Black necessitous migrants and poor Black people in the Global South. Our anti-racist movements cannot merely condemn the colonialism of the past, they must also denounce the ongoing colonialism that is evident in the fact that the darker-skinned two-thirds of the global population are at much greater risk of poverty, disease, premature death and the effects of climate crisis.

It's disappointing to note how infrequently Black peoples of the Global South are brought into conversations about anti-Black racism. Around 40 per cent of those who die at Europe's borders are Black migrants from African states. A large proportion of those who live undocumented in Europe, with limited access to employment, healthcare and housing, are Black. And the vast majority of those who live in extreme poverty are Black people from sub-Saharan African countries. I have heard people argue that BLM is a movement that was founded because of police brutality, and takes that as its focus, but border police are also police, and people are driven to deadly borders by hunger, medical need and environmental devastation.

Nor can 'Black Lives Matter' stop at Black lives. If the movement is grounded in the idea that racism and colonialism are unjust and must be challenged, then it has obvious links to other struggles against related injustices. Yet these connections are not always made strongly enough, and those who have brought BLM into more mainstream conversations haven't necessarily used those opportunities to show solidarity with related causes.

In 2020, universities across the UK starting releasing statements with text such as the following, from my own institution: 'We stand in solidarity with those now struggling for justice. We affirm that Black lives matter.'[61] Most of these statements were tokenistic gestures to respond to or stave off criticism at a time of acute sensitivity, though some institutions made and kept promises of material support for Black staff and students. Then, in May 2021, Israel started bombing the Gaza strip, following an uprising after attempts to evict Palestinian families from their homes in East Jerusalem. My students wrote to the senior administration of the university, asking that they issue a statement condemning the actions of the Israeli state and supporting the Palestinians' struggle for justice. They pointed out the asymmetry of the 'conflict': the Israeli military is extremely powerful and well-funded, and even when it isn't bombing Gaza, the Israeli government enacts a system of racist apartheid which occupies Palestinian land and violently subjugates Palestinians in Israel, the West Bank and the Gaza strip.[62] They reminded the university of its statement on BLM, which made a commitment to anti-racism (whataboutery can be put to good use in calling out moral inconsistency). The vice-chancellor replied that the university could not get involved in 'political activities or campaigns' and 'must remain neutral'. It was a baffling response, not least because it was an admission that the institutional commitment to BLM had *not* been intended as a political statement, and was supposed to be 'neutral', which begs the question of what on earth they meant by it. Presumably they had in mind whatever Washington DC mayor Muriel Bowser was thinking when she had 'Black Lives Matter' painted in huge yellow letters on the road leading to the White House, and then increased the city's policing budget.[63]

That 'Black Lives Matter' unsettles so many powerful people is an indication that it's working. But we should not be content to see these discussions stall around the acceptability of a single phrase. We have to ask how the material world would have to change for Black lives to matter, and those who take that question seriously will find themselves looking back through history, across borders and right into the heart of the economy.

# 6

## Who Should We Believe?

[S]ometimes a white man will tell a black boy anything, everything, weeping briny tears. He knows that the black boy can
never betray him, for no one will believe his testimony.

James Baldwin, *Playboy* (1985)

Every cell in the human body contains minuscule threads of deoxyri-
bonucleic acid: the spindly molecule better known as DNA.* They're
long, coiled molecular scrolls on which the constitution for that
particular body is spelled out. In humans, this information is organised into forty-six chapters, known as chromosomes, which are
arranged into twenty-three pairs. We know this because, equipped
with a suitably powerful microscope, it's possible to examine human
cells, and under certain conditions you can count the number of pairs
of chromosomes. One of the earliest attempts at this was carried out
by Texan biologist Theophilus Painter, who in 1921 announced that
there were twenty-four pairs of chromosomes in human cells,
amounting to forty-eight in total.[1]

Counting chromosomes is fiddly (like peering into a pan of boiling
spaghetti and trying to count the strands), and getting so close is laudable. Yet remarkably, a number of other scientists repeated the experiment and kept getting the same erroneous number as Painter. He was
a well-regarded biologist, so if another scientist counted a different
number of chromosome pairs, they were liable to repeat their tally
until their result matched the accepted number. Painter's mistake was

* Except mature red blood cells and cornified cells in the skin, hair and nails.

perpetuated from 1921 to 1956, which means that in a field which prides itself on replicability, whose methods and technologies were continually improving, a Great White Man's error went unquestioned for thirty-five years. Curiously, textbooks in this period published microscopy photographs showing the *correct* number of chromosomes (twenty-three pairs) accompanied by captions stating the *incorrect* number (twenty-four pairs). People couldn't imagine a scientist of Painter's stature being wrong.

Alice Catherine Evans faced the opposite problem. Born in 1881 and raised on a farm in Pennsylvania, Evans initially trained as a schoolteacher, one of the few professions open to women. On the side, she took free classes in biology and went on to obtain degrees in bacteriology. While working as a scientist at the United States Department of Agriculture, Evans investigated a bacterium known as *Brucella abortus* which caused severe illness and miscarriage in animals. Evans wondered whether this bacterium could also be the cause of a human illness known as 'undulant fever',* and suspected that infected cow's milk was responsible. She confirmed that the two bacteria were indeed identical, and suggested that undulant fever could be eliminated if milk was boiled before use.

In her memoirs, Evans describes the backlash to her discovery, noting that the 'reaction to my paper was almost universal scepticism, usually expressed by the remark that if these organisms were closely related, some other bacteriologist would have noted it.'[2] In other words, if such a major finding was correct, surely a man would have already figured it out? A prominent scientist named Theobald Smith (who Wikipedia describes as 'America's first internationally significant medical research scientist') vociferously opposed her work. Evans wrote:

> Scientists are probably the most objective of researchers. Unfortunately, they can be influenced by their social system. I was a newcomer in the field where he was regarded as an authority . . . and he was not accustomed to considering a scientific idea proposed by a woman.[3]

---

* The modern name is brucellosis.

Three years later, she was vindicated when several other groups of credible scientists (i.e. men) confirmed her findings. Around the same time, Evans contracted undulant fever, which was at that time incurable. For the next twenty years, she struggled with pain, fevers and sweating.[4] Her symptoms were not taken seriously and many people believed her illness was imaginary. (We'll return to the discrediting of illness in women in due course.) She wrote: 'To be ill and regarded as an imposter is to be in an almost intolerable situation.'[5] In 1930, a law was passed requiring the pasteurisation of milk, which effectively eliminated undulant fever in the United States.

Evans was a trained bacteriologist who had conducted careful scientific research and arrived at a highly plausible result. Yet her findings were met with doubt and suspicion. Just as Painter's contemporaries couldn't see how he could be wrong, Evans' scientific colleagues couldn't imagine her being right. We are liable to have too much confidence in some people and not enough in others. And the way that falls is far from accidental.

## Who Is Credible?

Gwyneth Paltrow urged customers of her lifestyle brand to insert egg-shaped stones into their vaginas in order to 'increase vaginal muscle tone, hormonal balance, and feminine energy in general'. Gynaecologists warned against it.[6] Residents of Flint, Michigan, sniffed the discoloured water coming out of their taps and complained to city officials. Michigan's Department of Environmental Quality insisted that the water was safe to drink. Ernesto Araújo, Brazil's minister of foreign affairs under Jair Bolsonaro, described climate change as a left-wing conspiracy to 'suffocate the economic growth of capitalist, democratic countries'.[7] Ninety-seven per cent of climate scientists believe that global heating over the last century is primarily due to human activity.[8] It is sometimes obvious who we should believe, but what is it that makes them believable?

The confidence we have in the knowledge of another person is captured in our estimations of their 'credibility'. Credibility is an

integral part of human life. It has two ingredients: being knowledgeable and being trustworthy. A person who is competent but
dishonest is not credible. Bill Clinton told the world he didn't have
sexual relations with Monica Lewinsky. His credentials suggest he's
clever and he's knowledgeable; his semen on Lewinsky's dress indicates he's also a liar. A person who is truthful but not competent
may also lack credibility. Lenny in *Of Mice and Men* is honest, but
believes whatever his friend George says, which mostly consists of
reassuring lies.

Credibility is often scarce and competitive, not least because we
need to be able to settle disagreements. Scientists and healthcare
workers tell us that a vaccination will reduce the risk of serious illness
and contribute to herd immunity, while anti-vaxxers on YouTube
caution us that the government is trying to implant microchips in our
bodies. I choose to believe the medical experts, because I deem them
to be more knowledgeable and because their professions have measures in place to guard against dishonesty (e.g. peer review, clinical
records). Courtrooms present the most obvious case of having to
decide between differing reports of the same set of events. If two
witnesses give conflicting accounts, we must infer that at least one of
them is lying. Their perceived credibility determines who is believed.
We tend to trust people who've been shown to be correct and honest
in the past, or who give us the sense of being well-informed and
trustworthy.

Credibility is important because most human communication
consists of the exchange of knowledge. When I ask you what time it
is, or which companies are the greatest carbon emitters, I am asking
you for your knowledge. When you explain the difference between
grime and garage or confide in me about your sexual assault, you
offer me your knowledge. If I consider you to be credible, I believe
what you tell me and absorb it into my own store of knowledge. If I
don't, I'll nod along and then discard what you've told me, or else
challenge you on it. In this way, we continually swap knowledge with
each other. As a university lecturer, my ability to do my job – to teach
students and develop novel ideas – depends on people seeing me as
credible in my subject area.

It's hard to overstate the importance of being perceived to be credible. People who appear to be credible get more out of life. They have a better chance of getting a job, being respected at work, winning arguments, accruing followers on social media, influencing other people's ideas, having the police and courts take them seriously, and succeeding in public roles, including politics and journalism. Importantly, they also have a better chance of being listened to when they say they've been treated unfairly.

We rarely know for sure how credible a person is, so we find ourselves estimating how credible they *seem*. In making that assessment, we take shortcuts. I can't fact-check every article I read online, so I judge the credibility of the text based on the reputation of the publication or the writer. We take similar shortcuts with people. I believe the pharmacist that a particular cream will soothe a wasp sting, trust the book recommendations of authors whose work I've enjoyed, and take seriously my well-dressed sisters' comments about my appearance. I could be wrong in any of these instances – undoubtedly I often overestimate some people's testimony, and underestimate others' – but I don't have the time or energy to establish each person's actual credibility, and it isn't always possible to do so.

Working out who knows what and who is being honest is a difficult business, and we often get it wrong. Sometimes we undermine our own credibility. Consider Matilda, protagonist of the 1907 cautionary poem, who calls the London fire brigade, pretending there's a fire in her home. A few weeks later, a fire *does* break out and, despite her shouts for help, her neighbours ignore her and she is burned to death. Because of her track record, Matilda wasn't credible with regard to house fires.[9] Those who disbelieved her weren't necessarily blameworthy. Yet often, even when someone doesn't have a poor personal track record, we assign them a low credibility anyway, based on stereotypes associated with a social group to which they belong.

## Seeking Credibility While Black

While waiting for a bus in Southeast London in April 1993, Black teenager Stephen Lawrence was racially abused and then stabbed twice in the shoulder and collarbone by a group of six white men with a history of racist violence. With his lung collapsing and four major blood vessels ruptured, he and his friend Duwayne Brooks attempted to flee. After sprinting 130 yards from the scene of the attack, Lawrence collapsed and died of blood loss on the pavement before the ambulance arrived. The ensuing case was horrifically mismanaged, and an inquiry published in 1999 came to the historic (but unsurprising) conclusion that London's Metropolitan Police Service was institutionally racist. It wasn't until 2012, nearly two decades after Lawrence's death, that two of the men involved were finally found guilty of murder.

Among their many blunders and wilful missteps, the police failed to take seriously the testimony of the one eyewitness, who was also a victim of the racist attack: Duwayne Brooks. The police saw a young Black man, and regarded him with immediate suspicion and distrust. They did not ask for his assistance when searching the area, even though he had the best knowledge of the attackers and their movements. Officers mistakenly assumed that the attack had been the result of a fight, and thereby underplayed the fact that Brooks had also been a victim of the violence and a witness to the death of his friend. No one at the scene asked him what had happened or whether he was okay. Not only was he mistrusted and neglected, Brooks was subject to an attempted smear campaign. He was surveilled by police who were tasked with finding 'dirt' that could be used to undermine his credibility.[10] The eventual inquiry concluded that Brooks had been subject to injustices that jeopardised the case:

> We are driven to the conclusion that Mr Brooks was stereotyped as a young black man exhibiting unpleasant hostility and agitation, who could not be expected to help, and whose condition and status simply did not need further examination or understanding. We believe that

Mr Brooks' colour and such stereotyping played their part in the collective failure of those involved to treat him properly and according to his needs.[11]

Philosopher Miranda Fricker points to the case of Duwayne Brooks to illustrate the ways in which the credibility of people who belong to marginalised groups is often automatically downgraded.[12] Regardless of how knowledgeable or trustworthy a person *actually* is, the degree to which they are believed tends to be unfairly low if they belong to a marginalised group. As we've already seen, taking shortcuts when judging credibility is understandable. The problem is that those shortcuts often ride on stereotypes, and stereotypes relating to marginalised groups tend to focus on their members being unintelligent, dishonest, overly emotional, unable to be objective, or some combination of these. In other words, the shortcuts we take when it comes to marginalised people tend to suppress their credibility.

Fricker has a term for the particular injustice of having your credibility systematically downgraded: *testimonial injustice*. A person offers their account of the world – their testimony – and they are unfairly disbelieved or their account is taken less seriously than it should be. As a result, they are prevented from being a full member of the community of knowers in which they live.

Duwayne Brooks experienced testimonial injustice on account of being a Black teenage boy. His status as an eyewitness and the best friend of the victim was overlooked and he was typecast as a violent and aggressive Black man who could therefore not be conceived of as a victim in need of support or a key testifier who could help the investigators. The police acted on stereotypes and Duwayne Brooks was subject to what Fricker calls a *credibility deficit*: he was treated as somebody who was much less credible than he actually was.

Credibility deficits based on race and gender are particularly obvious in the way public figures are treated. In 1987, the first politicians of colour were voted into the UK parliament. Among them was just one woman, Diane Abbott. She'd been the only Black pupil at her grammar school and the only Black student in the Faculty of History at the University of Cambridge, and she was now the first and only

Black woman MP.[13] She'd won the votes of the people of Hackney North and Stoke Newington, in London, but struggled to find support among other politicians. While her face featured prominently on all the opposition's flyers (code for: *vote for the other side and you'll end up with a Black woman*), her own party kept her candidacy quiet, treating her as an embarrassment and a liability. Once elected, she was offered no policy briefing or media coaching, because, as she put it, 'they would rather I fucked up than have any credibility at all'. During a television debate shortly after her election, the presenter announced that the Labour Party was unelectable 'and one of the reasons for it is Diane Abbott and people like her'.[14] The racist dog whistle rang out loud and clear.

Right from the get-go, politicians, the public and the media were eager to see Abbott trip up and corroborate their insistence that she was unfit for power. They attempted to hasten her failure, to force an error, by ridiculing her relentlessly, using established misogynoir tropes to present her as hypersexual and angry.[15] Her appearance was continually cross-examined. She was subjected to rape and death threats. Despite her hefty workload – she managed a large volume of racism-related casework in addition to her regular tasks – she was presented as being lazy and incompetent. A feature in the *Sunday Telegraph* sneered that 'Gossip columnists have made the odd remark about her hips . . . In fact, her only truly outsized attribute is the massive chip on her shoulder.'[16] This was a reference to the common charge that she had secured her position by 'playing the race card', an accusation she weathered while handling hate mail littered with the words 'bitch' and 'n*****'.

Abbott admits that the persistent abuse and lack of support had made her question her career choice. She has shared samples of the messages she receives: 'Pathetic useless fat black piece of shit Abbott. Just a piece of pig shit pond slime who should be fucking hung (if they could find a tree big enough to take the fat bitch's weight).'[17] Tory councillor Alan Pearmain was disciplined for posting the comment 'Nice lips kid. But a shade too much rouge' under an image of an ape wearing lipstick with the caption 'Forget the London look, get the Diane Abbott look.' (He later commented: 'Why is it particularly offensive? People will take offence about everything, won't they?'[18])

Diane Abbott is painted as an Angry Black Woman ill-suited to political life. Her own colleagues have contributed to this perception. In 2015, politician Jess Phillips, who makes a big song and dance of her (very white) feminism, boasted to the *Independent* that she told Abbott to 'fuck off' during a disagreement, asking her: 'Who the fuck do you think you are?' Phillips added that 'people said to me they had always wanted to say that to her, and I don't know why they don't as the opportunity presents itself every other minute.'[19] Abbott was baffled by this tale, responding that 'Jess Phillips MP never told me to fuck off. What was extraordinary is that she made a big deal about telling people she had.'[20]

In 2017, thirty years after she was first elected, Abbott messed up the numbers when asked about the policing budget in a radio interview, venturing an implausible underestimate, and then correcting herself when she found the right page in her notes. Here was the racists' long-awaited proof that this outspoken, uncompromising Black woman was above her station and out of her depth. With shameless glee, she was savaged on social media and slammed in the press. Her detractors paid no attention to the fact that the bungled conversation was her sixth or seventh interview in a row, on an empty stomach, and that she has diabetes and was struggling to maintain safe blood sugar levels. In that election cycle, 45 per cent of all the abusive posts sent to women MPs were aimed at Diane Abbott, most of them making reference to her gender and race, and many containing threats of sexual violence.[21]

Despite all this, in 2017 Diane Abbott won an impressive 75 per cent majority in her London seat (the difference between her votes and those of the runner-up exceeded the number the then-prime minister Theresa May scraped together in total). Abbott is one of Britain's longest-serving MPs and is in the top 3 per cent when it comes to vote share. She is one of Britain's most successful politicians. And yet she's still widely seen as being unworthy of her position.

Diane Abbott's struggle to be taken seriously is an archetypal example of the ways in which gender and race affect a person's credibility. (US politicians Ilhan Omar and Rashida Tlaib have had similar experiences.) We can also now see that Theophilus Painter was subject to a *credibility excess* and Alice Catherine Evans to a credibility *deficit*.

At a basic level, being disbelieved or mistrusted on occasions when you should be believed or trusted is exasperating. But that's the least of it. A credibility deficit can destroy a person's life. Border officials are trained to assume that asylum seekers are making fraudulent claims. Worse, linguistic barriers and the suppression of traumatic memories can lead to minor discrepancies which are readily seized upon as evidence that their claims are bogus, resulting in detention and deportation. Similarly, for those accused of committing crimes, credibility can make the difference between freedom and incarceration, length of sentence, or even life and death.

Being systematically disbelieved means being prevented from taking part in the core human activity of producing and exchanging knowledge. A person's knowledge is downgraded, their attempts to share, inform, teach, argue and correct are undermined. They are elbowed even further into the margins.

## How Stereotypes Discredit

One way of elevating your own apparent credibility is to discredit others, especially those who pose a threat to your account of the world. Over the last few centuries, there have been sustained efforts to present marginalised people as less intelligent and less trustworthy. One could argue that race and gender were constructed precisely with the aim of smearing particular people in order to exploit them more easily.

In 1768, Carl Linnaeus, widely known as the father of modern biological taxonomy (the Linnaean system – consisting of kingdoms, phyla, classes, orders, families, genera and species – is named after him\*), devised a system for classifying humans which characterised Europeans

---

\* Humans are classified as: animalia, chordata, mammalia, primates, hominidae, homo, sapiens.

as 'gentle', 'inventive' and 'governed by laws', while Africans were described as 'crafty, sly, lazy, cunning, lustful, careless . . . and governed by caprice' and African women specifically as 'lacking shame'.[22]

In the nineteenth century, scientists sought to link this race-based behavioural hierarchy to the shapes and sizes of skulls. When that fell out of fashion, they turned their attention to intelligence testing, pointing to differences in IQ between different racial groups. By the mid-twentieth century, most scientists had concluded that social and economic factors explained any observed differences. Yet every twenty years or so, a white man publishes a new text which claims to have found that Holy Grail of white supremacy: evidence that genetic differences make Black people less intelligent.[23] (Note that when white children underachieve in the UK, commentators go straight to the assumption that white people's educational needs are being neglected, or that poverty is responsible.[24]) Such texts often come from disgruntled right-wing ideologues, and are easily debunked – most often because they cite low-quality, biased studies, neglect to consider contextual factors or involve strategic misinterpretations – but the embers of racist myths about differences in intelligence have never been fully extinguished.

Scientists have also frantically sought to prove that women have smaller, less powerful brains, governed by hormonal fluctuations, which make them apt to lie and exaggerate. Aristotle was an early adopter of this view, writing in 350 BC that women are 'more void of shame or self-respect, more false of speech, more deceptive [than men]'.[25] This set the tone for the next two and a half thousand years. In 1886, the president of the British Medical Association worried not only about women's intelligence, but that educating them would be detrimental to their sexual and reproductive health and marriageability, leading to 'anorexia scholastica'.[26]

French anthropologist and psychologist Gustave Le Bon was one of several scientists determined to find that women's brains were smaller than, and cognitively inferior to, men's. In 1879, he wrote that: 'There are a large number of women whose brains are closer in size to those of gorillas than to the most developed male brains . . . This inferiority is so obvious that no one can contest it for a moment.'[27]

These speculations were eventually countered by mathematician Alice Lee, one of the first women to graduate from the University of London. She devised a formula for calculating skull capacity, which was at that time thought to be a proxy for intelligence. She tested her formula on a group of women students, a group of male university staff, and thirty-five prominent anatomists. A leading anatomist turned out to have one of the smallest heads, and many of the women students had larger skulls than the famous scientists. Many staunch adherents of the skull size–brain power hypothesis quietly abandoned the theory, and Lee's mentor (the eugenicist Karl Pearson) wrote a paper eight years later firmly repudiating the idea of a correlation between cranial capacity and intelligence in humans.[28]

Menstruation has also long been a candidate for explaining the cognitive inferiority of women. During the Second World War, doctors warned women pilots against flying when they were affected by the 'dysfunction' of their menstrual cycle. (Many women got around this rule by claiming their periods were highly irregular so they could fly throughout their cycles.[29]) Recruits also had to be thirty-five or younger, 'to avoid the irrationality of women when they enter and go through menopause'. A study led by endocrinologist Brigitte Leeners is the latest of many to show that menstruation has no effect on cognitive function.[30] Yet mistrust persists: a 2013 survey revealed that 51 per cent of British people would not trust a woman pilot.[31]

The idea that women are led by feelings and men by reason is also still widespread. A 2019 study required participants to respond to gendered words quickly as they flashed up on a screen (e.g. uncle, brother vs aunt, sister) along with words associated with thinking (e.g. rational, logical) and feeling (e.g. emotional, intuition). The experimenters found that the concept of 'reason' is more readily associated with men, while feelings are associated with women.[32]

The supposedly superior rationality and competence of men conveniently falters in just one area: the domestic realm. Here, men are often taken to be inherently inept at housework and care work, and irrational and reckless in relation to sex. A man's rationality can be overruled, we are told, by the 'uncontrollable' male libido, which leads him to 'think with his dick'. His competence is inadequate to the demands of childcare or housework. (An entire comedy film and television genre is devoted to the ineptitude of men as they attempt to care for children and perform basic domestic chores.)

This myth of domain-specific incompetence liberates men from sexual responsibility, care work and household chores without having any bearing on their fitness for power and responsibility in other domains. This frees up men's time for leisure or higher-status paid work, while women are burdened with additional unpaid labour and responsibility.

Similar observations can be made about people of colour. A migrant domestic worker in Lebanon once told me that it never ceased to amaze her that the family she worked for trusted her to care for their young children and prepare their meals, but not to keep hold of her own passport. I could poison them all, she joked. We are inconsistent about who we trust and the domains in which we trust them.

That stereotypes about people of colour and women should cluster around their incompetence in relation to skills and roles that are held in high esteem is no accident. If they are less intelligent, then their suitability for positions of power and influence is automatically called into question. Power is best protected by presenting anyone who poses a threat as being biologically unfit to hold it.

## Credibility Penalties in Action

Once you start looking, credibility deficits that arise from stereotypes are everywhere. Studies have shown that when people are asked to judge the quality of scientific research articles, they rate the same texts more highly when told they were written by men.[33] Likewise, juries find male expert witnesses more trustworthy, likable and believable than their female counterparts.[34] The same is true for social media posts: political tweets are thought to be more credible when respondents believe they were posted by men.[35] And identical CVs are deemed to be more impressive when the name at the top is assumed to be that of a man or a white person.[36] In a 2014 study, researchers set up an online live-chat course and found that when they were perceived to be men, instructors were judged to be more professional, more knowledgeable and more enthusiastic than when students thought they were bring taught by women.[37]

Accents are also strongly determinative of credibility. Americans tend to perceive British accents as indicating intelligence, while those with Latinx, Midwest and New York accents are perceived to be less intelligent.[38] Similarly, British people associate received pronunciation English and Network American with greater intelligence compared with regional British and American accents.[39] (Comparable associations are observed for German speakers, where regional accents lead to lower assessments of competence and reduced employability.[40]) In one study, non-native English speakers with stronger foreign accents were deemed to be less believable when asked to repeat trivia statements.[41] The stronger the accent, the more marked the credibility deficit. Another study showed that foreign-accented job applicants were discriminated against for high-status jobs, and deemed to be better-suited to low-status jobs.[42] Accents are often a proxy for socio-economic class and ethnicity, and accent prejudice is usually a form of classism, racism, or both.

Confidence is often taken to be a proxy for credibility. A psychology study gave a group of 242 students a list of historical figures and events, and asked them to indicate only the ones they had heard of. Some were real events and some fabrications. Ticking fake events and figures was understood to be a sign of overconfidence. The researchers then asked the students to rate each other's academic performance. Those who had claimed to know the greatest number of fake facts were rated the cleverest by their peers.[43] We are more likely to see people as being credible when they project self-assuredness.[44]

Reading off credibility from confidence is worrying, because self-assuredness is heavily gendered: men and boys tend towards over-confidence, while women and girls tend towards under-confidence. This trend has been observed across many contexts. Women are likely to apply for jobs or promotions only when they meet all of the listed requirements, while men apply if they think they can meet around half of them.[45] Male students overestimate their test scores compared with their actual performance, while female students underestimate theirs, and this effect is stronger where respondents also indicate agreement with gender stereotypes.[46] This suggests that the more sexist a man is, the more overconfident he's likely to be.

If it sounds as though women are holding themselves back and men are helping themselves out, note the ways in which these confidence disparities arise. Women are not only treated as though they are less competent, which often leads to 'imposter syndrome' and low confidence, but they also face social *penalties* for projecting confidence. A recent meta-analysis established that when women display confident, dominant behaviours, their likability (and employability) dwindles.[47] Yale Professor Victoria Brescoll has studied this effect, and found that when participants were asked to consider a woman CEO who talked more than her colleagues, they judged her to be less competent and a worse leader than a male CEO who spoke the same amount. When they were instead told that she spoke less than other people, her competence was rated more highly.[48] Taking all this together, if you're a woman, you need to pipe down to be taken seriously, but unless you're confidently speaking up, you risk being treated as less competent (one of many 'double binds' that are characteristic of oppression).

Similarly, psychologist Madeline Heilman led a study in which participants were asked to rate the competence of two fictional assistant vice-presidents of a company, James and Andrea. In the first part of the study, participants read James and Andrea's *identical*, fairly average personnel files. While they were rated as being equally likable, 86 per cent of participants thought James was better at his job. No surprise there: James gets a credibility excess, and Andrea a credibility deficit. That's sexist testimonial injustice for you. In the second part of the study, the files reveal that James and Andrea are both in the top 5 per cent of performers in their companies. While James and Andrea's perceived competence equalised (there's no arguing with the fact that they are both excellent at their jobs), 83 per cent of people found James more *likable* than Andrea.

Women participants are just as likely to hold these biases as men.[49] As philosopher Kate Manne puts it:

> Regardless of their own gender, people tend to assume that men in historically male-dominated positions of power are more competent than women, unless this assumption is explicitly contradicted by further information. And when it is so contradicted, women are liable to be disliked and regarded, in particular, as 'interpersonally hostile,' . . . being perceived as conniving, pushy, selfish, abrasive, manipulative, and untrustworthy.[50]

The upshot is that as a woman, you can be competent, or you can be likable, but you can't be both. It is assumed that women are less competent than men, but when we are forced to admit that they are just as capable, we don't like them any more. Competence is required of those in positions of power, and reducing one's approval of a person who is undeniably proficient is a way of discouraging such people from seeking high-status positions. The trends mentioned here are exacerbated for women of colour. The attacks on Diane Abbott have always been deliberately hostile: they intend to warn Black women that they are not welcome in politics.

In short, a range of stereotypes relating to our social identities operates to pigeonhole each of us in terms of competence and trustworthiness. Unsurprisingly, confident white men do particularly well, and you end up with absurd statistics, like the fact that there are fewer women at the helm of major UK companies than there are men named John.[51]

## The Cost of Disbelief

One of the most pernicious instances of the collective failure to believe women is the widespread myth that women lie about rape. As recently as 2003, the sex crimes investigative division in Philadelphia was colloquially known as the 'lying bitch unit', while a 2016 report on the Baltimore City Police Department found that the testimonies of those reporting sexual assault were regarded with 'undue scepticism'.[52] This is despite the fact that the data show that women are no more likely to lie about rape than people are to lie about any other crime. Recent data from the UK over a seventeen-month period recorded 5,651 prosecutions for rape and thirty-five prosecutions for false allegations, meaning that less than 1 per cent of allegations were false.[53] This is in a context in which rape victims are frequently disbelieved and in which low reporting rates mean the number of prosecutions is much lower than the number of actual rapes.

That women are at risk of sexual harm is axiomatic, a fixed point around which the rest of our lives must turn. For at least eight hours each day, and in most of the world's streets, parks, countryside and leisure sites, unaccompanied women are not safe. We do not ask for explanations as to why the world is like this. Rather, women are warned that half of the day and more than half of the world is for the exclusive use of men. In 2021, a YouGov poll indicated that 86 per cent of women in the UK aged between eighteen and twenty-four have been sexually harassed in public spaces, which gives the lie to the notion that things are getting better.[54] Only 4 per cent of those who had been harassed reported the incident.

Speaking up is costly and the returns are slim. Outlandish questions are asked of the victim:* 'Are you lying? What did you do to bring this on? Don't you realise what this will mean for him?' Kate Manne describes this last question as being motivated by 'himpathy': the excessive sympathy that is spontaneously extended to the purported perpetrator, rather than the victim.[55] (Though note that himpathy is much less enthusiastically extended to men of colour, a point I'll return to later in this chapter.) There is a widespread tendency to place the horror of being a man who is falsely accused above the horror of being a woman who is abused, and thereby to lean towards the suspicion that she might be lying. No other life experience, no other crime, is met

---

* I use the term 'victim' rather than 'survivor' because not everyone survives sexual wrongdoing. I acknowledge that not everyone is comfortable with this term, but hope it will encourage readers to think of sexual wrongdoing as a form of wrongdoing more generally.

with such clamorous and automatic distrust and such reluctant sympathy. Those who speak up become cautionary tales which leave the rest of us feeling safer in our silence.

It is instructive to take a closer look at the small number of falsified allegations of sexual assault. First, these cases rarely amount to anything; they're almost never situations that end up derailing the life of the accused. Studies from the United States show that half of these claims are made by someone other than the victim herself (often a parent, typically in cases in which a child has lied to avoid getting into trouble for staying out late). A fair proportion of false reports are attempts to access medical care or psychiatric help, and are dropped once this end is achieved. Those who pursue false claims are usually people with a history of fraud and fabrications, in most cases individuals leading difficult lives with various unmet financial, emotional and medical needs. Some struggle with untreated mental illnesses which can cause a break with reality, so that 'lying' wouldn't be the right word anyway.[56] The lesson is therefore not that women lie, but that societies fail to take care of those most in need. And the grim irony is that it is precisely those people whose urgent needs are unmet and who lack support networks (unhoused people, poor people, LGBT people, people with criminal records and people who are physically or mentally ill) who are most vulnerable to sexual assault.

The effects of the myth are grave. Even when sixty women had come forward accusing Bill Cosby of rape, the idea that he was an abuser was still regularly doubted. What if they were just lying, all sixty of them? What if they wanted vengeance? (No one ever seems to ask *why* a bunch of women who don't know each other might wish to take revenge on a particular man.) That such a ridiculous hypothesis seemed reasonable gives a sense of how desperately people cling to the idea that women lie, and how reluctant we are to confront the reality that men, including (and perhaps *especially*) successful men, rape.[57] Similarly, Harvey Weinstein harassed and assaulted at least eighty women over the course of three decades before his behaviour was taken seriously.[58] And with the accusations of at least a dozen women in his sails, Donald Trump breezed into the most powerful position in the world.

Being routinely subject to a credibility deficit means having to work harder than others in order to be believed. Writing in the *Los Angeles Review of Books*, Sarah Banet-Weiser notes that 'performing believability is yet another extra shift in women's work'.[59] Starting from the position of a 'burden of doubt', women must toil to prove they are credible before any of their claims are heard. This can mean treading the line between showing too much emotion and being cast as irrational, or insufficient emotion and being seen as cold and calculating. It can mean going over a traumatic incident with a fine-tooth comb to gather the strongest possible evidence, knowing that the authorities will probably fail to do the requisite investigatory work, while keeping in mind that a glut of evidence may make one's claim look too orchestrated to be believable.

It isn't only when a man's reputation is at risk that women's testimony is met with doubt and suspicion. As a rule, when we talk about our bodies in any context we are liable to experience testimonial injustice. My mother practically has to be strong-armed to the doctor when she is unwell, because she has been made to feel that her medical problems are trifling or exaggerated (my father has the same doctor and no such trouble). I was told by a gastroenterologist that my symptoms were common in 'high-achieving young women'. That's doctor-speak for: 'maybe it's all in your head?' (Six months later a biopsy confirmed that my small bowel had been damaged by coeliac disease.) These anecdotes are instances of a wider problem.

Women are between 13 and 25 per cent less likely to receive analgesics for abdominal pain, even when they have the same reported pain scores as men, and they typically wait longer for any medication to be given.[60] Women who are admitted to hospital with irritable bowel syndrome are more likely to be offered sedatives and lifestyle advice, while male patients with the same symptoms are offered X-ray imaging of the digestive system.[61] In general, women are more likely than men to have their pain attributed to psychological causes, and to be given mental health referrals rather than physical investigations and treatments.[62] The myth that boys really mean it when they say they're in pain, while girls may lie or exaggerate, is applied even to infants, which suggests that people believe that girls are *born* malingerers.

Studies show that adults rate the pain of a crying baby as being more serious when they are told the child is a boy than when they're told the child is a girl.[63] Disparities have also been established in relation to race. A 2015 study led by Monika Goyal demonstrated that Black children with appendicitis were less likely to receive painkillers for moderate pain, and less likely to receive opioid painkillers for severe pain, which suggests that their pain reports were subject to a credibility deficit (or their pain was deemed to be more endurable).[64] Similarly, a set of studies published in 2022 found that adult participants tend to believe that toddlers from poor families feel less pain than their wealthier peers, which suggests that poor children are also subject to credibility deficits.[65]

This research points to a broader trend: marginalised people's accounts of their own bodies are very often discredited, which is one of several ways in which oppression limits the health and wellbeing of particular communities. In the UK, access to abortion services requires that two doctors deem a termination to be necessary. In the absence of physical health risks, pregnant people must be at risk of mental illness or be deemed unfit to parent in order to have their abortion approved. This means that the law requires that pregnant people present themselves as vulnerable to mental illness if the pregnancy continues, or as lacking the capacity to care for a child.[66] Similarly, trans people's testimonies about their own genders are not only deflated, but are often denied outright. Even when legal and medical recognition is available, it tends to require that trans people conform to a narrow sense of what gender consists of, and to report a particular attitude towards their own bodies in order to access the services they need. Their own testimonies are deflated, while medical professionals' assessments of their identities are inflated. Philosophers Miranda Fricker and Katharine Jenkins also note that the characterisation of trans people as experiencing a psychiatric disorder makes them additionally vulnerable to having their testimony dismissed on the grounds that they are thereby unreliable, unstable or dishonest.[67] There is no way to win; credibility deficits ensnare marginalised people.

## Faking It

I've gone to some effort in this chapter to dispute the myth that women are liars. The awkward truth is that women do appear to be more dishonest than men. Forty per cent of women report lying on a daily basis, as opposed to 20 per cent of men.[68] (Though it may be that women are more honest or self-aware when it comes to their dishonesty.) Some women admit to lying as often as thirty times every day. In more than half of cases, women lie in order to 'make someone feel better'. The second most common reason is so as 'not to get into trouble' and the third is because 'life is complicated'. The most common context in which these lies are told is the home, where women lie in order to smooth things over with the people they live with and care for.

In the 1989 film *When Harry Met Sally*, Harry insists, over lunch in a Manhattan deli, that he would know if a woman was faking an orgasm. Sally calls bullshit, contending that men cannot tell the difference. When Harry scoffs and insists that *he* knows when it's the real thing, Sally responds, 'It's just that all men are sure it's never happened to them and most women at one time or another have done it, so you do the math.' She begins a series of highly plausible ascending coital moans, slapping the table and throwing her head back as she reaches a loud and head-turning climax. Having made her point, she calmly eats a forkful of salad. (The scene closes with the immortal line, from Estelle Reiner – the mother of the film's director, Rob Reiner – 'I'll have what she's having.')

The fact that women sometimes lie about orgasms when they have sex with men is usually presented as a humorous one, a private joke between women about the ways in which we hoodwink men, and how easily they're fooled. But it's not funny. When women lie about orgasming, they put their partner's feelings ahead of their own pleasure, and, as a trend, that's troubling. Women also frequently report faking orgasms as a strategy to end bad sex.[69] As Lili Loofbourow noted in a 2018 article in *The Week*, 'bad' sex for women often means coercive or physically painful sex, while 'bad' sex for men means uninteresting or unexciting sex.[70] A 2015 study found that 30 per cent of women experience pain during penis-in-vagina sex, and almost three-quarters during penis-in-anus sex. In 43 per cent of cases, women keep quiet about their discomfort, and in half of the cases where they do speak up, neither partner does anything about it. The authors of the study note that painful sex is 'the norm' for women, who often feel a duty to grit their teeth and please their partner regardless.[71]

Women not only lie within sex; they also lie to avoid sex. A 2012 survey found that sixty-one per cent of women report lying in order to get out of having unwanted sex.[72] The age-old, seemingly apocryphal, feigned headache, is in fact the third most common excuse, just behind being too tired and having an early start the following morning.

Lying about sex and suffering in sex are ways of meeting our needs in an imperfect world. Power compels us to conform to its desires, and when we cannot meet those desires, it forces us to lie to avoid its rage. Women lie about orgasms to avoid humiliating men who believe they are able to satisfy women's sexual desires. It is better to feign sexual pleasure because men's displeasure is potentially dangerous. As Katherine Angel points out in *Tomorrow Sex Will Be Good Again*, this affects women's conceptions of their own pleasure, so that the question of what women want in sex (and elsewhere) is a vexed one. We do not exist under conditions in which women can easily form desires that are legible even to ourselves.[73]

Strategic dishonesty is deployed in other, non-sexual contexts. When a man starts mansplaining, it is often safer and easier to let him unspool his boring monologue uninterrupted than to interject to tell him you already know, or that he's got it wrong. An interruption could be met with hostility or aggression. Literature scholar and cultural critic Koritha Mitchell speaks of the 'know-your-place' aggression that people from marginalised groups, and people of colour in particular, face when their success or expertise unnerves those with privileged identities.[74] Sometimes it's safest to let someone believe they know more.

Tolerating mansplaining is one part of a broader trend in which women pretend to be less intelligent than they are. A girl in my younger sister's class at school handed back a test that she had peer-marked and pleaded with my sister to deduct a few points. She was concerned that her cleverness would threaten her social cachet. This is a common concern, and with good reason. A 2014 study by sociologist Maria do Mar Pereira found that by age fourteen, boys in the UK have acquired the belief that the intelligence of women undermines their masculinity and, accordingly, the girls in their peer groups downplay their aptitude.[75] These pressures persist into adulthood. A 2016 study conducted in the US showed that men tend to find intelligent women less attractive, and are prepared to make an exception only if an intelligent woman is also exceptionally beautiful.[76] Many girls and women respond to this reality by feigning 'ditziness' and allowing men to believe they are more intelligent, cultured and knowledgeable. In some contexts, being seen as inordinately clever can affect a woman's life options. I have a Chinese friend whose parents were opposed to her doing a PhD lest she thereafter be seen as cold, frigid, and anti-family, and end up becoming one of the unmarried *shengnu* (leftover women). Writing about this phenomenon in *Quartz*, journalist Lily Kuo describes a popular joke in China, which posits that there are three genders: men, women and women with PhDs.[77]

And then there are the 'lies' we tell to make our bodies more acceptable. A 2017 survey showed that 63 per cent of men believe that women 'mainly wear make-up to trick people into thinking they're attractive.' Just under half of the women polled agreed with this statement.[78] In other words, make-up is widely understood to be a fraudulent form of presentation. Similar forms of bodily 'dishonesty' abound: dyeing hair, wearing push-up bras or compression underwear, depilation, surgical enhancements and tanning or lightening skin. Women of colour often feel an even greater pressure to 'lie' in these ways through the use of skin-bleaching creams, wigs or hair extensions, and cosmetic surgery to reshape noses, eyelids and jaw-lines to approximate 'white' beauty standards more closely.

Oppressed people are often required to lie in order to survive in a world that is hostile to their flourishing on honest terms. When another party has power over a person's life, including perhaps whether they can live at all, dishonesty becomes necessary to survival. Consider the phenomenon of plea bargaining in the US criminal justice system, which compels innocent people (often people of colour) to lie in order to save themselves from lengthier jail sentences. Or the ways in which asylum seekers, desperate for refuge, are sometimes incentivised to lie in order to conform to the narrow range of suffering that is intelligible to hostile Global North governments. Writing in the *New Yorker*, Suketu Mehta describes this pressure to embellish:

> It is not enough for asylum applicants to say that they were threatened, or even beaten. They have to furnish horror stories. It's not enough to say that they were raped. The officials require details. Inevitably, these atrocity stories are inflated, as new applicants for asylum get more inventive about what was done to them, competing with the lore that has already been established.[79]

We can understand this strategic dishonesty through the work of philosopher Kristie Dotson, who describes the way in which marginalised people often remain silent, or modify their testimony, because their honesty might lead to consequences that are dangerous to them. Those from oppressed groups are therefore motivated to give a distorted or partial account of their experiences. Dotson refers to this as 'testimonial smothering'.[80] It's a form of self-censorship that silences people, limiting their access to successful, productive exchanges with others in which they can voice their needs and thereby increase the chance of having them met.

Drawing on the work of Kimberlé Crenshaw,[81] Dotson offers the example of Black women's experiences of domestic violence. Black women may be reluctant to speak out or seek help when they experience violence at the hands of Black men, because they fear (quite understandably) that their reports will be taken to confirm racist stereotypes about the violence of Black men, and thereby lead to worse outcomes for Black communities as a whole (racial profiling, being shot by police). They may therefore smother their testimony, which is also harmful to them, but may be the least bad option. Not only are those from subjugated groups compelled to smother the truth, in many cases they must provide *false testimony* in its place. They have to lie as a form of self-preservation. Those who lie in this way bargain with the violent forms of power that constrain their existence.

We often think about the negative effects of lying on those who are lied to, but what about the cost to a person who has no choice but to lie? Lying has adverse effects on physical and mental health,[82] including elevated blood pressure, heart rate and cortisol levels.[83] It leads to neurological adaptations which facilitate future, larger lies.[84] Producing and upholding lies is tiring and stressful,[85] and can also affect a person's conception of the truth, as they attempt to minimise cognitive dissonance by pruning off memories that contradict a lie.[86] And if deception is suspected or discovered, there can be serious reputational costs that further limit their credibility and that of others who share their identities.

There might therefore be an additional layer of testimonial injustice to consider: not only does oppression reduce a person's credibility, it also tends to deprive them of the ability to be honest in scenarios where being so endangers their safety or comfort, making them less credible still.

## Credibility in a Complex World

While it's often the case that women are disbelieved when they shouldn't be, and men are believed even when they shouldn't be, the real world, with its intersecting dimensions of oppression, defies this gloss. The most common exception occurs when the credibility deficit faced by men of colour collides with that faced by white women.

In the UK, there is a widespread stereotype that South Asian men are sexual predators. A couple of high-profile cases of child sexual abuse rings with South Asian members have been used by racist commentators to foment a moral panic. In 2017, Sarah Champion, the equalities minister for the Labour Party, wrote an article in a major newspaper which began with the statement: 'Britain has a problem with British Pakistani men raping and exploiting white girls.

There. I said it. Does that make me a racist?'[87] (For the record, yes Sarah, it does.) The term 'Muslim grooming gang' has played a major role in British public discourse in the past five years, often accompanied by the claim that people are too afraid to report or punish these crimes for fear of being accused of racism. In fact, women are probably more likely to report rape when the perpetrator is a man of colour, because in those cases they have a better chance of being believed. In 2020, a government report concluded that child sexual abuse networks are primarily composed of white men under the age of thirty.[88] How could Champion and the British media have got it so wrong? They were primed to underplay the sexual wrongdoing of white men and overblow that of Brown men.

Women and girls are *under*-believed when it comes to sexual abuse and assault, yet Brown men are often *over*-suspected of committing those offences. Brown men are not the only group to be over-suspected. Black men have long been represented as violent, hypersexual and a threat to white women. This has often been put down to biology, or else to the peculiar, victim-blaming idea that Black men rape white women as revenge for racism. In *Women, Race & Class*, Angela Davis describes the history of this trend. She points out that during the American Civil War, when white men were away fighting, not a single Black man was publicly accused of rape by a white woman. The idea that Black men cannot control their impulses to rape white women arose after the abolition of slavery, as a justification for lynching.[89] Lynching made little sense when Black men were enslaved, as this would amount to the destruction of one's own 'property', but after abolition, lynching was a way of continuing to suppress Black people with violence, and protecting a woman's honour was the most socially acceptable defence for savage murders.

Unsurprisingly, white women played their role within this violent set-up. One of the most famous cases is that of Carolyn Bryant, who, on 21 August 1955, served fourteen-year-old Emmett Till in her grocery shop. He bought chewing gum, and put the money in her hand instead of onto the counter, as Black customers were expected to, and is then reported to have whistled, before leaving.[90] Four days later, Bryant's husband and his brother kidnapped Till at gunpoint, tortured him, shot him dead, weighted his body and threw him in a river. At Till's murder trial, Carolyn Bryant alleged that Till had made verbal and physical advances. The two killers were acquitted. In 2017, she admitted to historian Timothy Tyson that she fabricated her courtroom testimony.[91]

You can draw a line from Carolyn Bryant in 1955 to Amy Cooper in 2020, calling the police when asked to put her dog on a lead in a restricted area of Central Park, and telling them 'There is an African American man . . . recording me and threatening myself and my dog. Please send the cops immediately.' Cooper made the preposterous claim (on video) because she felt confident that her testimony would trump that of a Black man.

Even so, to pit white women against men of colour is too simple. In our efforts to dispel the myth that men of colour have a propensity to rape, we should not feed the myth that women have a propensity to lie, nor *vice versa*. Rather, we are all positioned within a system that primarily protects capital, and does so partly through the supremacy of whiteness and of men. We are liable to disbelieve women and girls until the alleged transgressor is a man of colour, and to believe men unless they are Brown or Black and the accuser is white. Then we are apt to be excessively eager to believe. The impulse in both cases is the same: protect white men and their interests; protect a system whose unchallenged functioning requires that people of colour and white women are kept in their places.

A second complexity also bears mentioning. One of the hashtags of the #MeToo movement is #BelieveWomen. Opponents of the movement have railed against this slogan, on the grounds that believing *all* women is ridiculous. Of course women lie and get things wrong; everybody does. And due process *is* important, even if those processes are clearly in need of an overhaul. Yet #BelieveWomen doesn't mean 'believe *all* women'. Like 'men are trash' it's a *generic* generalisation. It means 'women are, as a general rule, credible'. And that follows from the fact that *people*, as a general rule, are credible. Everyone deserves to be given a fair hearing and the benefit of the doubt. The only reason we have to make that point in relation to women is because they're treated as *lacking* credibility on account of being women.

Writing in the *New York Times*, Susan Faludi points out that right-wing commentators have deliberately inserted an 'all' into the statement and then criticised the doctored hashtag #BelieveAllWomen.[92] And unsurprisingly, the rigged version is now sometimes uncritically reproduced by those who care about women's credibility. We must resist this. It's just a slogan, but its imprecision not only threatens to discredit our demands, but also to marginalise those who may be harmed by the testimonies of (e.g. cis, white, middle-class) women. Obviously we should not believe *all* women, nor should we believe *all* men of colour, but we can start by owning up to the troubling patterns in our allocation of credibility, and the differential harms they're causing.

## The Testimony of Trees

In 2020, more than 8,000 wildfires burned over 4 million acres of California. They have two major determinants. One is climate change, which is extending the fire season and pushing temperatures to new records, leaving forests parched to within a spark of disaster. The other is a century-long policy of total fire suppression. North American Indigenous wisdom prescribes burning off the forest understorey every decade or so to eliminate the tinder that foments larger, less predictable blazes. The growth rings of ancient trees bear the marks of these precautionary burns, which periodically singed their bark without killing them. If, centuries from now, there are any trees left to tell the tale, or dendrochronologists to read them, the testimonial injustice experienced by Indigenous people will be legible in the 100-year absence of fire scars in the rings of old trees.

The science of Indigenous people has long been ignored and discredited in order to uphold the idea that Europeans brought science and rationality to 'primitive' places. Over the past two decades, as the threat of global heating has ratcheted up, it has been ever harder, and more foolish, to deny the expertise of Indigenous scientists, whose knowledge is essential to returning the planet to good health. Rangers from Aboriginal and Torres Strait Islander groups in Australia have been critical to developing fire management practices that have reduced the areas affected by blazes, resulting in a dramatic fall in carbon emissions.[93] Tiwi islander Willie Rioli said that 'people need to listen to science – the success of our industry has been from a collaboration between our traditional knowledge and modern science and this cooperation has made our work the most innovative and successful in the world.'[94] Similarly, Maori and Pacific Islander scientists have long been tracking the behaviours and slipstreams of whales and dolphins, and hold knowledge that is essential to understanding changes to their populations and the profound dangers of commercial fishing and mining.[95]

Indigenous peoples are wronged by testimonial injustice, and a consequence of that wrong is the broader failure to heed the precious, expert knowledge that is vital to averting, mitigating or surviving climate crisis, and imagining ways to live in balance with the rest of the biosphere. Likewise, when we downgrade the credibility of women, people of colour, trans people, disabled people and people of other marginalised identities, we wrong them because we deny them participation in the core human activity of producing and exchanging knowledge, but we also eliminate vital accounts of what is wrong with this damaged and divided world, and how we might go about fixing it.

This epistemic impoverishment has measurable effects. To take just one example, 80 per cent of 'experts' quoted in online news articles in the UK are men, and this trend, which is particularly pronounced in relation to business and economics, hasn't changed over the last decade.[96] This perpetuates the harmful idea that women are not able to speak authoritatively. But there's a bigger issue: certain perspectives are excluded. A 2018 study showed that the gender of an economist tends to be predictive of their views on economic policy. Men often favour market solutions, while women lean towards government interventions, and are more likely to prioritise protecting the environment and opposing austerity measures.[97] Women's life experiences inform their political and economic views. Platforming male economists has shifted public opinion as to which policy suggestions are most tenable, influencing political decisions in ways that entrench certain ways of living together to the exclusion of others.

Challenging testimonial injustices requires us to destabilise the stereotypes on which they rely and radically revise how we apportion credibility. That doesn't mean believing uncritically. Rather, we must face up to the fact that our assignments of credibility are already uncritical. Consciously breaking away from the received views about who is believable promises to move us all towards something more like the truth.

# 7

## Where Does a Mansplainer Get His Water?*

As a rule the man who has been led to believe that he is a brilliant and interesting talker has been led to make himself a rapacious pest. No conversation is possible between others whose ears are within reach of his ponderous voice . . . There is a simple rule, by which if one is a voluble chatterer . . . one can at least refrain from being a pest or a bore. And the rule is merely, to stop and think.

> Emily Post, *Etiquette in Society, in*
> *Business, in Politics, and at Home* (1922)

There is a scene in Aldous Huxley's 1925 novel, *Those Barren Leaves*, in which a bumptious older man, described as 'potentially anything he chose to be, but actually, through indolence, unknown', periodically breaks off droning on about his own ideas to turn to the young woman beside him, an accomplished novelist, and say: 'I give you the notion, gratis, as the subject for a story.' She replies that she is 'most grateful' for his suggestions, but the reader senses her toes curling in annoyance.[1]

The act of mansplaining long predates the term, which was coined by feminist bloggers following the publication of Rebecca Solnit's article (which later spawned a book of essays) 'Men Explain Things to Me: Facts Didn't Get in Their Way'.[2] Solnit gave an account of an incident at a party in which a man asked about the books she'd authored. She started to describe her most recent work, a monograph

---

* From a well, actually. (Internet joke, source unknown, *c.* 2016.)

on the photographer Eadweard Muybridge, but was cut short by the man's interjection: 'And have you heard about the very important Muybridge book that came out this year?' He proceeded to describe the book (which, it transpired, he hadn't actually read) while Solnit's friend repeated over and over again: 'That's her book.' Solnit was so stunned by his mansplanation of her own work that she momentarily believed that someone else had published a book on the same topic that year.

Solnit's essay lifted the lid on the antisocial behaviours of those who explain, pontificate, and correct others where these interventions are unwelcome and patronising. We have all had our brushes with mansplainers, and if characters in novels are anything to go by, they were just as common and tiresome in centuries past. But what's actually wrong with an inapt explanation? Is there anything *morally* amiss? Is it fair to chastise others for explaining things without invitation?

Explaining is, in the general case, a morally laudable activity. It's useful, generous and essential for learning. Explanations are the central engines of knowledge, supplying the 'hows' and 'whys' that allow us to make sense of the world. But it is precisely this property that means they are readily coopted as instruments of hierarchy, manipulation and injustice. The question of who gets to do the explaining is a political matter.

## What Is an Explanation?

A child and parent walk down a street. They pass an unhoused man in a shop doorway who asks, 'Excuse me, can you spare any change?' While the parent looks away, the child gapes in puzzlement, glancing back a few times, and once they're out of earshot, asks, 'Why didn't we give him any money?' Her parent doesn't miss a beat: 'Lots of homeless people are drug addicts and if we give him money he'll just spend it on drugs.' This explanation percolates through the child's mind, forming new connections and pinching off old ones. The beginnings of a prejudice take shape as the explanation does what explanations do and reorders her prior understanding of the world.

An explanation succeeds when it revises a person's initial assumptions in such a way as to allow them to make better sense of their observations. Sometimes we request explanations directly, in the form of questions, like the child in the example. In other cases, it's just obvious that someone would benefit from an explanation, even though they haven't directly asked for one. Consider the following exchange between two co-workers in a town in which a widely reported sexual assault occurred the week before:

PERSON 1: Apparently he attacked her not long after she left that new bar at the end of the high street.

PERSON 2: Poor girl. It's awful, isn't it? Such a shock. It's a nice part of town, too. My neighbour knows the family, and said she's a lovely girl.

PERSON 1: Well, the newspaper said she'd been chatting to him all evening, and I heard she was tottering on great big heels and wearing a very short dress.

PERSON 2: Had she been drinking?

PERSON 1: They said she could barely stand up, so, you know . . .

PERSON 2: Oh, I didn't know that. Well, I suppose that makes it slightly different.

Having previously believed that an 'undeserving' person had been attacked without provocation, Person 2 now understands the victim to have engaged in behaviours which encouraged the assault. Person 2 is perhaps a proponent of a common worldview, the 'just-world hypothesis', whose adherents believe that the world is fair and if bad things happen to somebody, it must be because they did something to deserve it. This worldview is threatened by the fact that something terrible has happened to a 'lovely girl', and is restored by Person 1, who *explains* that the girl was wearing revealing clothing, had been flirting with the rapist, and was drunk.

The question of which 'facts' feature in our background assumptions about the world is a highly political one, and they are liable to be those that stabilise existing distributions of power. They often originate in the direct or indirect messaging that we are exposed to daily through mass media, as well as in oppressive stereotypes that are rarely explicitly challenged. In the example above, the views held by the discussants are morally troubling and empirically questionable, but disturbingly common. A 2018 survey carried out by UK charity End Violence Against Women Coalition found that a third of men and one in five women believe that if a woman flirted on a date, then any subsequent sex is not rape, even if she doesn't consent to it. A 2019 survey carried out by the *Independent* found that 55 per cent of men, and 41 per cent of women, believed that 'the more revealing the clothes a woman wears, the more likely it is that she will be harassed or assaulted'.

Explanations work by converting surprising events into unsurprising events. They do so by introducing additional information which causes a person to revise her view of the subject under consideration. They are powerful interventions. In the cases just described, they are used to introduce or reinforce 'facts' about the world that harm unhoused people and victims of sexual violence. In this sense, explanations are an effective method for entrenching ideologies.

So far we've considered cases in which an explanation is clearly necessary. There are other situations in which the context makes it appropriate to offer explanations as a matter of course. I routinely offer my students explanations of various phenomena because that is expected within my role as a lecturer in the context of a university. Then there are the scenarios in which an explanation is neither requested nor appropriate. That's okay if it's a mistake; less so when we start to notice patterns in the kind of people who impose unsolicited explanations on others.

## Splaining

One of the most notorious misdemeanours of explanation is that of mansplaining, as well as its cognate forms: whitesplaining, cissplaining, etc. These forms of explanatory wrongdoing occur when a person supplies an unwanted explanation or unsolicited advice to someone who he deems, on the basis of their social identities, to be his intellectual inferior. He begins to expound, correct, or counsel, despite these interventions being inappropriate and unbidden. These unwanted interventions can be grouped together as instances of 'splaining'. Splaining is a subvariety of 'bayardism': the exercise of self-confident ignorance.

To be clear, the claim is *not* that white people and men can never be experts. Privileged people are often experts in the strict sense of the word, because they are afforded better opportunities in education and employment. They can even be experts in matters which predominantly affect marginalised people, allowing for some margin of error when it comes to experiential shortcomings and biases. Those who wield the terms in ways that exclude the possibility of certain groups having anything useful to say are usually overextending them. Splaining requires you to have less expertise in the topic under discussion than those around you, and to hold forth without any indication that your views are needed, having assumed that your audience is less knowledgeable than you are on the basis of their gender, race, class, etc. Of course, 'expertise' is a fraught notion, and I intend for the term to be broad enough to accommodate forms of expertise that have traditionally been undervalued: i.e. the sort of expertise a person might develop through particular experiences, rather than only that which is conferred through formal study or training.

Splaining is something privileged people are liable to do because privilege leads to feelings of authority and entitlement. Being a man and being white, and particularly being both at once, tends to give a person such a strong sense of security and belonging as to make him liable to overestimate the value of his contributions and underestimate the worth of others' knowledge. As we saw in Chapter 6, studies show that men systematically overestimate their expected and actual performance in tasks, while women are liable to underestimate themselves.[3] No surprise, then, that men go around thinking they know things they don't.

Consider the cis man who, in 2019, posted on Facebook that women should stop complaining about the cost of tampons, and then proceeded to present a weird and faulty set of calculations which culminated with the statement that those who menstruate need '90 tampons max' each year.[4] Or the response that woman photographer Laura Dodsworth received to her collection of candid close-ups of one hundred vulvas, intended to demonstrate – contrary to what one would conclude based on mainstream pornography – that vulvas come in many shapes, sizes and colours. The photo series was entitled 'Me and My Vulva: 100 Women Reveal All'. A man quickly swooped in to tell Dodsworth that, 'The correct word is vagina.' The correct word is, of course, vulva. He doubled down on his 'correction', and even when a gynaecologist intervened, still tried to explain why he was right after all. When told he was mansplaining, he tried to correct his accuser's definition of mansplaining. He got that wrong, too.

An often overlooked but commonly observed strain of splaining is that of wealthsplaining. In 2020, UK MP Ben Bradley (who was privately educated, and, as an MP, has a salary that is three times the UK average) argued against the provision of free school meal vouchers to families living in poverty by claiming that the money was essentially a way of diverting money to crack dens and brothels.[5] Free school meal vouchers can in fact only be spent on food, and his comments were clearly intended to vilify those in receipt of welfare payments. As part of the same broader discussion, politician and journalist Annunziata Rees-Mogg (daughter of a baron, and sister to multimillionaire politician Jacob) tweeted that fresh potatoes were cheaper than pre-prepared chips, explaining that: 'The oft repeated but inaccurate belief that low quality/unhealthy food is always cheaper than raw ingredients is part of the problem. It's why learning to buy/budget for food is important alongside learning to cook.'[6]

Yet this 'explanation' for poverty and hunger – that people buy items that are 53p more expensive because they are too stupid to cook or budget – is not only false, it misses the point entirely. As food campaigner Jack Monroe wrote in response, convenience food is chosen because poor people are also often short on time and energy, may lack cooking equipment and additional ingredients, may be living in temporary accommodation and are more likely to be mentally or physically unwell.[7] Pre-prepared chips are also delicious, providing much-needed pleasure and comfort.

Examples of whitesplaining also abound. As Black Lives Matter protests made the news in the UK in 2020, the then-foreign secretary Dominic Raab was asked whether he would ever take the knee. He responded:

> I've got to say, on this taking a knee thing, I don't know, maybe it's got a broader history but it seems to be taken from the Game of Thrones [*sic*], feels to me like a symbol of subjugation and subordination rather than one of liberation and emancipation.[8]

It's of course no accident that his whitesplanation trivialised and discredited the act of taking the knee, and, by association, the Black Lives Matter movement. He also added the gross detail (which hits the full house of endorsing racism, gender stereotypes, nationalism and monarchism all in one) that 'I take the knee for two people; the Queen and the missus when I asked her to marry me.'*

Mansplaining need not relate to experiences or body parts cis men have no personal experience of, and whitesplaining is not limited to unsolicited explanations relating to race. Splaining has much broader scope, and can occur in relation to almost any topic. (Though cases relating to marginalised identities tend to be the most unsettling and infuriating, a reminder that even personal and painful topics are fair game for explanatory domination.)

I once lived with a woman whose doctoral research was on the philosophy of our perceptions of time. It was a project in the philosophy of psychology, in which she was an expert, having already studied philosophy and neuroscience. We were at an event at which a (white man) physicist approached her and asked about her research. When she responded that she was working on the philosophy of perceptions of time, he cut her short to tell her 'You know, Einstein has some very important work on time' as though she might have somehow not heard of Einstein's work, which was in any case not relevant to hers. He went on, 'I myself have written several books that might be useful to you.' Then he proceeded to list the titles of his own work, which

---

* This is also an example of a dog whistle.

had no bearing on hers (he wasn't even a physicist who studied time), and she had to pretend to write things down, because he was anxious that she didn't forget.

Philosopher Casey Johnson theorises that cases such as this involve a particular variety of splaining in which a 'speech act confusion' occurs.[9] In these situations, a person attempts to make an assertion and another person misinterprets the kind of speech act they were trying to make. So instead of hearing an assertion, they hear, for example, a question, or assume that the person is requesting an explanation or a suggestion, and they respond as though some information was asked of them.

Johnson points out that men who hear women's assertions as requests for explanation or advice have incorporated gender into their assessment of the conversation, and have accordingly downgraded their appraisal of the person's authority. This is an instance of *testimonial injustice* (see Chapter 6): women are subject to credibility deficits simply by virtue of being women. Mansplaining occurs because men are liable to hear women's assertions as requests.

We make legitimate assessments about people's intentions in conversation based on their social roles and identities all the time (my boss asking if she can have a word and a man in a pub asking if he can have a word are two different things), but a person's gender is not legitimate grounds for deciding that an assertion is instead a request. It's an instance of sexism. More than that, women cannot fully participate in producing knowledge if their assertions and explanations are interpreted by men as requests for information, or an opening for a man to hold forth about his own views on that topic, however uninformed. Mansplaining is a sexist conversational habit which erodes women's ability to create and communicate knowledge.

I have plenty of personal experience of being undermined in this way, but one in particular stands out. A couple of years ago, I was watching the women's soccer World Cup with some friends in a pub. Another friend joined us at half-time with her boyfriend. The two of them were having a row about the Monty Hall problem, a simple but counterintuitive mathematical puzzle based loosely on the US gameshow *Let's Make a Deal*. I won't go into the details here, but it's fun to work through if you don't know it already.[10] I love this problem dearly. I spent weeks as a teenager figuring out different ways to reach the correct answer, and years later I taught it in logic classes when I was a graduate student.

My friend (a woman of colour) was arguing that the correct answer to the problem was, in fact, correct. Her boyfriend (a white man) was telling her she was ridiculous. I dug out some old receipts from my purse and started scribbling on them, explaining why she was right. The others (who had not seen the problem before) followed the explanation and saw why their intuitions were mistaken. But my friend's boyfriend told me I was wrong and that my work didn't make sense. I was unfazed; it's a non-intuitive problem – that's why it's interesting – and there is more than one way to demonstrate the result, so I set about detailing a second method. His girlfriend informed him that I have a background in mathematics. (He has a lay person's understanding of math.) He shrugged and carried on telling me I was wrong, insisting that the answer was obvious to him and he didn't get why none of us could see it. I lost it. I don't remember what I said but I do recall my tone: irate, furious, harsh. He laughed and asked why I was so worked up. It was just a math problem, no need to get so upset.

But there is every reason to get upset. After a certain level, math is very difficult. You have to work hard to get good at it. It's also an exceedingly sexist discipline to work and study within, and you have to fight your own internalised sexism to do it in the first place. I was not about to let my hard-won expertise be so easily devalued by a person whose qualification to dispute my knowledge lay only in his being a white man. His unwillingness to see me as an expert and his rejection of my attempts to explain something to him felt like an affront. (*He* brought the problem to our table that night; my explanation was entirely solicited.) In isolation it's a minor indignity, but I experienced it resting atop a mountain of similar affronts I'd endured from similar men. Splaining is, in this sense, often a micro-aggression. Each incident might feel insignificant, a slight that can be shrugged off and accommodated within the margin of inconsiderate behaviour we afford to those around us. But where should we draw that line, and at what cost?

Splaining is harmful because it is one of many ways in which some people assert their authority and deny others the opportunity to enjoy the credibility they deserve. Splaining is both a symptom of privilege and a cause of it. Over time, the act of splaining tends to embolden certain groups and shrink the conversational space for everyone else. In 'Men Explain Things to Me', Rebecca Solnit describes the far-reaching effects of mansplaining:

> Every woman knows what I'm talking about. It's the presumption that makes it hard, at times, for any woman in any field; that keeps women from speaking up and from being heard when they dare; that crushes young women into silence by indicating, the way harassment on the street does, that this is not their world. It trains us in self-doubt and self-limitation just as it exercises men's unsupported overconfidence.[11]

It gets worse. Mansplaining and whitesplaining are so common that people of colour and women are liable to begin to question their own authority. Even when we know we've trained hard to be experts, even when we know our experiences have taught us valuable things, the excessive confidence of another person can fan the flames of a nagging doubt. We start to feel like imposters.

There's another part to it, too. The expertise of marginalised people is often resented by others, who find it threatening, excessive, unbecoming. For all of these reasons, we are apt to wield our expertise more tentatively. Sometimes we are so tentative that we are not recognised as experts. We undersell ourselves. It's a double bind; we start to co-author our own diminishment. We use hedges, qualifiers, tag questions and intensifiers, little words peppered through our speech which soften our statements and make them sound less like assertions.[12] We say 'I think', 'sort of', 'like', 'maybe', and we sound hesitant; we shrink our expertise to match what our contracted confidence permits, and what society's narrow tolerance for the expertise of marginalised people can accommodate.

## Explanatory Injustice

Once uttered, an explanation can make the world a different place. Explanations *do something* to those who accept them: they revise our beliefs about the world and leave our understanding of it changed. This means that explanations are necessarily political. One aspect of this is in the question of what gets explained and what is left unexplained.

Television news programmes rarely explain the origins of the conflicts they cover. Doing so would implicate European colonial powers and Western imperialism. The wealth of particular states, institutions and individuals and the poverty of others are also rarely explained, and are instead taken for granted. The murderous acts of white men and boys are often explained in terms of loneliness, poverty and mental illness, while the equivalent acts of Brown and Black boys and men are not explained, beyond gesturing to their Blackness or Brownness, leaving us to infer some essential propensity to violence. As Shereen Marisol Meraji and Gene Demby point out on their podcast *Code Switch*, while migrants and people of colour are regularly expected to 'get' white cultural references without explanation, any reference to the cultures of racialised groups is expected to come with an explanation, thereby reminding listeners or readers of who is centred and who is marginal.[13]

We need to keep a very close eye on who gets to do the explaining. Explanations are central to some jobs and social roles; academics, writers, journalists and politicians, among others, exercise control over the explanations that reach everyone else. I provide explanations of various kinds to hundreds of students every year, and I'm explaining right now. Explaining is also a significant part of the role of a parent, though parents' influence is limited to their own children, and of the role of a schoolteacher, though teachers are often constrained by centralised curricula.

Those who work in the roles just mentioned tend to belong to the same social class. Almost all of the explanations we receive, and the ways in which they shape the world for us, come therefore through the filter of a small group of privileged people. These people have access to a range of platforms (public speaking, television appearances, social media) through which they reach large numbers of people. Accordingly, they're able to create, curate and communicate dominant, conventional explanations that determine how we understand the world. Not only are their experiences fairly limited, but they are liable to favour explanations that stabilise the status quo from which they benefit. Or at least, those who do so are most likely to hold on to their platforms in the future.

Those with a monopoly on explaining are unlikely to be able or willing to develop explanations which serve the explanatory needs of people from marginalised groups, including those explanations that are needed to challenge their oppression. As a result, members of marginalised groups often lack the conceptual resources to explain their experiences or to challenge inaccurate explanations which relate to them. They are subject to an *explanatory* injustice.[14]

## 'No, I Don't Get It': Resisting Oppressive Explanations

In the 2017 series of the UK reality television show *The Apprentice*, a group of women discussed a sales strategy for maximising the revenue of their burger stand in London's financial sector. Celebrity businessperson Karren Brady eavesdropped on their conversation with the aim of later reporting back to business tycoon Alan Sugar.[15] One contestant remarked that since the financial sector is male-dominated, they should ensure that the team members chosen to sell the food were 'attractive'. Here, Brady cut in: 'What do you mean about "attractive"?' The contestant, now more tentatively, responded that the salesperson must be 'good at selling and . . . they have to be good to sell to men, if you see what I'm saying.' Brady pressed her: 'No, I don't know what you're saying. What are you saying?' The team of hopefuls fell silent.[16]

Brady clearly *did* know what was being implied. We all did. The contestant was saying that lots of men would enjoy being approached by a young, attractive woman, and would accordingly be more likely to part with their money. Since the aim of the game is to make money, she was suggesting they capitalise on this obviously sexist reality, and send their most conventionally attractive team members out as the salespeople. It makes perfect sense. If your only aim is to maximise profits, it's a winning strategy.

Yet Brady was doing something clever and powerful. She was *feigning* misunderstanding in order to force the contestant either to admit she'd been willing to make use of, and thereby strengthen, sexist norms, or simply to confront how problematic her assumptions were. It worked. The silence that followed Brady's interrogation was one of realisation and embarrassment. It was a teachable moment. Pretending not to understand can be a powerful manoeuvre, not least because we are regularly called upon to understand, and thereby comply with, a system that harms us.

In the 1980s, shop owners in New York City starting using buzzer systems to screen customers at the door and refuse entry to those who looked 'undesirable'. Undesirability was primarily determined by race; they were trying to keep out Black customers, on the basis of the racist stereotype that they were dangerous to be around and likely to steal.[17] Black law professor Patricia J. Williams described the way in which the public debate was characterised by Black people being implored to *understand* the reasoning of white shopkeepers and retail assistants. She referred to a letter in the *New York Times*, whose white authors asked Black readers to admit that they too would exclude themselves. Williams wrote that there was a 'repeated public urging that blacks put themselves in the shoes of white store owners, and that, in effect, blacks look into the mirror of frightened whites [*sic*] faces to the reality of their undesirability.'[18]

Black people were asked to *understand* the discriminatory policy, to admit that it made sense for people to exclude them. They were asked to cheerlead their own rejection and accept lines of reasoning which positioned them as violent and threatening, and presented racial profiling as reasonable and justifiable. This is typical of conversations in which marginalising comments are made. Speakers often deploy common expressions which enjoin the listener to see the sense and obviousness of what is being said, e.g. 'put yourself in the shoes of . . .', 'you have to understand that . . .', 'surely you can see that . . .', 'it goes without saying that . . .', 'you get me', 'you know what I mean'. This is what the *Apprentice* contestant tried to do, and it's what the shop owners in New York in the eighties tried to do. It's a way of gesturing towards the oppressive assumptions that are being made without having to state them directly. There are countless other examples of this common dialogical strategy.

In a 2009 television appearance on Fox News, presenter Brian Kilmeade declared he had once asked a Muslim:

> 'How do you feel about the extra scrutiny, clearly, you're getting at the airports?' And he said, 'I'm all for it, because I want to get home to my family, too.' And that's really got to be the attitude. So, if you're Islamic, or you're Muslim and you're in the military, *you have to understand* . . . and that's just the fact right now in the war that was declared on us.[19]

Note my emphasis on the 'you have to understand'. Kilmeade asks that Muslims endorse their racial profiling and, worse, that they have the 'right' attitude towards it, i.e. one of acceptance and empathy with the assumptions underwriting the practice.

In *Bad Feminist*, Roxane Gay recounts a visit she made to her landlord's office to pay her rent.[20] A few weeks before, a group of Korean students had vacated another apartment in her building. The landlord's secretary informs her that the company has gone to great lengths to ventilate the apartment, because 'you just wouldn't believe the smell'. Lost for words, Gay nods in shock, prompting the secretary to whisper, conspiratorially, by way of explanation: 'You know how those people are.' Horrified by this addendum, Gay responds with 'I have no idea what you mean.'

As we saw in the previous section, an explanation is a speech act which, when accepted, succeeds in changing how the listener understands the world. The process of explaining is a collaborative enterprise. Realising this opens up new vistas for resisting explanations that are racist or sexist, or otherwise false or marginalising. When an explanation is provided, it can be rejected. This rejection can take the form of a simple 'No, I don't get it', or 'I have no idea what you mean.' The powerful method employed by Karren Brady and Roxane Gay corners the explainer into reiterating their problematic view, often in stronger, clearer terms, which makes it easier to call them out, or lets them see their own shortcomings more starkly. Explanations for marginalising actions or perspectives often rely on vague, euphemistic phrases. When a person is forced to explicitly state their assumptions, they must reflect more closely on what they're actually saying, and whether or not they can justify it.

In my work, I call this strategy for resisting explanations 'disunderstanding' (a portmanteau of 'deliberate' and 'misunderstanding').[21] When you *disunderstand* you urge a person to expose the dubious assumptions underwriting their explanation.[22] Of course, a person's ability to disunderstand is critically dependent on who she is. Resisting an explanation, like resisting anything, is risky. Powerful people, in particular, are liable to become defensive or nasty when their authority is challenged and they are denied the superiority that comes of having successfully explained something to others. Those who are most likely to feel the need to resist are also those for whom resistance might turn out to be costly or dangerous.[23] People of colour and white women, in particular, are often expected to play the role of explainee, not challenger. For this reason, in certain cases some of us may quite reasonably feel compelled to go along with an explanation that is marginalising and indicate our assent even though inside we are vehemently refusing the revision of our background assumptions. As we saw in the last chapter, playing along – whether by faking orgasms or tolerating mansplaining – can be the safest way out of certain situations. We can practise solidarity by posing challenges where others cannot easily do so.

Leaving a morally troubling explanation unchallenged permits it to act on the world in ways that perpetuate harm. The possibility of rejecting explanations suggests a very clear duty, the realisation of which not only promises to make the world a fairer place, but also to make our knowledge of it keener and more powerful. It's sometimes said by those campaigning against victim-blaming that 'a dress is not a yes'. A dress is also not an explanation.

# 8

## Who Is Cancelling Whom?

> Unlike some on the left, I have never doubted that 'cancel culture'
> exists, fuelled by political intolerance and the toxic anonymity of social
> media. The great myth about cancel culture, however, is that it exists
> only on the left.
>
> David Olusoga, *Guardian* (3 January 2021)

About a decade ago, I was loading up a film on my laptop with my
friend Sol when they recoiled in horror: 'I can't believe you have
Woody Allen as your background.' When I'd recovered from my
puzzlement, I burst into laughter. The photograph on my computer's
desktop of a wrinkled, bespectacled man in a flat cap, with thick-
rimmed glasses perched on an unusually large nose was my Kurdish
grandfather, Farajollah Shahvisi, who had died in Tehran the year
before, and who – I realised, in that moment – was the spitting image
of the elderly Woody Allen.

Allen stands accused of having sexually abused his seven-year-old
adopted daughter, Dylan Farrow. He also began an affair with another
of his girlfriend's adopted daughters, Soon-Yi Previn, when she was
in high school and he was in his mid-fifties.[1] I didn't know any of this
as I worked through his back catalogue in my late teens. Sol's reaction
to what they had assumed was Allen's picture made me wonder about
the possibility of separating the art from the artist. Would it be wrong
to revisit his films? If I did, should I find a way to watch them without
further lining his pockets? Similar questions hang over the two
hundred blockbuster films whose credits are sullied with Harvey
Weinstein's name.

Questions about disgraced celebrities lead inevitably to conversations about 'cancel culture'. Have Woody Allen and Harvey Weinstein been 'cancelled'? What does that mean for men worth hundreds of millions of dollars, whose influence and legacies are vast and pervasive? This invites broader questions: is being 'cancelled' morally distinguishable from merely experiencing consequences for causing harm? Is an apology enough to avert 'cancellation'? Should we seek to punish people, or create conditions under which they can learn? Are our responses to wrongdoing constructive? Are they proportionate?

On the one hand, it seems undeniable that 'cancel culture' is a tactical moral panic cooked up by conservatives to enable their bigotry, while on the other hand it seems that those who call out wrongdoing often do so in ways that are troubling and unhelpful. Something isn't right about how we deal with the harms we cause each other. And as with most things we're still figuring out, social media tends to fan the embers of uncertainty into a haphazard inferno that damages us all.

## Clay Pot Cancel Culture

Two and a half thousand years ago, a person could be expelled from the ancient democratic city-state of Athens if they had caused offence or were deemed to pose a threat. Each winter, citizens were given the opportunity to name a person they would like to see expelled. Since most people were illiterate, a scribe would record these names. The technology of paper had not yet been developed, and imported papyrus from Egyptian Nile grass was expensive and scarce, but there was plenty of broken pottery lying around which served as an early form of scrap paper. The scribe would scratch the name of an unwanted person on a shard of pottery. These shards, known as *ostraka*, were then arranged into piles corresponding to each name and totted up. If the largest heap consisted of 6,000 *ostraka* or more, the person in question would be cast out of Athens. No case needed to be made against the person, and they had no opportunity to protest or appeal against the expulsion. Political rivals could be banished in this way, but an annoying or unpopular person might meet the same fate. (Compare with the ruthless, arbitrary ways in which hopefuls are voted off reality television shows.) Mercifully, only one unlucky soul would receive this strange sentence each year. An ostracised person was given ten days to put their affairs in order and leave Athens, and would be executed if they remained. After a decade of exile, they were permitted to return.* The word 'ostracise' derives from the *ostraka* on which the exile's name was engraved.

Formal ostracism is still practised in some communities. Jehovah's Witnesses can be 'disfellowshipped' from their church for moral transgressions, which means being cast out of the congregation and shunned by friends and family within the religion. In Bali, an individual or entire family may be subjected to *kasepekang*, a severe form of social punishment that excludes them from communal life. Ostracism can take place more privately, within a friendship group, family or between two people. Giving someone the 'silent treatment' by refusing to speak to or acknowledge them is a common form of ostracism in interpersonal relationships. In Iran, a form of ostracism, known as *qahr*, sometimes occurs between a parent and their teenage or adult children when a difference of opinion or values leads to a period of mutual silence. Its resolution, *ashti* (peace), often requires the intervention of a third party.

Ostracism is distinguished from other forms of social exclusion by its application to individuals on the basis of their individual actions or traits rather than their social identities. Trump's 'Executive Order 13769', which blocked the entry of refugees and visitors from six Muslim-majority countries, was a racist policy that banished people irrespective of the details of their lives as individuals. The systematic exclusion and marginalisation of particular groups of people is properly described as oppression, rather than ostracism. In practice, ostracism and oppression are often hard to untangle. Perhaps a particular woman really is so unpleasant that excluding her from social gatherings is reasonable; maybe her colleagues are being sexist. This chapter

* A similar system was adopted in the Italian city-state of Syracuse, and was known as 'petalism'.

focusses on the ostracism experienced by people we would not typically describe as being oppressed, and does not explore the ways in
which ostracism can be used as a tool of oppression.[2]

Ostracism occurs when a person is deemed to have acted in an
antisocial or immoral way. It is a form of retributive justice, and,
indeed, one might think of the criminal justice system, and incarceration in particular, as an extreme, state-sanctioned form of ostracism.
Ostracism has several purposes. It deprives a person of some of their
usual social interactions or connections, with the aim of making them
suffer and encouraging them to change their behaviours, as well as
acting as a deterrent to others; it also excludes or discredits a person
so that the influence of their actions is limited.

One common and visible form of ostracism in the modern world
is 'cancelling',* which is often described as occurring within a broader
'cancel culture' or 'consequence culture'. Cultural studies scholar Eve
Ng defines 'cancel culture' as:

> the withdrawal of any kind of support (viewership, social media
> follows, purchases of products endorsed by the person, etc.) for those
> who are assessed to have said or done something unacceptable or
> highly problematic, generally from a social justice perspective espe-
> cially alert to sexism, heterosexism, homophobia, racism, bullying,
> and related issues.[3]

The term 'cancel culture' has its roots in Black Twitter.† In its
original formulation, it generally involved Black people, and predominantly Black women, calling out racism and misogynoir online in the
knowledge that their call-outs were probably the only kind of justice
they'd see.[4] Accordingly, media studies scholar Meredith D. Clark
describes calling out as a tool of the Other.[5] Social media is where
people go to report harms and mete out a form of crowdsourced

---

* 'Dragging', or 'calling out', are sometimes used as synonyms, but these are forms
of critique which tend to precede cancellation.
† That 'cancelling' derives from a tool and term that was first used by Black people
explains some of the automatic scorn it is met with ('woke' is similarly mocked).

justice when the official channels for reporting wrongdoing do not serve them.

'Cancel culture' gets a lot of bad press, but the studies indicate that opinions are mixed. Of those surveyed in the US in 2020, 46 per cent of people felt that 'cancel culture' had 'gone too far', while 27 per cent of respondents thought that it had a positive, or very positive, effect on society.[6] When the word 'cancelling' isn't used directly, support for the practice is more pronounced. Just over half of those surveyed agreed with the statement 'people should expect social consequences for expressing unpopular opinions in public, even those that are deeply offensive to other people', and 54 per cent of people reported that their opinion of a person would change if that person had made an offensive statement within the last year. As many as 40 per cent of people – and 55 per cent of those under the age of 35 – reported having personally participated in the process of cancelling.[7] In short, there's plenty of support for the idea that a person should face consequences for harmful statements or actions, especially among younger people, and many people are already engaged in doling out these reprisals, but there's also a feeling that the consequences should be proportionate.

An episode of 'cancellation' typically proceeds in several stages. First, there's the transgression: a person says or does something morally troubling, or is accused of having done so. Usually, though not always, their words or actions harm a subordinated social group. They are called out, often by multiple people, who may demand particular consequences, e.g. an apology, the termination of an employment contract. The call-out may end up being amplified, particularly if the transgressor is a public figure or organisation. There may be a 'pile-on', in which the transgressor is subject to a high volume of criticism. (At this stage, there's often some backlash, as others defend the transgressor, or express a more general concern that 'freedom of speech' is imperilled or that 'cancel culture' has 'gone too far'.) The transgressor may attempt to clarify, apologise, or make amends. Depending on the nature and timing of this response and the supposed wrongdoing, this may or may not quell the condemnation. Related parties may withdraw their association by, e.g. removing sponsorship, revoking an employment contract, withdrawing a book deal, axing a television programme. Even if there is no formal, specific deprivation, the alleged transgressor may find their social and professional opportunities diminished.

Importantly, this schema could also describe the course of action when one individual harms another, or is accused of having done so. There is nothing new-fangled about cancelling: it's a scaled-up version of how we hold each other to account. That said, the scaling up, which is usually facilitated by social media, tends to raise the stakes in ways that generate secondary moral problems.

## 'Cancel Culture' or 'Consequence Culture'?

One difficulty with the term 'cancel culture' is that it means so many different things. When I worry about being cancelled (and I do), I am primarily concerned about getting sacked from my job for speaking out about whiteness, masculinity and the violence of the Israeli state. Others have been fired or disciplined over these issues, and they're topics on which I am likely to express my anger publicly. When corporate brands and celebrities express concerns about 'cancel culture', they're nervous about losing customers and followers. Politicians and right-wing commentators often use 'cancel culture' interchangeably with 'wokeness' or 'political correctness' as a way of gesturing towards a host of issues associated with the 'culture wars', i.e. the toppling of colonial statues, being asked to use considerate language or school pupils learning about racism. Since Chapter 2 explored this last set of cases, I'll set them aside here and focus on the 'cancellation' of ordinary people and celebrities.

In July 2020, *Harper's Magazine* published 'A Letter on Justice and Open Debate', signed by over 150 public figures who expressed concerns about 'a new set of moral attitudes and political commitments that tend to weaken our norms of open debate and toleration of differences in favor of ideological conformity.' This was a letter about 'cancel culture'. (Many have speculated, convincingly, that the missive was more specific than that, and was in fact an indirect defence of J. K. Rowling, whose transphobia has been widely criticised.) The list of signatories at the foot of the letter was star-studded: Noam Chomsky, Gloria Steinem, Margaret Atwood, Salman Rushdie and Malcolm Gladwell, among others. People who have no trouble making their voices heard, and whose collective online following runs into the billions. It's not entirely clear what *they* were worried about, and it looked a lot like a plea for unconditional exaltation, or immunity from criticism. The prominence of 'cancel culture' as a flashpoint in public discourse derives in part from the efforts of a small number of people who are fiercely protective of their power and influence. As with 'political correctness', this seems to reflect a desire to speak and act without consequences.

One of the clearest examples of how claims about 'cancelling' relate to a yearning for adulation is that of British author and schoolteacher Kate Clanchy, author of the prize-winning 2019 book *Some Kids I Taught and What They Taught Me*. In 2021, Clanchy experienced a Twitter pile-on after racist, classist and ableist passages within her book came to wider attention. In 2022, her publisher dropped her. On those facts alone, it sounds as though Clanchy was cancelled, which isn't to say that such a cancellation would have been unwarranted. However, on closer inspection, something much stranger happened. In the summer of 2021, a reviewer on *Goodreads* criticised Clanchy's book, quoting racist snippets of text from within it. Outraged, Clanchy herself shared the review on Twitter, claiming that the quotes were 'all made up', that she was being wrongfully accused of racism and urged her 37,000 followers to report the review so that it could be taken down and her reputation reinstated.[8] The quotes were *not* made up, they came straight from her book, and by the time Clanchy realised this her wrongdoing had doubled: she'd not only written a book in which she made racist and classist remarks about her students, she'd also falsely accused others of attacking her, and openly tried to use her vast platform to silence them. (For what it's worth, I believe that Clanchy genuinely thought she had not written those words. She could see they were racist, and as a 'well-intentioned' white woman, was so unable to understand herself as holding racist views that she felt confident posting before bothering to do a quick *Ctrl+F* in her own copy of the manuscript.) There's a lot to say about this case. Why didn't her editors flag the bigoted content at the draft stage, and what does this tell us about the publishing industry? But the most important point is that Clanchy's expectation of total reverence is what catalysed her cancellation. She brought it on herself. Further, Clanchy was picked up by a second publisher immediately after being dropped by the first. That's not what we typically mean when we say a person has been 'silenced' or 'cancelled'.

Anxious celebrities have allies among conservatives. 'Cancel culture' is presented as a form of left-wing authoritarianism that threatens the right to free expression. As we saw in Chapter 2, the idea that left-wing authoritarianism has reached a tipping point and is poised to extinguish open debate has been around for decades, and long precedes social media. It's another faulty 'slippery-slope' argument: if we let these instances of 'cancelling' go unimpeded, totalitarianism awaits! It's hard to see what the slippery-slope mechanism might be in this case; J. K. Rowling isn't invited to speak at a book festival, and the next thing you know . . . publishers are trampling one another for the rights to her next book.

The ramping up of 'cancel culture' into a moral panic is an instance of what writer Nesrine Malik calls 'frequency scrambling'.[9] This phrase describes scenarios in which the attempt to attend to a genuine grievance (i.e. the bigoted comments of a public figure) is overshadowed by a manufactured grievance ('people are being cancelled!'). So much time and energy is invested in rebutting the false grievance that the real grievance ultimately flies below the radar, and attempts to resolve a genuine problem end up looking as though they *are* the problem.

Let's consider some of the finer details of 'cancellation'. First, public figures are more vulnerable to being called out because their wrongdoing has greater influence, which means there's a stronger case for *containment*. Many of us have a racist aunt or father-in-law, but our relatives' comments are of no interest or consequence to anyone outside their social circle, even when they express those views on public social media accounts. The ability to be 'cancelled' therefore assumes some initial degree of power and influence. A famous person's racist utterance has the potential to normalise racism in a way that our aunts' words do not.

Second, the opportunities that are withdrawn when a person is 'cancelled' are typically those that were only afforded to wealthy, powerful individuals in the first place. We are not generally talking about people losing their homes or livelihoods (though more on that in the next section), we're talking about prestigious and lucrative roles that are not essential in order to lead a dignified life, and apply only to a select few. Further, provided we're not acting upon biases that stem from broader forms of oppression, it's usually morally acceptable to have preferences about who we support and appoint, and to withdraw that backing when a person acts out. I used to respect the political activism of Radiohead's Thom Yorke, but his failure to show solidarity with Palestinians ruined that for me.[10] To the extent to which I was ever a 'fan', I'm not any more. To be cancelled is not to cease to exist socially, or to be cast out of Athens for a decade because someone doesn't like the look of you. In most cases, a very privileged person has some of those sizeable privileges reduced, and often only temporarily. J. K. Rowling may complain of being cancelled on account of her transphobia, but she still regularly tops the list of the world's richest authors, and has 14 million Twitter followers. Those who care about the marginalisation of trans people have simply decided to distance themselves from her and her work.

Call-outs are common, but material consequences are very rare. On the contrary, many people actively court controversy as a way of staying in the public eye in an increasingly competitive attention economy. Far-right controversialist Milo Yiannopoulos seems to live by this credo. He has stated that 'rape culture is a myth' and wrote an article entitled 'Would You Rather Your Child Had Feminism or Cancer?' He has promoted conversion therapy for gay people (this is made even more complicated by the fact that Yiannopoulos used to be gay, and now refers to himself as 'ex-gay'), whipped up a Twitter storm of racist, sexist abuse directed at *Ghostbusters* actor Leslie Jones, calling her a 'black dude', and has links to neo-Nazi groups. Not only did 'cancel culture' leave Yiannopoulos unscathed, but a publishing house was salivating at the chance to capitalise on his hate: he was given a $250,000 advance by Simon & Schuster *precisely* so that he could elaborate on the racist, sexist and homophobic views that are his sole claim to fame. Eventually, the book contract was revoked after he asserted that thirteen-year-olds were able to consent to sex with adults, and that older men could help young boys to 'discover who they are'. He'd finally found the line and crossed it. (The self-appointed protectors of free speech sat this one out: more evidence that their battle is for the *specific* right to engage in oppressive behaviours without consequences. It's also illustrative of the 'won't somebody please think of the children* (or foetuses)' tendency of the political right, particularly when whipping up moral panic.)

In a letter to his Instagram followers in 2021, right-wing broadcaster Piers Morgan claimed to have become the 'latest "victim" of cancel culture', after he left his job at *Good Morning Britain* following a series of emotional outbursts on air in which he splutteringly rejected Meghan Markle's reports of the racism she experienced from the British royal family, and the effects it had on her mental health.[11] Yet Morgan was not fired from the show; he resigned after storming off set in a rage. It's not clear whether he'd have been permitted to keep his post if he'd tried to – 41,000 complaints were made to the UK communications regulator – but leaving a job after a very public breach of contract is not the same as being 'cancelled'. Further, his period of unemployment didn't last long. In February 2022, advertisements began to appear on buses across the UK announcing Morgan's appointment by right-wing tabloid the *Sun*. The wording of these billboards was telling: 'When you can't believe he just said that'; 'When Piers is saying what we're all thinking'; 'Piers joins the *Sun*. Ready for Fireworks?' In other words, the *Sun* took him on precisely to give a platform to the sort of belligerent, reactionary views he claims to have been cancelled for.

Kanye West has at least been candid about the fact that his 'cancellation' hasn't actually amounted to much. In 2018, he faced a backlash for his support for Donald Trump and his remark that 'when you hear

---

* As originally spoken by Mrs Banks in *Mary Poppins* (1964) and then Helen Lovejoy in *The Simpsons* (1996).

about slavery for 400 years . . . that sounds like a choice'. In the aftermath of this ruckus, when discussing a performance based on his latest release, West remarked that 'half that audience that was there last night, half the people that are listening to the album are supposed to not listen to the album right now. I'm canceled. I'm canceled because I didn't cancel Trump.'[12] (What might it mean to 'cancel' a *president*, short of impeaching him or voting him out of office?) West had been 'cancelled' but pointed out that people were still showing up to his concerts. The two albums he's released since have both reached number one on the US *Billboard 200*.

Finally, the idea that 'cancellation' is a tool of the left or a practice that only targets the powerful is a serious misapprehension. In 2013, US scholar Steven Salaita was prevented from taking up his post at the University of Illinois after criticising the actions of the Israeli government during 'Operation Protective Edge', in which over two thousand Palestinians were killed. He has since found himself effectively unemployable in academia, but continues to write in between shifts as a school bus driver in Washington, DC.[13] This is a dramatic instance of cancellation having real, material consequences, yet it rarely features in these conversations, because the moral panic about cancellation is orchestrated by those on the right. A year later, Saida Grundy, a Black sociologist of race at Boston University, tweeted a series of critical statements relating to the inheritance of slave status and the culture of white male privilege in US universities.[14] Conservative student groups threatened Grundy, accusing her of reverse-sexism and reverse-racism, and tried to get her fired.[15] She kept her job, but the president of Boston University (an engineer by training) issued a condescending letter expressing sympathy with her detractors, and condemning her posts. In other words, a powerful white man publicly discredited a junior Black woman employee about an issue that falls within her area of academic expertise, resulting in serious reputational damage.

Sometimes an instance of 'cancelling' appears to be focussed on some laudable social justice objective, but is really just a misunderstanding that has gained such magnitude and momentum as to be devastating to its victim. In 2019, Natalie Wynn, of the popular philosophy YouTube channel ContraPoints, noted that she finds the request to share her pronouns awkward. Her comments related to her experiences as a trans woman, and she is far from the only one who is troubled by mandatory pronoun sharing.[16] Yet she was sharply criticised for sidelining non-binary people, and the backlash quickly cascaded into a feverish Twitter pile-on, which left her no choice but to disable her account and publicly apologise. Many of those who contributed to the pile-on presumably did so in error, not having properly read or understood her comments. Thanks to social media, there's no limit to the damage such mistakes can cause. In other cases, attempts to cancel are deliberate acts of sabotage, spearheaded by those with access to large platforms, and are intended to activate and harness outrage in others in order to settle some personal squabble or undermine a rival (e.g. the 2021 Slumflower vs Florence Given spat on Instagram[17]).[18] Cancelling works exceptionally well in these cases because when it comes to people who work on social justice issues, nothing sticks and stinks the way accusations of oppression do.

And then there's everybody else: people who aren't celebrities or academics, whose opportunities to be heard by others are very limited. As we saw in Chapter 6, our access to platforms is strongly determined by our social identities. The more serious problem that discussions about 'cancel culture' successfully overshadows is the systematic exclusion of particular groups from public discourse, especially in relation to issues that concern them deeply and on which they are experts. Trans people are rarely asked to speak about threats to their safety and dignity; Palestinians are seldom invited to share their experiences of subjugation; refugees are almost never given chances to describe what drove them from their home countries and the violence they experience at European borders. More to the point, financial insecurity, and the ways in which it tends to consume a person's time and energy, and compel their subjugation to powerful people, is a much bigger threat to freedom than 'political correctness' or 'cancel culture'.

'Cancelling' occurs across the political spectrum. But conservative public figures have always been close to the centres of power – through their links to corporations, print and broadcast media, religious groups, and politicians – and have therefore long been accustomed to speaking without consequences. The internet and, in particular, social media, has democratised public discourse and made reprisals much easier than ever before, allowing the left to begin to close the gap. Those on the right have felt the erosion of their previous discursive immunity very keenly, and have therefore panicked and decried 'cancel culture' in ways that those on the left haven't felt the need to.

Taking stock, what we call 'cancel culture' is often just the super-sized celebrity version of what the rest of us experience all the time: consequences for our mistakes and bigotries. You do something shitty and people distance themselves from you, especially if you refuse to acknowledge your wrongdoing and make amends. There's nothing new or unusual about that, but there are important additional complexities. Sometimes cancellation lines up with broader forms of racist and colonial silencing, as with Salaita and Grundy; on other occasions it is deliberately misused to humiliate or discredit a person who is envied, disliked or misunderstood, as in the case of Natalie Wynn. Very often, it reflects profound shortcomings in our conceptions of how to deal with wrongdoing. The rest of the chapter turns to this last issue.

## Casting Out the Scapegoat

In 2021, the England men's football team made it to the final of a major tournament for the first time since 1966. The squad was noted for its high-profile Black players, many of whom were outspoken about racism in the sport. Theirs was one of the only teams in the tournament to take the knee before every match. The final was tense, and after the full ninety minutes and thirty minutes of extra time, the score stood at 1:1. England lost the championship title after three players failed to score the last three penalties in the shoot-out: Marcus Rashford, Jadon Sancho and Bukayo Saka. All three players are Black. This is relevant because they were also some of the most inexperienced players on the team, with an average age of just twenty-one and a half: not the obvious choice for such a nerve-wracking responsibility. It's likely that they felt under pressure to be 'model minorities', to step up to prove themselves to a nation that still struggles to accept the Britishness of Black people. We also know that Black players feel heightened pressure when playing in front of crowds who are poised to respond to their errors with racist abuse. A recent study shows that the performance of Black players improved when they were forced to play in empty stadiums during the Covid-19 lockdown period; there was no difference for non-Black players.[19] As with any high-profile role in the UK, there's no room for error if you're a person of colour: one wrong move and your claim to Britishness and basic humanity is called into question.

I watched with horror as Saka's attempt was saved by the Italian goalkeeper. His was the last; it was all over. I could see what was coming. So could Saka: 'I knew instantly the kind of hate that I was about to receive,' he wrote afterwards. The abuse was swift and predictable. Racist messages, slurs and emojis were directed at the players' social media handles, leading Twitter to delete 1,000 posts and permanently remove a number of accounts. (There was also an outpouring of support for the three footballers, which was critical in ensuring that action was taken in response to the abuse.)

Among the alleged offenders was a thirty-seven-year-old estate agent named Andy Bone, who seemingly posted on Twitter 'N[******]s ruined it for us' (though he has subsequently claimed he was hacked).

Contrary to actor Roseanne Barr's claim that taking sleeping pills (or, similarly, getting upset about the football) can unleash random, isolated racist utterances, such outbursts generally point to even deeper reserves of hate.[20] Accordingly, some kind of consequence is apt, if only as an act of containment. Andy Bone's employer fired him (though he maintains his innocence), which seems like a reasonable measure in terms of protecting his colleagues and clients, but leaves the background problem untouched. This difficulty brings us back to Amy Cooper, who lied to the police about a Black man threatening her. She lost her job at an investment firm and faced criminal charges for filing a false report. Christian Cooper, the Black birdwatcher who was her victim, was not in favour of, and did not pursue, prosecution. He said:

Any of us can make – not necessarily a racist mistake, but a mistake. And to get that kind of tidal wave in such a compressed period of time, it's got to hurt. It's got to hurt. I'm not excusing the racism. But I don't know if her life needed to be torn apart . . . She went racial. There are certain dark societal impulses that she, as a white woman facing in a conflict with a black man, that she thought she could marshal to her advantage. I don't know if it was a conscious thing or not. But she did it, and she went there. If we are going to make progress, we've got to address these things.[21]

What should we do with the likes of Andy Bone and Amy Cooper? It's hard to shrug off their wrongdoing as mere 'mistakes'. Better to acknowledge, as Christian Cooper did, that their outbursts opened a brief window on to 'dark societal impulses' that are harboured and expressed in interpersonal encounters, but which reflect broader hostilities. To what extent are those systemic problems improved by tearing apart the lives of individuals?

Our responses to individual instances of structural oppression seem to serve as *scapegoats*. The idea of a scapegoat first appears in the Old Testament. The moral transgressions of the people of Israel were symbolically loaded upon the head of a goat who was then cast out into the wilderness to carry away their sins and thereby purify them. It was an expedient way of being seen to have dealt with a problem without having dealt with it at all. The ancient Greeks (in addition to ostracism) also performed the ritual of *pharmakos*, which involved expelling, beating or executing human scapegoats (usually slaves, disabled people or those deemed to be criminals) as a way of purging the community in times of crisis.

Consider the case of David Shor, an election data analyst at consultancy firm Civis Analytics. In May 2020, Shor wrote a tweet citing an academic paper written by Black political science scholar Omar Wasow, which argued that nonviolent protests in the 1960s were more effective in winning over Democratic voters than 'violent' demonstrations.[22] George Floyd had just been murdered and BLM protests were gathering momentum. Later that day, writer and activist Benjamin Dixon criticised Shor's tweet as an instance of 'concern trolling', i.e. focussing people's concern on electoral turnout in order to distract from the issue of Floyd's death and the vicious racism that underwrote it. More than a thousand people liked Dixon's post. Shor apologised for the tweet, but within a week, Civis Analytics had fired him. Dixon made an important point and Shor probably needed to do some thinking about race, protest tactics and the timing of his posts. But firing Shor was a cynical response. The insensitivity of his post likely reflects the need for culture change in his organisation or sector, but dismissing one person does not bring about that change. The firm was able to wash their hands of Shor's blunder by making him a scapegoat.

We focus unduly on individual scapegoats because we don't know how to deal with structural problems and the very personal pain they inflict. People become symbols onto which we load our frustration at a society that offers few other remedial pathways. That said, structural injustices emerge from the combined actions of individual people, and there have to be ways of ensuring, in the immediate term, that instances of harm are confronted.

## The Apology Dilemma

When I was a teenager, I freely used the word 'gay' as a slur. My best friend was gay, and I did it in front of him without compunction. I can recall making remarks I'd now classify as rape apologism, ableism, racism and classism, too. Those words and comments felt normal at the time, but like the ship of Theseus – whose wooden boards are replaced one by one until it's unclear whether we'd call it the same vessel – I have changed so much over the last two decades that it'd be absurd to hold me responsible for the oppressive acts of my earlier self. As writer Asher Perlman joked on Twitter in 2022: 'There is no one I have less in common with than the me who wrote my Facebook statuses circa 2008.'[23] Fixating on the historic wrongdoing of individuals ignores the fact that we're all constantly changing and learning.

Between 2011 and 2014, grime artist Stormzy, who was then in his late teens and yet to release his debut EP, posted a series of homophobic tweets. In response to two women's mutually supportive Twitter comments, he wrote that their behaviour was 'so gay'. He described a gay character on TV soap *EastEnders* as a 'fucking f★★'. The f-word (the second, genuinely offensive one) crops up again and again in his tweets from this period, as does the derogatory use of the word 'gay'.[24] Just a few years after posting these homophobic tweets, Stormzy began to use his new-found fame to raise awareness of social and economic inequality. When these posts were unearthed in 2017, he issued an apology:

> I said some foul and offensive things whilst tweeting years ago at a time when I was young and proudly ignorant. Very hurtful and discriminative views that I've unlearned as I've grown up and become a man . . . The comments I made were unacceptable and disgusting, full stop. Comments that I regret and to everyone I've offended, I am sorry, these are attitudes I've left in the past . . . I take responsibility for my mistakes and hope you can understand that my younger self doesn't reflect who I am today.[25]

Stormzy made those comments between the ages of eighteen and twenty-one, and was twenty-four when he wrote this apology. While only a few years had passed, those tend to be formative years, and he describes a relatable trajectory towards greater maturity and sensitivity. Not everyone was convinced, and detractors suggested that he'd apologised in order to protect his reputation and record sales. Regardless, his public persona has since been much more thoughtful.

In recent years there's been a trend for manufacturing scandals by exhuming the old social media posts of public figures. Among those who have been caught out are the comedian Trevor Noah, cricketer Ollie Robinson and rapper Azealia Banks. (In response to this trend, an app called 'Vanilla' has been developed to help people screen their old posts for oppressive language, so they can be deleted.[26]) Some of these cases point to broader cultural issues in their industries – since Robinson's racist tweets were discovered, the extent of racism in British cricket has been revealed through various other scandals – but most reflect the fact that many of us were crass, small-minded adolescents whose various bigotries were largely unchecked. Social media fossilises teenage foolishness, whether or not it has since been disavowed.

It seems unproductive and uncharitable to insist that a person's past actions define them now, especially if they have repudiated those actions and given no other reason for concern. As Judith Butler said in a 2020 interview:

> I have made some significant errors in my public life. If someone then said I should not be read or listened to as a result of those errors, well, I would object internally, since I don't think any mistake a person made can, or should, summarise that person. We live in time; we err, sometimes seriously; and if we are lucky, we change precisely because of interactions that let us see things differently.[27]

Apologies are important, but they pose a dilemma. On the one hand, apologising seems too easy, and can be done strategically. On the other hand, refusing to accept an apology and the possibility of growth seems uncharitable except in the most egregious cases, and ignores the fact that none of us is perfect, it is both possible and good for people to learn, and oppressive behaviours are linked to oppressive structures, so that our bad behaviour is never ours alone. Besides, a good apology is not easy; it requires ownership of the wrong and a commitment to do better. Behavioural scientists have shown that the most important components of an effective apology are acknowledging responsibility and then offering reparation.[28]

It's hard to see what could be gained by refusing Stormzy's apology. But it's even harder to see how we should respond to more direct or recent cases of wrongdoing, or instances where an apology isn't offered. And it's also important to acknowledge those cases in which a person's genuine attempts at atonement are refused, leaving them no route back from their ostracism.

## *Do We Know What Justice Looks Like?*

A few years ago, a man groped me in a busy market. I whipped around and punched him, but it was such a weak blow that he just laughed and walked away. I wish I'd hit him harder, broken something, left a mark. Even so, I don't want perpetrators of sexual assault to be physically harmed as a matter of course. I certainly don't want the state to hurt them. There is a gap between what I do when I am harmed, and what I feel is a defensible course of action in the more general case. Similarly, the fact that the relations of victims sometimes want murderers to be put to death is understandable, but is less of an argument for the death penalty and more of an argument for not asking victims' families to determine the forms that justice takes.

While it is obviously important to listen to those who have been harmed, unaddressed pain does not confer some instinctual gift for imagining decent solutions to that pain. Quite the opposite. As philosopher Olúfẹ́mi O. Táíwò writes: 'Contra the old expression, pain – whether borne of oppression or not – is a poor teacher. Suffering is partial, short-sighted and self-absorbed. We shouldn't have a politics that expects different: oppression is not a prep school.'[29] When people are hurting, they often want others to hurt, too. Unless this tendency is kept in check by a community that offers *care* rather than cheerleading our escalatory retaliations, the end result is liable to be more pain for everyone.

More generally, we should be critical of the view that oppressed people are automatically more likely to identify, and see ways out of, injustice. 'Feminist standpoint theory' tells us that our positions within social hierarchies affect the sort of knowledge we can acquire. This urges the careful consideration of the experiences of marginalised groups, who are liable to bear important insights on matters relating to their oppression. But there are complexities to this. A standpoint is not automatic; it is, rather, an achieved stance that is often attained through collective political struggle, as a matter of necessity, since it is in the interests of oppressed people to understand the inner workings of their oppression. As philosopher of science Sandra Harding writes:

'A feminist standpoint is not something that anyone can have simply by claiming it. It is an achievement [and] differs in this respect from a perspective, which anyone can have simply by "opening one's eyes".'[30]

People of colour are often able to offer insights about the experience of racism, but not every person of colour will be an expert: many people don't have the time or motivation to work towards developing a standpoint; others internalise racism especially deeply and strive to be the 'model minority' while pouring scorn on those who don't; some decry racism against their own community but contribute to other forms of racism. Further, racism comes in many different forms and degrees, and is enmeshed with other identities. The accounts of racism that we're most likely to hear are those that affect people of colour who have the platforms to speak out, which is to say, those who are famous, wealthy, well-educated. Meghan Markle faces anti-Black racism, but it would be absurd to suggest that she can speak for the experiences of Senegalese migrants in Europe (who will have more in common with other destitute people who aren't Black). Standpoint theory does not mean that every, or any, person of colour should be taken to be authoritative about the most effective anti-racist strategies. It certainly doesn't mean that oppressed people are, by the mere fact of their identities or experiences, able to provide constructive responses to wrongdoing.

Oppression can lead to an illuminative standpoint, but it can just as easily set a person's moral compass spinning. In a 1996 book exploring the effects of life experiences on conceptions of morality, philosopher Claudia Card explains that:

> The oppressed are liable to low self-esteem, ingratiation, affiliation with abusers (for example so-called female masochism), as well as to a tendency to dissemble, fear of being conspicuous, and chameleonism – taking on the colors of our environment as protection against assault.[31]

As I write, a worrying example of this misdirected vengeance is unfolding. In recent years, there's been a rise in 'gender critical' or 'trans-exclusionary radical' feminism in the UK, which amounts to groups of cis women (usually older, white, middle-class women) devoting considerable time and energy to demonising trans women and attempting to ensure that women-only spaces (such as rape crisis centres, domestic abuse refuges, prisons, changing rooms and bathrooms) exclude trans women. These people have caused great damage to the public discourse on trans people's rights, and have in some cases harassed and attacked (or incited others to attack) individual trans people. Those harms cannot be excused, but there is something perturbing at the heart of their tactics which deserves closer analysis. Many of the cis women involved have experienced particularly traumatic sexual abuse at the hands of cis men, and appear to be directing their pain at trans women, on the basis of two mistaken assumptions: that the violence of men is encoded in genetic or genital sex, rather than in the operation of gender, and that cis women are uniquely vulnerable to violence by cis men, rather than having that vulnerability in common with trans women. My sense is that transphobia in the UK stems, at least in part, from a systemic failure to respond appropriately to sexual assault and its long-term harms. This has led to misplaced acts of hatred towards trans women, who are an easier target than cis men and the institutions that facilitate their violence.

Trauma and oppression can also lead to call-outs in which the person doesn't *want* the perpetrator to do better. A common coping strategy for managing oppression is to carve up the world in ways that appear to make sense of pain and injustice. Believing that some people – whether individually or because of social groups to which they belong – are incorrigibly bad is a comforting thought, because it means that as long as you can avoid those people, you'll be safe. Countenancing the idea that they might be able to change destabilises that reassuring schema: the buffer between people who might hurt you and people you can trust dwindles, and the world becomes a more complicated and frightening place. This yearning for simplicity sometimes translates into the need to ossify a person's label as a transgressor and make them pay endlessly. Similarly, people sometimes use call-outs as a way of buttressing a personal identity that gives them acceptability and a sense of belonging in an alienating world.

These points may explain the singular wrath that is reserved for those who were understood to be 'woke' but have fallen short in some way. A book full of sexist and racist stereotypes written by someone like Boris Johnson (see his 2004 novel *Seventy-Two Virgins*) is met with a shrug: he's a douchebag. The rogues tend to get away with it. But if a 'good' person slips up, the tumble from their pedestal is rough and merciless. This makes sense if you understand that the determination to divide the world into the perfectly virtuous and the irredeemably evil requires that those who err are booted into the depths of hell to sustain the binary. The upshot is that those who espouse some kind of liberatory politics walk a tightrope: the only way is down. Of course, it makes sense to hold people to the values they profess, and it is understandable to feel disappointed when they fall short. It might also be that an oppressive act is more damaging when committed by a person who professes commitment to social justice. Nonetheless, we are all fallible and unfinished, and need to be offered conditions under which learning is possible.

All of the above leaves people frightened of getting things wrong. To some extent, that's okay: we should be mindful of our behaviours towards others. But the threat of humiliation or exclusion has the counterproductive effect of discouraging careful, critical thinking, and motivating people to adopt, wholesale, the views of those they assume have got it right. This is one of the ways in which 'echo chambers' emerge; repeating the received view within a particular social milieu is the safest way to avoid the stress and embarrassment (or worse) of being called out.[32] And this is bad news for social justice movements, which must nurture bravery, creativity and dissent if they are to imagine and enact alternative ways of living, as well as an understanding that resistance is always an ongoing practice.

In calling for greater care and patience towards one another, I am not advocating for the dubious idea of 'civility', which often amounts to tone-policing and 'both sides' discourses that are not only inattentive to power but are more likely to be weaponised against people of colour. Anger is often the right tool for the job; as Audre Lorde wrote: 'Before I give it up I'm going to be sure that there is something at least as powerful to replace it on the road to clarity.'[33] And there's nothing wrong with ruthless take-downs when occasion demands. As media studies scholar Meredith D. Clark points out, social media call-outs often amount to free feminised labour in the service of social justice. People are exasperated and their time is short, so their responses cannot always 'come wrapped up in niceties and polite speech . . . Sometimes, the urgency and weight of oppression require us to immediately cry out.'[34] Nor am I suggesting that people who cause harm should be let off the hook. I'd just rather we were more careful at sifting those who make mistakes from those who are deliberate aggressors, and that in the former case (and sometimes, also the latter) call-outs were offered as generous acts of clarification and challenge that suggest pathways for vindication.

Talking about 'cancel culture' leads us to broader questions about how we respond to wrongdoing, formed as we are by the system we seek to resist. Claudia Card asks, 'How is it possible for us as damaged agents to liberate ourselves from the damage?'[35] Our attempts at liberation are liable to carry forward the harms we are trying to cast off. We can be more specific in articulating this: 'cancel culture' feels a lot like an instance of everyday 'carcerality', which legal scholar Sarah Lamble summarises as:

> logics and practices that normalise punitive responses to harm. It's the 'common sense' logic that equates justice with punishment. When a harm occurs, carceral logics encourage us to locate the cause of the problem in an individual (bad choices, inherent evil, poor upbringing, cultural deficiencies, monstrous otherness, etc) and then isolate and punish that individual . . . Sometimes this is done overtly – by the state and the criminal justice system or when someone calls the cops on someone else – but it's also done in more subtle everyday ways that normalise vindictive or punitive behaviour or celebrate redemptive violence. These punitive logics seep into our daily interactions at work, at school, at home, in our neighbourhoods and in our organising communities.[36]

Carcerality is what makes the practice of locking up 'criminals' seem a normal, sensible method of dealing with those who violate the social contract, rather than an unwise and inhumane escalation.[37] It makes us believe that we have no choice but to focus on individuals, mark them as irredeemably bad, and add to the ledger of harms by punishing them, without asking whether such a strategy addresses the deeper problems that motivated their actions. Accountability is important, but it doesn't need to mean 'making people pay'. If we're prepared to be bold and imaginative, my wrong-doing might instead mean my 'giving account' as sociologist Melanie Brazzell suggests, allowing and encouraging me to 'critically examine the web of relations and structures that underpin my story and consti-tute me, and to *restory* myself with new lines of agency to make new choices without violence'.[38]

We are products of the cultures and milieus in which we live. And some of us have more opportunities than others to stay abreast of changes in anti-oppressive language, behaviours and movements. For example, people differ in their use of 'survivor of sexual abuse' or 'victim of sexual abuse': survivor is thought to be more empowering, but not everyone feels empowered, and not everyone survives. Some people of colour reject the term 'people of colour' in favour of (say) 'racialised peoples', and I've encountered many older people who recoil at the use of the term on the assumption that it is as offensive as the term 'coloured'. Meanwhile, in South Africa, almost one in ten people self-identify as 'coloured', by which they mean multiracial. Acting as though these issues are simple or obvious (even with the help of Google) is unhelpful and disingenuous. It's often difficult and confusing, and many of us are doing our learning (and making our mistakes) in public, on social media, which is ruthless and has a long memory. If we're not willing to help to move everyone along together, then it instead looks as though we're just in this for the thrill of the call-out and the moral high ground. We should be attentive to the occasions when we find ourselves overreaching in order to inflict punishment, exact revenge or win attention (often in the form of upvotes and reposts).

Philosopher Kate Manne provides an important insight in her book *Down Girl*. In reference to the use of the word 'misogynist' she points out that it's tricky to know when to deploy such a damning word in a society that is misogynistic by design. Manne suggests that we only refer to a person as a misogynist when:

their misogynistic attitudes and/or actions are significantly (a) more extreme, and (b) more consistent than most other people in the relevant comparison class (e.g. other people of the same gender, perhaps race, class, age etc., in similar circumstances).[39]

We might borrow this strategy when it comes to responding to other instances of oppression, and recognise both the degree and consistency of the harm, and the positioning of the perpetrator before subjecting them to damaging forms of ostracism. A journalist, politician or television presenter ought to know better than a person who has had fewer educational and professional opportunities. Stormzy's teenage homophobia is not the same as Trump's fully grown racism.

I think it's fair to say that social media isn't bringing out the best in us when it comes to being thoughtful and cooperative in these matters. Part of what goes wrong with both oppressive online behaviours *and* cancelling is that most of us *perform* on social media in ways that lead us not only to forget that the people we are interacting with are real, but to forget that we're real, too. Academics Waleed Aly and Robert Simpson point out that:

> it's part of the nature of these phenomena that the people involved in them don't see themselves as part of a mob . . . People engaged in these practices will tend to think of themselves as merely expressing their feelings, figuring out their political views, talking with friends, criticising unjust practices, or simply passing time.[40]

The platforms on which call-outs take place are designed to capitalise on our inattention and our thirst for validation through likes and shares. They encourage us to form ourselves as brands, which means engaging in self-caricature, and making our friends and enemies cartoonishly clear cut. They are not designed to encourage reflection on their limitations and the ways in which they fall short as tools for justice. Real or perceived acts of harm are easily amplified into monstrous battles, culminating in each of us yelling at each other's avatars until it's no longer clear who our friends are, what our common goals may be and how any of it relates to the material world and the ways in which it constrains us. As writer Jia Tolentino puts it in *Trick Mirror*: 'The internet is governed by incentives that make it impossible to be a full person while interacting with it.'[41]

This chapter is concerned with the actions of *individuals*, not states or institutions. The distinction is important because states, corporations, institutions and their representatives are extremely powerful and influential and have substantial resources at their disposal. The strategies we choose when we oppose the oppressive acts of governments and their agents (e.g. the police and army) or corporations should be directed at undermining their authority. The very tactics that seem troubling and disproportionate when applied to ordinary people – shaming, discrediting and refusing to engage – are therefore apt and effective when it comes to destabilising power.

Cancellation can be an important strategy for ensuring that individual contributions to structural injustice are contained and met with constructive consequences. But we mustn't get so ensnared in the process of holding each other to account as to forget that our bad behaviours are almost always rooted in harmful structures which only the most powerful have the capacity to dismantle. Focussing too intently on dishing out individual justice can leave us too fractured and dispirited to take on graver nemeses.

## Art and the Artist

There is still the question of what to do about the artistic products of those who harm or exploit others without acknowledgement or apology. Some people contend that boycotting the creative products of those who have committed wrongdoing is misguided. The argument goes that while we should hold people responsible for their actions, their character or conduct shouldn't affect how we relate to their artistic outputs. We should adjudicate their art on its own merits, and take care to separate the art from the artist.

But it's so often the case that the artist has not separated his art from himself. Rather, his sexualising or racist perspective is so often all over the artwork. In 1993, R. Kelly wrote and produced the song 'Age

Ain't Nothing but a Number' for singer Aaliyah. It's a song about a young girl entreating an older man to enter into a relationship with her. In 1994, Kelly, then aged twenty-seven, married Aaliyah, who was fifteen, by bribing a government official to create a forged document with an altered date of birth (the marriage was later annulled). Consider also sculptor, printmaker and typeface designer Eric Gill. Gill sexually abused his daughters and performed sex acts on his pet dog. In encountering Gill's work, it's impossible to subtract him from it. He has a wood engraving of a young woman with long hair leaning down, naked, in a tub. It's entitled *Girl in Bath: II* and is the likeness of his daughter Petra, who he sexually abused. Then there's a woodcut print which depicts a dog holding a flaming torch in its mouth entitled *Hound of St Dominic*, and it's hard not to think of him fucking his dog. Even for those works whose subjects are further removed from his abuses, there are other barriers to enjoyment. One thinks of the smoothing hands of the sculptor, and holding that thought tends to ruin more or less all his work.

I have watched a couple of Woody Allen films more recently. (I saw them on pirate DVDs while I was living in Beirut without an internet connection, so at least he didn't make any money out of it.) On revisiting them, it turned out that the sexual abuse he stands accused of didn't matter one bit. His films are awful in their own right. They're billed as the cerebral Hollywood choice, and as a pretentious, undiscerning teenager they seemed fine to me. Watching them as an adult, I found them so preposterous that once I'd got over my mortification they were hilarious in ways Allen didn't intend. The plots generally revolve around attractive young women (in one case a seventeen-year-old schoolgirl) fawning over the middle-aged Allen or a character written to represent him. Some older men might find the films a friendly place to indulge their fantasies, but for the rest of us, it's a bit like stumbling across morally dubious porn that's clearly meant for someone else. They're bad films. But seen in the context of Allen's life, they're chilling, and it's hard to believe that anyone could watch them without being reminded of his abuses of power.

We are formed by the cultures we live within and the art and media we engage with. The average person in the US spends eight hours per day – half the time they're awake – streaming online content.[42] That's aside from any time spent reading books or magazines or scrolling through social media. We're consuming vast amounts of information, and it shapes our perspectives. A steady diet of misogynistic writing dulls a person's ability to spot the misogyny around them. Mainstream pornography influences sexual expectations in ways that tend to dehumanise women, as well as leading to a reduction in egalitarian beliefs, an increase in violent attitudes and behaviours, and a greater propensity towards misogyny in young men.[43] Hollywood films can be just as troubling, and they too often provide templates for our social and romantic aspirations. Women account for just 10 per cent of the writers and 5 per cent of the directors of the 2,000 highest-grossing films since 1994.[44] Two-thirds of speaking or named film characters are men,[45] and women are four times more likely to be depicted naked.[46] Analyses of thousands of books and films reveal that men's lives are usually portrayed as being adventure-oriented, while women's are represented as being centred on romance.[47] Black characters are often the best friend or sidekick, rather than the protagonist, and are more likely to be killed off. Latinx, East Asian and South Asian people generally only feature as vehicles for the repetition of racist stereotypes. Only 2 per cent of films explicitly include LGBT characters or content.

The works of the likes of Allen and Weinstein are the staples of our cultural canon, and other voices and perspectives that might serve as a foil or counterweight are minimal, marginal or absent. Rather than thinking about it as 'cancelling', we might consider extending some quality control into the art, media and information we consume, choosing our encounters with a view to diversity, challenging and bolstering our capacity for independent thought. After all, it's not as though we currently encounter art 'organically'. Rather, our consumption is carefully curated to be profitable, with the help of algorithms whose objective is to anticipate and influence our tastes.

Disengaging from someone whose values you find objectionable does not amount to that person being 'cancelled'. Being discerning about whose works we engage with is no more troubling than being selective about our friends and partners.[48] It can be an effective way of applying pressure, of refusing to provide your time, attention or money in order to avoid complicity in perceived harms, and a way of contributing to the containment of that person's influence. It can also allow a person to avoid the needless discomfort of having to anticipate, endure or confront bigoted behaviour. I don't watch stand-up comedy unless I'm reasonably sure at the outset that the performer isn't racist, sexist, homophobic, transphobic, classist or ableist. Enjoying comedy requires a certain degree of relaxation; I don't want to be tense, waiting for a joke that might make my blood boil. That's not fun. Our values are important to us, and we make all sorts of choices in light of them. Doing so is an exercise of moral agency, of thoughtfulness, of self-protection, of resistance. As novelist Celeste Ng wrote in a Twitter thread on this issue:

> Maybe I consider a guy to paint my house, then find out he's super racist and don't hire him. Saying 'Oh, but he's a GREAT painter, who cares if he's racist!' means you think I weighed *my own* values – good painting job vs. dislike of racism – and got *my own* priorities wrong.
>
> 'But if everyone refuses to work with X, no one will hire him!' Yes, that is how consequences and societies work. If my guy X is an asshole to *everyone*, no one will hire him. There's no rule guaranteeing assholes work, or friends. This is one way societies discourage assholery.[49]

This returns us to the discussion about cancellation. It may not be the best first-line treatment, and there should generally be a door left ajar for those who change their minds, but ostracism – whether through boycotting creative products, refusing to hire a person or otherwise – can be a powerful tool for discouraging assholery.

# 9

# Are We Responsible for Structural Injustice?

It happens that every man in a bank hates what the bank does, and yet
the bank does it. The bank is something more than men, I tell you. It's
the monster. Men made it, but they can't control it.

John Steinbeck, *The Grapes of Wrath* (1939)

On the hottest day of 2021, I sat in the garden at my parents' home on
the north coast of the Thames estuary. In gloomy tones, we talked
about the weather. That week, Turkey had recorded its highest
temperature on record: 120°F. Wildfires raged through Siberian
forests, releasing thousands of years of sequestered carbon into the
atmosphere in acrid, lung-scarring plumes. Five hundred people had
just died in a heatwave in Canada in temperatures that reached 121°F,
eight degrees hotter than any previous record. Finland and Estonia
had also just recorded historic highs. Floods were wreaking havoc in
Germany, Poland, the Netherlands and the Czech Republic (and by
the end of that week, the UK, too), claiming hundreds of lives. We
were glad of the cloudless sky, but in the context, the dazzling sunshine
felt like a threat.

As we talked, my father balanced on a stepladder, attaching a
tarpaulin to the back of the house to cast some shade for us to sit in.
He used cable ties to fix its corners to the garden fences. Irked by the
use of disposable plastic, and true to my role in the family dynamic as
sanctimonious know-it-all, I asked why he couldn't use rope instead,
gesturing to a ball of twine that sat atop a pile of odds and ends. He
laughed. 'You do realise that's made of plastic, too?' I picked it up and
noted its shiny nylon weave. 'Besides,' he added,

do you really think what *I* do makes a difference, when factories are making hundreds of these every minute, and oil companies are selling them gallons of petrol to make the plastic? I've given up on worrying about what I do. Why should I bend over backwards for nothing?

I sighed, and settled back into the patch of shade as the midday sun yellowed the grass and shrivelled the leaves on the fruit trees. The world was burning and I was chastising my father for using a few centimetres of plastic as he tried to keep us cool. I sympathised with his despondency. The greatest threats to life globally – environmental destruction, global inequality – are vast, systemic problems, while our responses are often trifling, and focus on scolding others and wracking ourselves with guilt. Ditching drinking straws, carrier bags and cable ties isn't going to save the planet. Yet a planet of people whose lives are premised on the untrammelled consumption of nonrenewable materials – in the form of straws, carrier bags and cable ties, but also phones, jeans and cars – is not one that *can* be saved.

It's tempting to resign ourselves; declare the mess intractable. Life is already so hard; shouldn't we be forgiven for taking the path of least resistance? It's an easy line to take from a well-kept garden in a wealthy nation. In the UK, the effects of global heating have so far been comparatively manageable, well-funded infrastructure will provide some defence against rising threats, and most livelihoods don't depend on the weather. Such detachment is a luxury few others can afford. On the Pacific Island of Kiribati, where per capita carbon emissions are negligible, fresh water is already being polluted by rising sea levels, farmland is shrinking as soil is poisoned by saltwater and homes are being submerged. More than two million Kenyans, whose contribution to climate change is smaller still, face starvation as droughts threaten their food security.[1] In recent years there have been dramatic reductions in global crop yields and micronutrient contents, pushing the world's poorest people towards greater risk of malnutrition.[2] The stakes could not be higher nor the deadline for action more pressing.

Environmental destruction, like poverty and racism, is a *structural* problem; it is part and parcel of our economic system. But structures are not ephemeral: they are constituted by the combined effects of our individual actions and choices. How should we, as individuals, respond to structural problems? This is a philosophical and practical problem that bothers me more than any other. I haven't managed to answer it here, but what follows are some thoughts on how philosophy can help us to find our way through some of the complexities.

## Don't Blame Me, Blame the Structures!

Identifying who is responsible for large-scale injustices is a complicated matter that's best illustrated through a real-life example. Fifteen years ago, British surgeon Mahmood Bhutta visited the city from which his parents had migrated to the UK in the 1970s. Sialkot, in the Punjab province of Pakistan, was an ancient metropolis that was razed by Alexander the Great and rebuilt into a thriving city noted for its production of silk and swords. It was later home to paper factories and ironworks, and became a major steel producer under British colonialism, producing surgical instruments which were used throughout colonial India. Today, it is a leading producer of scalpels, scissors, forceps, needles and other instruments, accounting for 80 per cent of the metal tools that are critical to safe surgery globally.[3] Bhutta, a colleague of mine who specialises in ear, nose and throat surgery, and was in Sialkot to visit relatives, was asked by his cousin whether he'd like to see where his surgical instruments were made.[4] They walked through the city's industrial district, where people toiled in makeshift units that were open to the street. Here, unregulated workers are subcontracted by large companies to make components of products which are assembled elsewhere and sold on to health services globally, including the UK's National Health Service (NHS).

Bhutta was shocked by what he saw. Children as young as seven operated metal-grinding machines, amid exposed wiring, metal dust, excessive heat and noise and hazardous chemicals. He was told of people working eleven-hour shifts for a third of Pakistan's minimum wage, of limbs being cut, burned and crushed in occupational accidents, of the absence of personal protective equipment.[5] After further investigation, he realised that the surgical instruments he uses were often made under sweatshop conditions by desperately poor Pakistanis, many of them children, who work excessive overtime, are paid wages too meagre to live on, have insufficient health and safety arrangements, and are often prevented from joining unions. Bhutta was improving and saving lives in the UK with the help of tools whose production was destroying lives elsewhere. Clearly he isn't to blame. Yet figuring out precisely who is responsible is far from straightforward.

It seems reasonable to assume that the fault lies with the factory owners. But paying workers more and offering them additional occupational protection is costly, so either prices must rise or profits must fall. Raising prices might lead the NHS procurer to choose the cheaper products of a rival company in order to optimise funds for other areas of essential healthcare. Holding prices fixed and allowing profits to drop could result in insufficient funds to update machinery and improve products, and a competitor company with inferior working conditions might instead win the contract. (Shareholders are also likely to kick up a fuss if their returns take a hit.) In both cases, if the company were to fold, many jobs would be lost. While governments could improve the regulation of these industries, NHS procurers might then source products from countries whose protocols are laxer and prices are lower. Everyone ends up being constrained to do the *wrong* thing regardless of their intentions or values, because the incentive structure of capitalism makes normal, rational behaviours calamitously harmful, especially to the world's poorest people.

This is what is known as a *structural* problem.* Nobody actively wants products to be made under such awful conditions, yet if everyone does what best serves their immediate interests, they end up collectively reproducing and bolstering a system that is ruinous for workers and the environment. Ours is a world replete with structural problems that take this form.

As we saw in Chapter 1, structures act as sets of imperceptible constraints on our actions that are enforced through norms, manners,

---

* Large-scale problems that are difficult to characterise and address are also sometimes known as 'wicked' problems.

laws, bureaucracies, material realities and institutions. They encourage or incentivise certain attitudes and behaviours, and make others difficult or impossible. Imagine a trek through dense woodland. Almost all hikers opt to follow the path which has been trampled and bushwhacked by many others before them. There are other possible routes through the trees, but you'd have to thrash at thickets and be grazed by thorns, and your progress would be slow and halting. When we say a particular social reality is *structural*, we mean that it is caused by people taking the well-trodden path, and that each time a person takes it, it becomes more well-trodden. (In philosophy we say that structures are *recursive*.) Even if a person is determined to take another route and succeeds in doing so, their efforts are unlikely to break through the undergrowth sufficiently to create a trail that is noticeable or appealing to the next hiker.

A structural injustice occurs when structures motivate people to unintentionally act in ways that cause harm to others. Let's extend the analogy of the trampled route. Imagine that a group of subsistence farmers plant their staple crop on the only fertile strip of land in town. This sliver of earth happens to be the shortest route for townspeople to reach the train station. Every day, as they hurry to work, commuters trample the struggling crops, leaving the farmers with dangerously low yields and the threat of starvation. Structural injustices occur when a group is mistreated through the combined actions of large numbers of people who, for the most part, do not intend to cause harm, but whose actions are strongly incentivised by the constraints and pressures of the broader system, and their attempts to meet their own needs within that system.

Examples of structural injustices in our everyday lives abound. Consider Yezda, a young woman who lives in a society in which young people, and young women in particular, feel pressure to wear the 'right' clothes. Fashions change fast, and she buys cheap versions of the latest styles from a budget retailer whose clothes are stitched by sweatshop workers in Indonesia, and are made from cotton that is causing water stress and environmental devastation in Uzbekistan.[6] Yezda does not intend to contribute to harmful practices, but by leading ordinary lives constrained by particular social and material realities (gendered social norms about clothing, the retailers whose clothes she can afford), she and her peers bolster an unjust industry. After watching a documentary about the harms of fast fashion, she stops buying new clothes, even though her friends tease her for being peculiar and puritanical. Nothing changes for the workers in Indonesia or for the dried-up basin of the Aral Sea; fast fashion hurtles on. In what sense was Yezda responsible for the harms caused by high-street fashion? Did her attempt to take responsibility make any difference?

Sam, a white airport security officer, faces similar issues. Though there are protocols about when to frisk passengers and search their bags, there's informal pressure to err on the side of caution when a passenger seems suspicious. The airport director is anxious that the airport should prioritise security, even if that means being overzealous. A young, brown-skinned man with a large beard approaches the security area. He avoids making eye contact and seems tense and uncomfortable. Sam directs his colleague to take the man aside to be searched while he pulls the bag off the conveyor belt and examines it thoroughly, undoing the passenger's careful packing. He doesn't find anything suspicious, and as the man repacks his jumbled belongings, he tells Sam that he is always searched, and finds air travel very nerve-wracking as a result. Sam worries that he is making unfair assumptions about people and causing them further stress, yet he reasons that any of his colleagues would have done the same and that it would be disastrous if he ever allowed a person with malevolent intentions to get through, so he isn't able to change anything. Sam contributes to Islamophobia through his racial profiling, but his job seems to require that he does so.

Mahmood Bhutta, Yezda and Sam play a role in the injustices that harm Pakistani metal-grinders, Indonesian textile workers and Muslim air passengers. Yet it's not clear that they can easily correct these injustices through the narrow range of individual actions that are within their power. How should we conceive of their contributions and responsibilities, and the actions they should take to tackle them?

## The Invention and Limits of Individual Responsibility

While the major moral problems we face are structural, there is a widespread tendency to fixate on individual solutions such as donations to charity, eating Fairtrade chocolate and using ecologically kind detergent. This serves capitalism very well. Focussing on our own privatised culpability and that of our neighbours averts our gaze from the failings that are core to the system itself. Such an approach has been described as a 'neoliberal diversion'.[7] Persuading us that saving the planet depends on our individual decisions also opens opportunities for new markets: people can give $3 a month to be relieved of any guilt about global poverty and pay a premium for less exploitative coffee or less toxic shampoo.

There's good reason to be cynical. For many of us, it's now second nature to think of our daily decisions in terms of their 'carbon footprint': cycling instead of driving, cooking a vegetarian dinner, turning down the temperature when doing laundry. We end up with a score which captures the extent of our individual contribution to the devastation of our planet. Yet the idea of a 'carbon footprint' was a con from the start. While the concept of an ecological footprint for a nation or industry dates back to the 1990s, the 'carbon footprint' of individual people gained prominence as a notion in 2000, when UK-based oil corporation British Petroleum (BP) paid PR firm Ogilvy & Mather to push public discourse towards the idea that individuals, rather than fossil fuels companies, were responsible for climate change.[8] They sensed that with growing awareness of environmental devastation, the tide of opinion would turn against them, leading to a PR disaster. Publicising the idea of individual responsibility was a pre-emptive strike. By 2004, the BP website boasted a user-friendly carbon footprint calculator, resulting in the absurd situation of having ordinary people compute the measure of their responsibility for global warming at the online home of a company that extracts 3.7 million barrels of oil every day.

The propaganda campaign succeeded: carbon footprint figures and calculators have become mainstream, urging us to direct blame and anxiety at our own decisions and those of our peers. While the idea of a 'carbon footprint' and the practice of 'ethical consumption' can be useful starting points for thinking about environmental destruction and labour transgressions, they tend to distract us from the more determinative levers of change, and they fail to account for the contexts in which we live. A person who lives in an affordable suburb that isn't well served by public transport has no choice but to drive to the job that keeps them afloat. In 2019, asthmatics were confronted with the bewildering fact that the greenhouse gas emissions of the inhalers which help them to breathe comfortably have a carbon footprint equivalent to that of meat.[9] Many people *can't* escape contributing to structural harms, and some of us are less able to choose more 'ethical' options.

Growing up in a family of six on a small income, we saved money by buying eggs laid by caged hens, chicken from battery farms and cleaning products thick with pollutants. We bought the cheapest electronics, and when those low-quality items inevitably broke, we'd buy the same short-lived products again, because the cost of getting them fixed outweighed the cost of replacement. Sticking to a budget was essential to our ability to live without continual anxiety. I'd note the smug assertions of the more 'ethical' items on the supermarket shelves, but they were often as much as three times the price. It adds insult to injury if most people are priced out of making morally good decisions, while those with more disposable income can buy their way to a cleaner conscience. That can't be a way to solve serious structural problems.[10]

Yet if we are prepared to let people off the hook because their contributions to large-scale harms are minuscule and are compelled by prevailing structures, what does that mean for racism, sexism and other forms of oppression? Sam the airport security officer acts on Islamophobic biases every day. Should we let it go? We can raise the stakes: what about a police officer, socialised in a racist society and trained in a profession that facilitates violence against racialised communities, who shoots a Black girl dead because he mistakes the glint of a chocolate-bar wrapper for a weapon? If racism is a form of *structural* injustice, what moral traction do we have in blaming any individual?

As we saw in Chapter 8, we have to strike a balance between understanding ourselves as blameworthy and holding each other to account, while at the same time recognising the conditions under which our choices are made. It is essential that we acknowledge that the system constrains our actions, but we must stop short of being so forgiving as to stabilise those structures of inequality.

It is helpful to recognise that different forms of structural injustice make different demands of us. Using a racist slur directly harms another person in a way that using a disposable drinking straw does not. (A single drinking straw is, in fact, a literal drop in the ocean compared with, say, the 705,000 tons of plastic dumped in the sea every year by the fishing industry.[11]) In both cases, injustices are strengthened, and injurious behaviours are normalised. But while environmental injustice stems from the combined effect of individual acts of environmental disregard, racism is caused through both aggregated harms *and* individual harms. When a Muslim woman is told to 'go home' by a passer-by, not only does that act normalise racism for those who witness the incident, and affirm the abuser's sense of superiority and entitlement, it also frightens the victim, makes her feel even less welcome in her community, and raises her cortisol levels, increasing her vulnerability to a range of health conditions. Some of these effects are interpersonal, in that they involve individuals directly harming other individuals, but all of these effects also indirectly bolster unjust structures.

Making this distinction is vital, because while it is difficult for most ordinary people to appreciably reduce their role in causing environmental destruction, it is comparatively easy for each of us to minimise our interpersonal contribution to racism and sexism – by, for example, being more thoughtful about language and firmly challenging harmful utterances – and thereby make a substantial and immediate difference to the lives of those in our communities.

We must be mindful of the pitfalls of individualising responsibility, but also beware of the opposite extreme, and avoid piling all the responsibility on the structures and letting ourselves off too lightly. Talking about structural problems too often involves gesturing towards an abstract, amorphous, insurmountable force. There was a 2021 article in the *Guardian* entitled: 'Don't Blame Men for the Climate Crisis – We Should Point the Finger at Corporations'.[12] It acknowledged that men have a heftier footprint when it comes to meat and driving, but closed with the statement 'We are not going to fix the climate crisis by shaming largely powerless individuals or getting men in the west to eat more plant-based burgers; it can be fixed only through systemic change.' I think I agree with this, but I'm not entirely sure what it means. Like bringing up religion,[13] bursting into tears or saying 'it's complicated', the label 'structural' or 'systemic' tends to act as a conversation stopper.

We need to find a way to acknowledge the structural and individual without over-emphasising either. Structural problems are scarcely influenced by individual actions, but are perpetuated by the sum total of those actions. At the same time, each of us can only directly change our own actions.

## Taking No More Than Our Share

Two decades ago, I gave up meat. I had no grand moral justification, I was just one of those teenagers who forges an identity through the indiscriminate rejection of norms. (To complete the picture, at the same age, I wore a beret and never smiled in photos.) It wasn't a difficult transition. My family didn't eat a lot of meat to start with: ours was a culturally Muslim household, so that ruled out pork, and the mad cow disease crisis struck when I was a child, so that ruled out beef.

My reasons for staying vegetarian as an adult relate to the environmental costs of meat production. Here, I'll focus on the land use issue.[14] Grazing cattle requires vast areas of agricultural land. Once you subtract oceans, glaciers, deserts, beaches and mountains, only 21 per cent of the world's surface is habitable. Half of that land is occupied by forests, urban settlements, lakes and rivers. The other half is used for food production. Eighty per cent of that limited supply of agriculturally useful land is given over to the grazing of animals for food, yet those animals provide only 20 per cent of the world's calorie needs.[15] We are not using the world's land very effectively, and some people are eating so much meat that the land available to feed others is diminishingly small.

Not all of this land is used for grazing; some of it is used to grow crops for animal feed. Soy, for example, is often planted on slashed and burned patches of previously ancient rainforest, and while it's often mistakenly claimed that vegans' demand for tofu and soy milk precipitates this destruction, in fact, 80 per cent of soy is fed to live-stock as high-protein meal.[16]

Meat poses serious ethical questions whose answers shed light on how we should respond to other forms of structural injustice. One way of working through the morality of meat consumption is to apply a highly intuitive mechanism for determining which actions are permissible. Eighteenth-century philosopher Immanuel Kant puzzled over the question of how to be good.[17] He devised a formula which was conceptually related to the Golden Rule, which is most commonly expressed in English as 'Do unto others as you would have them do unto you.' The Golden Rule is often traced to Jesus Christ's Sermon on the Mount, but in fact dates back four thousand years, to the Middle Kingdom of ancient Egypt, and was also articulated in the ancient Sanskrit epic the *Mahābhārata* as: 'One should never do some-thing to others that one would regard as an injury to one's own self.' Kant's heuristic (known as the 'Categorical Imperative') asks that each of us makes sure our actions are steered by rules that it would make sense for *everyone* to follow in similar circumstances. When deliberating on the morality of a course of action, we must ask: is this action universalisable?

Suppose I'm thinking of breaking a promise. To work out whether doing so is morally permissible, I must ask whether I can coherently think that everyone else should also always break their promises. This doesn't seem possible. If promises were always to be broken, they'd become unreliable, and then we've lost the core of what makes a promise a promise – that they are reliable guarantees about the future. Breaking promises is therefore not something that can be turned into a universal moral rule because doing so removes the conditions that make promising possible. Having a rule like this for promises would also make many important relationships and projects impossible. If my promise to meet you at an agreed time for a cup of tea can't be trusted, then you have no way of reliably arranging a social life with me; a promised ceasefire between two warring groups could not be relied upon and conflict would persist. So in addition to making no sense as a universal moral rule, breaking promises also undermines our ability to live in a society with one another. It's therefore morally wrong, and should be avoided.

With regard to meat, we must ask: would it make sense for everyone in the world to eat meat? How much meat should they be allowed to eat? There are several ways to answer these questions. Let's focus on land use. The world can be divided into three regions: (1) those countries in which moderate amounts of meat are eaten, so that if everyone followed those sorts of diets, less agricultural land would be used than currently is in use; (2) those countries in which a fairly large amount of meat is eaten, such that if everyone ate that way, it would take more land for agriculture than is currently needed (i.e. forests would have be felled to produce more arable or pasture land); (3) those countries in which so much meat is eaten that if everyone in the world tried to eat that much, *there wouldn't be enough land for this to be possible.*[18] Unsurprisingly, the categories tend to track the per capita wealth of nations: overconsumption of meat is primarily a Global North problem. Category (1) includes Thailand, China, Sri Lanka, Iran and India. Germany, the United Kingdom, Mexico and South Korea are in category (2). And the typical diets of the United States, Ireland, Canada, Sweden, France, Italy, Australia and New Zealand fall in category (3). It pays to examine some of the exact numbers. Half of the world's habitable land is currently used for agriculture, but if everyone ate the diet of an average person from India, only 22 per cent of land would be used, while if everyone ate the diet of a person in the UK, 95 per cent of habitable land would be needed. And if everyone ate the way an average person in the USA does, 137 per cent of the planet's habitable land would be necessary, which is of course, impossible.

Let's apply Kant's principle to the three categories. You can have a rule about eating little or no meat, and if everyone followed it, not only would it be possible for everyone in the world to follow a similar diet to you, but some existing farmland could be reforested. This would increase carbon capture and rejuvenate ecosystems, or the reclaimed land could act as a buffer for growing additional plant-based food, in view of the UN's recent warning that 30 million people are 'one step away from starvation'.[19] Or you could devise a moral rule which allowed people to eat meat with almost every meal, and while it would be possible at current population levels for everyone to eat this way, additional vast swathes of rainforest would need to be destroyed. Finally, your moral rule might seek to allow each person even greater quantities of meat, like the 273 pounds an average US resident eats every year,[20] but we know there isn't enough land for this to be possible.

We have to conclude that the people in this last category act immorally, because they choose to act in a way that is not universalisable. Eating anything other than a very modest amount of meat is a declaration of entitlement to more than your share of the world's resources. (And that's without getting into what non-human animals deserve, which is surely something other than a bolt to the brain.) Those looking for practical heuristics about meat consumption may wish to consult the 'planetary diet' recommended by medical journal *The Lancet*, which calculates that we can each eat one ninety-eight-gram piece of beef each week and a modest slice of chicken every day, and stay within Earth's boundaries.[21]

Meat isn't the only troubling food. Chocolate also poses moral issues, and here I lose the moral high ground. Meat wrecks certain rainforests, and chocolate destroys others. While industrial farming is gutting the Amazon, the dense rainforest of West Africa, which runs through Sierra Leone, Liberia, Côte d'Ivoire, Ghana, Togo, Benin, Nigeria and Cameroon, is being decimated by the demand for cocoa plants. Seventy per cent of the world's cocoa is sourced from this region, and in Côte d'Ivoire, the area of land covered by rainforest has decreased by 80 per cent since 1960.[22] Poor, small-scale farmers, often operating illegally in protected areas, topple ancient trees, burn their undergrowth and raise puny but lucrative cocoa plants among their mighty stumps. They will never see, nor could they afford, the confections their plants flavour. Not only do I eat about 40 pounds per year – well above the national average – but I have a taste for the darkest chocolate. I'm about as heavy an individual contributor to this harmful practice as can be found. You definitely couldn't make a moral rule which permitted everyone to eat as much chocolate as I do.

We can extend this principle of universalisability to other domains, too. There simply aren't enough precious metals in the Earth's crust for everyone to upgrade their electronics every couple of years. There isn't enough water to grow the cotton that would be needed for everyone to wear new clothes every season. Carbon emissions already exceed the biosphere's handling capacity, and Global North states, corporations and individuals have exhausted that budget with no regard for what is universalisable, racking up 92 per cent of excess emissions and leaving no leeway for Global South states to meet their people's basic needs.[23] The same disparity is seen at the individual level: a 2022 study showed that the annual emissions of the wealthiest 1 per cent exceed those that the poorest 10 per cent produce over more than two decades.[24] Most of the structural injustices to which we contribute depend on the world being carved up into those who take more than their share of the world's resources and those who shoulder more than their share of the world's burdens.

So what use is the test of universalisability in helping us to act in response to structural injustice? At first sight, it looks to be the wrong approach to problems of this sort. The principle assumes that individuals are the sole authors of their decisions, but since our 'choices' are instead forcefully constrained by broader structures, this guidance looks unworkable. Besides, me quietly giving up chocolate is unlikely to save a single tree. However, if we agree that checking whether our actions are universalisable is a reasonable strategy, yet can see that in practice we're rarely able to act upon that guidance, this tells us something important: the *system* is faulty in a much deeper sense. We knew that already, but armed with the categorical imperative, we are better able to explain why: a functional, morally defensible political and economic system shouldn't incentivise us to act in ways that are clearly non-universalisable and which tend to worsen inequality.

Thinking about universalisability therefore helps us to talk about why things need to change, and offers a powerful route to understanding why these issues are, at root, issues about supremacy and equality. We might call on governments to think about failures of universalisability as they incentivise or disincentivise particular industries. After all, how could it be morally acceptable for any democratic government, tasked with managing the needs of the populace, to encourage or permit some people to consume so much more of the world's resources than is their due?

## Individuals Build Collectives

Refraining from actions which are not universalisable makes moral sense, but structural problems would remain intact unless a great many people followed the same rule. One vivid illustration of this predicament was presented by philosopher Derek Parfit, who devised a thought experiment in which a person is hooked up to a torturing machine that delivers very mild electric shocks.[25] One person turns up the voltage by such a small increment that the victim doesn't notice the change, and then a second person comes along and turns the dial a little more, then another follows, and so on. Before long, the poor victim is writhing in agony and at risk of cardiac arrest. Each torturer contributed such a negligible amount to the increase in voltage that it would seem inaccurate to describe any individual as harming the victim, yet the overall effect is undeniably harmful. Parfit notes that individual refusal seems to make no difference: if one of these 'harmless torturers' refused to turn up the pain dial, the end result would be just the same – the person would still be writhing in pain.[26] Yet he concludes that even though the harm caused by any given individual is so slight as to be imperceptible, those who inflict those minute harms still act wrongly if they participate knowing that their actions cause considerable harm when *added* to the contributions of others acting similarly.[27]

Returning to the earlier example, Yezda wasn't just buying new jeans, she was buying new jeans knowing that others would *also* be buying new jeans, and that *collectively* they were buttressing a system characterised by poor labour practices and environmental destruction. There is no sense in adjudicating Yezda's actions in isolation. We must examine her purchases in the context in which they occur, and look for responses that account for the communal nature of the wrongdoing as well as the individual actions that constitute it. Doing so sheds light on a possible solution. If the 'harmless torturers' collectively decided to refuse to turn up the dial – if they went on strike from their horrible work – the victim would remain unharmed. And if Yezda and others could somehow expose and challenge the labour practices and environmental costs of fashion brands, their refusals would have greater efficacy. What options might there be for such collective action?

Many of us work out our responsibilities in relation to structural injustices by considering what it would take for the problem to be resolved – e.g. for everyone to reduce their meat consumption and take the bus – and then trying to do our bit. Yet in the absence of a collective, organised effort to make these changes, our efforts have almost no effect. It's a bit like wanting a fence to be repaired after a storm, and nailing a single plank of wood and merely hoping that each of your neighbours will do the same. No fence gets built. Philosopher Elizabeth Cripps calls these individual slices of responsibility, which are often causally insignificant, 'mimicking' duties.[28] They are the duties that would be required by a fair scheme, and they include sorting your recycling, using ecological laundry detergent and taking fewer flights. They are so-called because there is a (largely baseless) hope that if each of us simply *mimics* these duties, the structural problem will be fixed, and everyone will have done their fair share. All the planks will appear, and we'll have a fence. The problem is that in most cases, there is no fair, collective scheme. There's just your plank and maybe mine, and that is not a fence. Cripps recommends that we instead focus our efforts on a more important category of actions which she calls 'promotional' duties – duties to bring about the sort of collective action that would target the structural problem. Rather than fixating on sorting our plastic recycling, we should campaign for a ban on single-use plastic packaging. Instead of just taking the bus, we ought to organise or join a protest that closes the road to private vehicles, thereby disrupting motorists and capturing the attention of the press and government. Sometimes, a mimicking duty is also a promotional duty. When I state my pronouns at the start of a lecture, I put my single plank in the fence but I do so in a way that is highly visible, and has the effect of reminding others that gender is an unstable category that each of us can make and unmake.

Political philosopher Iris Marion Young offered a helpful model for understanding our responsibilities for structural injustice. She argued that it is right for each of us to be assigned some of the burden of working towards changing unjust structures, because we all have a particular relationship to the production or perpetuation of structural injustice. But she pointed out that the conventional understanding of responsibility as *liability* for past harms tends to lead us astray in the case of structural injustice. It is futile to try to work out what share of blame or guilt is yours to bear. We should instead think about the responsibilities we have to prevent harms in the future, and, given the nature of the injustices, those responsibilities will have to be discharged collectively if they are to be effective.

The burdens we bear depend on our levels of social and economic power. Powerful people and institutions can make changes overnight that we as individuals might not achieve in decades, or at all. Consider that in cities all over the world, well-meaning people are trying to help those who are unhoused by cooking and serving food, running shelters, providing healthcare, collecting donations and lobbying local and national government. Yet the rates of unhoused people rise with each passing year. The only European country in which there is a downward trend is Finland, and rough sleeping has been drastically reduced in its capital, Helsinki. The Finnish government's 'Housing First' policy makes the right to housing unconditional, addressing other issues (such as substance addiction) once a person has some-where secure to live.[29] Again, charities and local councils lobbied hard for the change, but ultimately the government had the power to enact it and radically improve the lives of tens of thousands of people in a single stroke. Leaving people unhoused is a political choice, and the greatest responsibility for change lies with governments.

A related response to the dilemma of structural injustice has been offered by philosopher Robin Zheng.[30] Zheng sets out to try to bridge the gulf between the individual and structural in order to figure out how our individual actions build structures. She argues that structures are composed of people acting within their *social roles*, which are, as she puts it 'the site where structure meets agency'. In order to bring about change we must push the boundaries of our social roles (as parents, teachers, partners, neighbours, etc.) and engage in behaviours that erode harmful structures from within. In doing so, we change the way others perform their roles and thereby influence the structures that constrain us all. Think of a society as a big fishing net, and social roles as the knotted nodes on the net. If you pull one of the nodes away from its initial position, the rest of the net will move, too, and the shape of the mesh around that node will have to change. Likewise, if we tug at our roles by performing them in slightly different ways, then other people's social roles must shift, too, and the whole of society is drawn, incrementally, in a different direction.

What would this look like in practice? A teacher might hang a South-oriented Gall–Peters map in the classroom and teach children about the colonial origins of global inequality. A politician might refuse to sing the national anthem. A doctor could declare, in a television interview or a newspaper article, that it is against the Hippocratic oath to treat patients differently based on their citizenship or ability to pay. An essential worker might organise or join in with industrial action. A museum curator might add annotations to exhibits, describing the colonial regimes that stole each artefact. A university administrator might accede to the demands of a student group and cease to serve beef in campus food outlets. To take a real-life example, Mahmood Bhutta returned from his trip to Sialkot and blew the whistle on what he'd seen, speaking to major newspapers about the sweatshop labour behind medical equipment.[31] He founded the Medical Fair and Ethical Trade Group, and works with the National Health Service, which has a budget of $177 billion per year, to tackle labour violations in healthcare supply chains.

Some of the acts just listed may seem minor, but our power and our social roles are supposed to determine the nature and degree of our responsibility, and their feasibility and visibility are part of the point: each act erodes the stabilising assumptions of this unjust world, and those who witness or are affected by it (including those who object, precisely because they object) are influenced, too. What Cripps, Young and Zheng have in common is that they encourage us to think carefully about *who* we are – in terms of the roles and power we hold, and our relationships to others – and take shrewd, strategic action from where we stand.

## Moral Awareness

Harmful structures are most obviously maintained by material incentives. My parents buy a new printer when the ink runs out because that's cheaper than replacing the cartridge. Yet cost and convenience aren't the only motivating factors. We also make decisions that are morally troubling because we are deliberately prevented from seeing the harms to which we contribute. Worse, we're often actively encouraged to contribute to those harms, because doing so keeps the cogs of capitalism turning. Whatever other strategies we might take, tackling structural injustices requires greater moral awareness. Examining the history of cigarettes provides some insights as to how we might be made to confront our wrongdoing.

Scientists first identified the link between smoking and cancer in the 1950s, leading to the British Medical Research Council's announcement, in 1957, of 'a direct causal connection' between the two. By the 1960s, the Royal College of Physicians had published a report which additionally implicated smoking in bronchitis and coronary heart disease, and advised that the government intervene by more tightly regulating the advertising and sale of cigarettes, and their use in public spaces. By 1971, all cigarettes sold in the UK had government health warnings printed on their packets. Over the ensuing decades, the medical case against smoking strengthened as studies showed that one in three smokers died of smoking-related illness, and hundreds of thousands of lives were lost each year as a result of second-hand smoke.[32] In 2003, new EU legislation mandated that the text 'Smoking kills' or 'Smoking seriously harms you and others around you' must cover at least 30 per cent of the area of the pack, and a second message, such as 'Protect children: don't make them breathe your smoke' or 'Smoking can cause a slow and painful death' must cover an additional 40 per cent. By 2006, smoking was banned in public places across the UK and, from 2017, all cigarettes and tobacco sold in the UK were required to be encased in plain packaging. Almost half of all adults in the UK smoked in 1974; in 2019, this had fallen to just 16 per cent.[33] Nowadays, cigarettes are readily associated with disease and death, and the data show that prominent health warnings are effective in promoting cessation of smoking.[34] Smoking in an enclosed space in the presence of a child or pregnant person would be regarded by most of us to be morally repugnant.

To be confronted with warnings of your potential 'slow and painful death' as you buy cigarettes is out of step with how the economy normally works. It seems unthinkable that consumers should be urged to consider the damaging effects of their choices on themselves and others. There is a lesson here. Our choices are constrained by the system in which we live (i.e. factory-farmed chicken and sweatshop-sewn clothes are cheaper), but our *desires* are also distorted by that system. We're made to believe that meat is essential to a healthy diet, that clothes look dated after a few months, and that owning new devices will make us happier. Any attempt at addressing injustice must account for both our constrained choices and our manipulated desires.

Social norms influence our desires and choices. In India there are more vegetarians than in the rest of the world put together, largely due to religious taboos on the consumption of some or all animals within the traditions of Hinduism, Jainism, Buddhism, Islam and Sikhism. In the West, meat consumption is as much about social permissibility as it is about flavour. Dog meat is supposed to be very tasty. It's been compared to beef or lamb: fatty, tender, fragrant. Cat meat is lighter, but sweeter and more succulent. Both are nutritious, and in the UK they're not in short supply; there are more cats and dogs than cows and pigs. Yet dogs and cats are so commonly domesticated in Western contexts that there is a taboo on their consumption. Eating a dog, even one reared for that purpose, would be seen as immoral. By contrast, cows, sheep, swine and fowl are routinely raised for human food, and a range of terminology is deployed to distance the living animal from its butchered flesh ('pork', 'beef', 'mutton', 'ham').

Social norms determine our attitudes and actions, but norms are continually shifting, and are sensitive to the information we have access to. What if, taking a lesson from the regulation of cigarettes, the packaging of animal products or fast fashion came with a *moral* warning?

> This item was sewn in a factory in Bangladesh by a worker who is paid no more than $90 per month. It is made of cotton, whose cultivation causes soil degradation and water stress, and acrylic, which is derived from fossil fuels. This garment releases microplastics into the ocean when washed.

I make this suggestion only half seriously; capitalist governments would be very unlikely to deter consumption in this way. You can imagine the tabloid headlines: 'Public to Be Guilt-Tripped Into Giving Up Meat'. But the information is true, and it's not quite right to contend that such a move would amount to excessive moralising, or would apply undue influence on our decision-making. The absence of accurate information about the costs of our consumption is *already* a moral position, and the way in which harmful products are advertised forcefully influences us in the opposite direction. The fact that we are encouraged to consume products without needing to consider any contextual information amounts to a moral statement about the low value afforded to the global industrial working class, non-human animals, and the planet.

To be clear, I don't think that shifting the responsibility onto consumers is, on its own, the right course of action. But as it stands, powerful individuals, governments and corporations have been permitted to draw us into their harmful practices, to rely on us to finance their exploitative schemes, without informing us of the true costs of our actions. Governments have the power to undermine the ability of corporations to make us complicit in causing harms, just as they did when they realised that smoking was lethal.

There's another lesson to learn from cigarettes. The advertising of tobacco products was banned in the UK in 2003, after more than two centuries of aggressive marketing. One particular promotional campaign stands out. In his 1928 book *Propaganda*, Edward Bernays, the 'father of public relations' (and a nephew of Sigmund Freud) wrote:

> The conscious and intelligent manipulation of the organized habits and opinions of the masses is an important element in democratic society. Those who manipulate this unseen mechanism of society constitute an invisible government which is the true ruling power of our country. We are governed, our minds are moulded, our tastes formed, and our ideas suggested, largely by men we have never heard of . . . It is they who pull the wires that control the public mind.[35]

Bernays drew on these sinister insights to produce highly effective US propaganda during the First World War, and continued to reflect on the 'engineering of consent' in peacetime. Most women at that time were reluctant to smoke cigarettes, due to widespread social taboos. Bernays set about opening up new markets for cigarette companies by promoting the idea that smoking was associated with women's liberation. He described cigarettes as 'torches of freedom' and linked their uptake to the casting off of other sex taboos, gesturing towards the 'men's work' that women had readily taken on during the war. He paid attractive, fashionable young women to smoke cigarettes at New York's Easter Parade in 1929, and later promoted the idea that smoking was good for weight control and throat health. (Despite all this, he cautioned his own wife against smoking.[36]) Rates of smoking among women tripled within a few years and rose sharply until the 1960s.[37]

How many women lost their lives because of Bernays? How many children were born prematurely, or with developmental difficulties, or later struggled with the effects of passive smoking? How many other people like Bernays are currently researching and implementing schemes to manipulate our yearnings in ways that harm us and others? Our behaviours are strongly influenced by advertising, which manufactures desires that vitalise markets, concentrating wealth in the hands of a few. Advertising is the propaganda wing of most of the structural harms we've explored in this chapter. It is an obvious and urgent target for any movement that intends to tackle structural injustices. Its eradication would open up space – both physical and discursive – to think about what our more authentic desires might be and how they should be tempered by our responsibilities to others.

Even though cigarettes are highly addictive, and even though the tobacco industry was one of the most powerful lobby groups in the world, scientists and governments managed to combine public messaging and the regulation of advertising to bring about a dramatic and continual decrease in the number of smokers, saving millions of lives. The case of cigarettes might be an exception; smoking endangers public health, which is costly to the health service and the workforce, while the harms of meat consumption and fast fashion mostly occur elsewhere, in places that are deemed not to matter. Still, there is a deeper lesson: we won't undo structural injustices without targeting capitalism's engines of spin.

## The System Injures Us All

A few years ago, a doctor from the international humanitarian organisation Médecins Sans Frontières told me a story that haunted him. He'd been caring for a group of severely malnourished children in a small hospital where the mortality rate was high. He became aware of a measles outbreak in the community outside the hospital and realised that without a rapid vaccination programme, many children would become infected and die. The doctor had a very limited budget (the charity runs on a shoestring and is always short of funds), and he realised that he would have to make a difficult choice: focus on treatments for the malnourished children under his care or instead use the money to pay for a vaccination programme and save greater numbers of children.

The doctor made the decision which seemed to optimise the number of lives that could be saved. In doing so, he made use of the highly intuitive philosophical idea of 'utilitarianism' which determines that the morally right decision is the one that produces the greatest 'utility', or happiness. One of its earliest proponents was John Stuart Mill,[38] who wrote in 1863 that 'Actions are right in proportion as they tend to promote happiness, wrong as they tend to produce the reverse of happiness.'[39] I didn't ask what happened to the children fighting for their lives on his ward. Presumably some of those who would have died anyway did so sooner; others who might have been saved wasted away. Years after this decision, the doctor regularly recalled the awful choice he'd faced, always with regret and sorrow. He knew he had made the 'best' decision, but nothing about it felt right.

In a 1984 book about the practice of nursing, philosopher Andrew Jameton described 'moral distress' as a state of unease that arises 'when one knows the right thing to do, but institutional constraints make it nearly impossible to pursue the right course of action'.[40] The doctor in the scenario above knew what was right: the malnourished children urgently needed sustenance and monitoring and the broader community needed an immediate vaccination scheme. Institutional constraints, in the form of scarcity so severe that meeting one set of needs necessitated foregoing the other, meant that the right decision was not available. He faced an awful choice and selected the best option of the two. Nonetheless, children starved and died, and their doctor was left with severe moral distress.

Those who are subject to repetitive moral distress may experience 'moral injury'. The term originated in the military, coined by Jonathan Shay, a psychiatrist writing about the trauma experienced by war veterans.[41] It has since been applied more broadly to refer to the damage to a person's sense of moral orientation as a result of enacting, witnessing or failing to intervene in, serious harms. Moral injury can lead to mental illness (common in both veterans and health professionals), but my concern here is its effect on a person's ability and motivation to function as a moral agent. Moral distress and moral injury are always the result of structural failures. They occur when the system does not permit us to be directed by our moral compasses, but instead places what is morally right beyond our reach. We are forced to act within rules and constraints within which what is decent is not possible.

We are all morally injured. The system that required a doctor to let his paediatric patients starve is the same system that floods us with propaganda for lifestyles premised on products that wreck the environment or are made in sweatshops. We have sufficient resources for every child to be nourished *and* vaccinated; these interests should never be in competition. That they and other basic necessities are so often mutually exclusive is the clearest symptom of system failure that I can imagine. It is not hard to produce food, clothes and other essential goods that do not destroy the planet and for which workers are fairly remunerated. This system rides roughshod over our most basic understanding of what is fair; it harms some people disproportionately and requires others to be complicit in those harms.

This chapter has focussed on environmental issues and global poverty as archetypal structural injustices. Of course, racism, sexism and other forms of oppression also derive from social structures. And these issues are anchored to one another: global poverty and environmental devastation are underwritten by racism and sexism. Sweatshops and environmental destruction are tolerated because those they harm most acutely – poor Global South people of colour – have been corralled into conceptual categories whose purpose is to mark them as inferior and enable their exploitation. Capitalism, which sustains itself by extracting value from people and the environment, is premised on the idea that it is acceptable and inevitable that some people should suffer and die so that others can have more. Yet we rarely confront these issues as instances of racism and sexism. It isn't just poor people who sew our clothes, it's poor *women of colour*. It isn't just unlucky people who die or are displaced by the effects of global heating, it's Global South *people of colour*. Global South peoples, low-wage workers and the environment are devalued because the economy is premised on their devaluing. It's axiomatic to the system. The factories of the world are located in the Global South, and their workers are primarily low-paid women of colour.

As long as this is the case, our Global North feminist and anti-racist movements are mere window dressing.

Oppression maintains a logic that makes exploitation possible. The subjugation of women ensures a supply of free or cheap domestic, emotional and gestational labour. Race grew out of the compulsion to steal the labour and resources of those from other lands. The violence and vilification faced by people of marginalised genders and sexualities is a way of disciplining those who threaten to destabilise the heteronormative nuclear family unit within which reproductive labour is privatised and devalued. Indigenous people whose epistemologies recognise the moral status of plants, non-human animals, rivers and mountains have been sidelined because they hinder the untrammelled extraction of natural resources to make consumer goods. Social identities are enmeshed in our material realities. Exploitation requires dehumanisation, and there is no better tool for the job than the categories and hierarchies of oppression.

If we are to address global poverty and environmental destruction, we first have to see these problems as the result of 'racial capitalism'[42] and ensure that our understanding of racism is capacious enough to move beyond the pockets of the Global North to which it is often limited. We need something like Ruth Wilson Gilmore's definition of racism as the 'state-sanctioned and/or legal production and exploitation of group-differentiated vulnerabilities to premature death, in distinct yet densely interconnected political geographies.'[43] The more familiar racism and sexism of our daily lives are instances of a broader trend that shapes our global economic system, and whose worst excesses occur in the Global South. We must identify flooding in Bangladesh and African migrants drowning in the Mediterranean as manifestations of racism, and understand the poverty wages of Thai electronics workers or the sexual harassment of garment workers in Lesotho as paradigmatic cases of sexism.

Figuring out ways to better conceptualise our relationships to structural injustice is important, but it is no substitute for the practical work of agitating the system. I wish I had more to say on the latter, but perhaps that is not the work of a philosophy book. As it is, my own complicity thickens by the minute, as every step I take in any direction compromises my most fundamental values. I wake up in the morning and lace up running shoes that were stitched in a factory in Vietnam by a woman who has no access to healthcare and will always struggle to eat, jog along streets choked with emissions from over-sized, under-occupied private vehicles. I return home and eat break-fast – a non-recyclable plastic tub of yoghurt made from the milk of a cow that was forcefully impregnated to ensure its milk supply – while my gas boiler burns fossil fuels to warm gallons of water for my shower. All of it is awful and on my own I can scarcely change a thing. Only one point is clear as day. Every formulation of the prob-lem leads to the same answer: 'not capitalism'. We are struggling along in a damaged world, and as philosopher Theodor Adorno wrote in 1951, a 'wrong life cannot be lived rightly'.[44] Our objective must be to rattle the joists of the system, destabilise the whole edifice and let the light in through the ruptures. It's a massive undertaking, but then again, there are masses of us.

# Conclusion: Your Nearest Barricade

I can't be a pessimist because I am alive. To be a pessimist means that you have agreed that human life is an academic matter. So, I am forced to be an optimist. I am forced to believe that we can survive, whatever we must survive.

James Baldwin, *The Negro and the American Promise* (1963)

It is customary to end a book about injustice on a positive note. Having laid out the problems in the body of the text, in tones that are often gloomy, the conclusion offers a pep talk that makes everything sound very tidy and exhorts the reader to get to work. The writer is careful to encourage realism, but cautions against the inertia of despair, falling back on words like those of the philosopher Antonio Gramsci, who urged a 'pessimism of the intellect and optimism of the will'.

To close with an optimistic pat would be disingenuous. I am drafting the last words of this book just as the 2022 United Nations Climate Change Conference comes to an end, having achieved nothing to slow the engines of consumption as they churn through the planet's resources, driven by the labour of the most wretched, heaping profits where they are least needed, in piles dammed by deadly borders. I can't see any reason to feel hopeful.

In the final stages of writing I had a baby, and like every other new parent, my relationship to time shifted. The future is now the place in which I will leave my child. Concerns about environmental destruction are often framed as anxieties about future generations, and it is standard practice to mention one's children and grandchildren, real or imagined, when trying to explain why staving off environmental degradation should be an urgent priority. I am sympathetic to this view, now more than ever, but it ignores the fact that this particular hell is already upon us, even if it is not evenly distributed. And while I am desperate for my child to know a world that is better than this one, I also want my parents to be soothed by signs of change, and I don't see why I should live the rest of my life in a world I'd be despondent about bequeathing to others. We should worry about the future, but not more than we worry about the present. We are people's children, too.

With this last point in mind, I'll sound a note of warning, if not optimism. However bad things are, we must not forget that there are barricades of resistance this very minute that are holding off something much crueller. Eight billion people are alive, and, for the moment, there are still trees and bees. Find your nearest barricade. As long as we can imagine something worse, we have a fight on our hands.

# Acknowledgements

Many of the arguments of the preceding chapters started out as responses to the difficult questions put to me by students at the American University of Beirut, the Brighton and Sussex Medical School and the Free University Brighton. Teaching is the best part of my week, and I am grateful to my students for bringing so much fun and hope to our discussions.

There would be no book without the big sister energy of Chanda Prescod-Weinstein, who set this project in motion and kept me on course, nor the cleverness and care of Jessica Papin, who has been this work's most ardent champion. Thank you to Gretchen Schmid and Kate Craigie for the enthusiasm and expertise that gave the book its initial momentum, and to Emily Wunderlich, Jocasta Hamilton and Caroline Westmore for shepherding the manuscript through its challenging final stages with kindness and understanding.

I am very grateful to Thomas Jones and Alice Spawls at the *London Review of Books* for being so welcoming and for letting me test my ideas across such a wide range of topics, and to Rebecca Liu at *Prospect* for commissioning the essays out of which this book grew.

One of the best things about writing a book is having somewhere to acknowledge the teachers who helped me to beat the odds: Neil Hooper, Beryl Pallin, Kate McDonagh, John McEachern, Barry Lucas, Rory Costello, Julie Rogers and Ed Tsang. I owe an enormous debt of gratitude to Owen Saxton for taking a chance on me and then cheering on my politics as much as my physics. Thanks to Jeremy Butterfield for the meticulous marginal comments that made me a clearer writer, and to Huw Price for urging me to take risks.

I have had the great fortune of working alongside decent people who have made my professional life a joy, leaving me to get on with thinking and writing while avoiding much of the ugliness of academia. Thanks to Samar Rawas, Ray Brassier, Bana Bashour, Hans Muller, Waddah Nasr, Pete West-Oram, Lisa Kearley, Mel Newport and Andrea Pepper, to name just a few. I am indebted to my dear friend and mentor Bobbie Farsides for modelling the good life, academic and otherwise, and for helping me to make a home for myself. Thank you also to my broader intellectual community, especially Agomoni Ganguli-Mitra, Brian Earp, Patricia Kingori, Lorna Finlayson, Ali Ghanimi, Priyamvada Gopal, Koshka Duff, Bob Brecher and Alastair Wilson.

Apologies and thanks to those who read some awkward early drafts, or otherwise helped with the text: Susan Shahvisi, Jojo Shahvisi, Sara Shahvisi, Neil Singh, Bob Brecher, Koshka Duff, Chanda Prescod-Weinstein, Pete West-Oram, Kamran Matin, Lena Zuchowski, and Jack Blaiklock. Special thanks to Hannah Loach, who looked through the whole book from her hospital bed when she had every excuse not to.

I am very grateful to the friends and family who talked to me about the book, waited patiently for me to be done with it, or helped to keep the rest of my life in order: Leena Al-Hassan, Ira Allen, Lisa Armstrong, Rav Athwal, Matt Bemment, Jon Bild, Jack Blaiklock, Dominic Burke, Fidaa Chehayeb, Annie Clements, Anna Cunningham, Tricia Curmi, Morna Dick, Nina Dodd, Bobbie Farsides, Tom Farsides, Esther Garibay, Maddie Geddes-Barton, Anna Gumucio Ramberg, Matthew Hanson-Kahn, Jason Hickel, Alaa Hijazi, Katharine Jenkins, Hannah Loach, Jayde Matthews, Kath Maude, Sol Soledad Miranda, Stuart Morris, Xina Moss, Fuad Musallam, Marija Pantelic, Louis Pilard, Becky Rowley, Rim Saab, Ghiwa Sayegh, Guddi Singh, Lily Singh, Bimal Singh, Mei Trueba and Lena Zuchowski.

Alan Bennett once wrote of his relief at having never 'trod that dreary safari from left to right which generally comes with age'. I am lucky to have been raised by parents who have kept going in the other direction, and always with such broad-mindedness and humility as to put the rest of us to shame. Thank you to my mother, Susan, who is the real writer in the family, for showing me the power of books, and my father, Masud, for making sure I know where I come from and urging me to make my voice heard. My wee sisters have always kept me on my toes: Jojo with the fierceness of her compassion; Sara with her unwavering integrity. My older sister Dana taught me so much more than she knows. Nothing brings me more joy than learning, and the greatest gift of my life has been doing so alongside Neil Singh. Thank you for looking after me with such tenderness and patience. You're still my best thing. Any errors in the text should be directed to Rayan, who is also responsible for reminding me that all a person really needs is a full belly and someone to make it shake with laughter. I hope you know a world in which we get those basic things right.

# Notes

## Introduction: Show Your Work!

1. Mary Midgley, *Owl of Minerva: A Memoir* (Routledge, 2007), p. xii.
2. Audre Lorde, 'The Master's Tools Will Never Dismantle the Master's House', *Sister Outsider: Essays and Speeches* (Crossing Press, 2007).
3. David Graeber, *The Utopia of Rules: On Technology, Stupidity, and the Secret Joys of Bureaucracy* (Melville House, 2016), p. 89.

## Chapter 1: Can You Be Racist to a White Person?

1. Vikram Dodd, 'Black People Nine Times More Likely to Face Stop and Search Than White People', *Guardian*, 27 October 2020, https://www.theguardian.com/uk-news/2020/oct/27/black-people-nine-times-more-likely-to-face-stop-and-search-than-white-people [accessed 26 November 2020].
2. Graham Ruddick, 'Ex-footballer Trevor Sinclair Loses BBC Role After Admitting Racial Abuse', *Guardian*, 2 January 2018, https://www.theguardian.com/world/2018/jan/02/ex-england-star-trevor-sinclair-admits-drink-driving-and-racial-abuse [accessed 26 November 2020].
3. Kick It Out, @kickitout, Twitter, 2 January 2018, https://twitter.com/kickitout/status/948200599727824896 [accessed 26 November 2020].
4. Kimberlé W. Crenshaw, 'Framing Affirmative Action', *Michigan Law Review First Impressions* 105 (2006).
5. Michael Harriot, 'The 5 Types of "Becky"', The Root, 29 August 2017, https://www.theroot.com/the-five-types-of-becky-1798543210 [accessed 23 October 2022].
6. Damien Gayle, 'People of Colour Far Likelier to live in England's Very High Air Pollution Areas', *Guardian*, 4 October 2022, https://www.

theguardian.com/environment/2022/oct/04/people-of-colour-likelier-live-england-very-high-air-pollution-areas [accessed 7 November 2022]; Harvard School of Public Health, 'Racial Disparities in Traffic Fatalities Much Wider Than Previously Known', 'News', 2022, https://www.hsph.harvard.edu/news/press-releases/racial-disparities-traffic-fatalities [accessed 7 November 2022].

7. Rosa Luxemburg, *The Accumulation of Capital* (1913), Chapter 26, 'The Reproduction of Capital and Its Social Setting', https://www.marxists.org/archive/luxemburg/1913/accumulation-capital/ch26.html [accessed 20 November 2022].

8. Sarah Green Carmichael, 'Women Shouldn't Do Any More Housework This Year', Bloomberg.com, 24 August 2022, https://www.bloomberg.com/opinion/articles/2022-08-24/women-shouldn-t-do-any-more-housework-this-year [accessed 18 November 2022]; UCL, 'Women Still Doing Most of the Housework Despite Earning More', Institute of Epidemiology & Health Care, 2019, https://www.ucl.ac.uk/epidemiology-health-care/news/2019/nov/women-still-doing-most-housework-despite-earning-more [accessed 18 November 2022].

9. W. E. B. Du Bois, *Black Reconstruction in America: An Essay Toward a History of the Part Which Black Folk Played in the Attempt to Reconstruct Democracy in America, 1860–1880* (Harcourt, Brace & Howe, 1935), p. 700.

10. 'When Did Marital Rape Become a Crime?' *The Week*, 6 December 2018, https://www.theweek.co.uk/98330/when-did-marital-rape-become-a-crime [accessed 17 December 2020].

11. Simon Duncan, 'Why So Many Women Still Take Their Husband's Last Name', The Conversation, http://theconversation.com/why-so-many-women-still-take-their-husbands-last-name-140038, [accessed 30 December 2020]; Ammar Kalia, ' "I Understand My Wife's Lived Experience Better": Meet the Men Who Have Taken Their Wives' Surnames', *Guardian*, 20 August 2019, http://www.theguardian.com/lifeandstyle/2019/aug/20/i-understand-my-wifes-lived-experience-better-meet-the-men-who-have-taken-their-wives-surnames [accessed 30 December 2020].

12. Saidiya Hartman, *Lose Your Mother: A Journey Along the Atlantic Slave Route* (Macmillan, 2008), p. 133.

13. Eric Williams, *Capitalism and Slavery* (1944) (University of North Carolina Press, 1994).

14. Kelly M. Hoffman et al., 'Racial Bias in Pain Assessment and Treatment

Recommendations, and False Beliefs About Biological Differences Between Blacks and Whites', *Proceedings of the National Academy of Sciences* 113, 16 (2016): 4296–301.

15. Monika K. Goyal et al., 'Racial Disparities in Pain Management of Children with Appendicitis in Emergency Departments', *JAMA Pediatrics* 169, 11 (2015): 996–1002.

16. This point is made particularly vividly by comedian Aamer Rahman, an Australian of Bangladeshi parentage, who frequently gets complaints from white audience members for his jokes about white people (which go along the lines of: 'Hey, what's the deal with white people? Why can't they dance?'). They accuse him of 'reverse-racism'. Rahman acknowledges that it might be possible, if certain conditions are met, for reverse-racism to take place. In a viral YouTube clip from one of his shows, he explains how this might work: https://www.youtube.com/watch?v=dw_mRaIHb-M.

17. Sara Ahmed, *Living a Feminist Life* (Duke University Press, 2017), p. 262.

18. Fiona Vera-Gray, 'Have You Ever Wondered How Much Energy You Put in to Avoid Being Assaulted? It May Shock You', The Conversation, 21 September 2016, http://theconversation.com/have-you-ever-wondered-how-much-energy-you-put-in-to-avoid-being-assaulted-it-may-shock-you-65372 [accessed 17 December 2020].

19. Marilyn Frye, *The Politics of Reality: Essays in Feminist Theory* (Crossing Press, 1983), p. 14.

20. Kevin Bright, 'The One with the Male Nanny', *Friends*, 7 November 2002 (Bright/Kauffman/Crane Productions, Warner Bros. Television).

21. One of many reasons why Ross is an awful person and *Friends* is an embarrassing cultural touchstone. See e.g. Rhiannon-Skye Boden, '20 Reasons Why Ross in *Friends* Is Actually a Terrible Human Being', *80s Kids*, 30 December 2019, https://www.eightieskids.com/ross-is-the-worst [accessed 23 December 2020].

22. Peter Towns, 'I'm Proud to Be a Nurse – So Why Do People Still Think It's Not a Job for a Man?', *Metro*, 8 July 2020, https://metro.co.uk/2020/07/08/male-nurse-sexism-12717345 [accessed 23 December 2020].

23. 'Not All Gaps Are Created Equal: The True Value of Care Work', *Oxfam International*, 2020, https://www.oxfam.org/en/not-all-gaps-are-created-equal-true-value-care-work [accessed 23 December 2020].

24. 'Study Finds English and Welsh Family Courts Not Discriminating Against Fathers', https://warwick.ac.uk/newsandevents/pressreleases/

study_finds_english [accessed 23 December 2020]. In fact, the really alarming finding in relation to custody is that women and children who have experienced sexual or domestic abuse often struggle to convince courts that the father's involvement is not in the child's best interests, which can leave children vulnerable to continued violence. See Sonia Sodha, 'The Idea That Family Courts Are Biased Against Men Is a Dangerous Fallacy', *Guardian*, 5 March 2020, http://www.theguardian.com/society/commentisfree/2020/mar/05/family-courts-biased-men-dangerous-fallacy-abuse [accessed 23 December 2020].

25. Cathy Meyer, 'Dispelling the Myth of Gender Bias in the Family Court System', *HuffPost*, 2012 https://www.huffpost.com/entry/dispelling-the-myth-of-ge_b_1617115 [accessed 3 November 2022].

26. Sarah Schoppe-Sullivan, 'Dads Are More Involved in Parenting, Yes, but Moms Still Put in More Work', The Conversation, 3 February 2017, http://theconversation.com/dads-are-more-involved-in-parenting-yes-but-moms-still-put-in-more-work-72026 [accessed 23 December 2020].

27. Katelyn Jones, 'We Parent Equally – But He's Seen as Super Dad and I'm Not Seen at All', Motherly, 4 November 2019, https://www.mother.ly/life/praise-the-dads-and-the-moms [accessed 30 December 2020].

28. '(1982) Audre Lorde "Learning From the 60s"', BlackPast, 12 August 2012, https://www.blackpast.org/african-american-history/1982-audre-lorde-learning-60s [accessed 8 December 2020].

29. Kimberlé Crenshaw, 'Demarginalizing the Intersection of Race and Sex: A Black Feminist Critique of Antidiscrimination Doctrine, Feminist Theory and Antiracist Politics', *University of Chicago Legal Forum* 1, 8 (1989): 139–67.

30. 'The Combahee River Collective Statement', 1977, https://www.blackpast.org/african-american-history/combahee-river-collective-statement-1977 [accessed 14 November 2022].

31. Amia Srinivasan, *The Right to Sex* (Bloomsbury, 2021), p. 17.

32. In the US, slavery would be abolished in 1865, denying a man the right to vote on the basis of race would be outlawed in 1870, and women would be granted the right to vote in 1920. In reality, of course, none of these dates was clear-cut and Black people were effectively unable to vote until 1965.

33. Leslie Podell, 'Compare the Two Speeches', Sojourner Truth Project, https://www.thesojournertruthproject.com/compare-the-speeches [accessed 21 December 2021].

34. The precise content of Truth's most famous speech, as well as the dialect in which it was spoken, is the topic of disagreement, but it is widely understood to have contained the spirit of the text quoted here.

35. Diane S. Lauderdale, 'Birth Outcomes for Arabic-named Women in California Before and After September 11', *Demography* 43, 1 (2006): 185–201.

36. Muslim non-binary people are generally invisibilised in these discourses: Islamophobia renders Islam as so uniquely oppressive that non-binary people are imagined out of existence.

37. Moya Bailey, 'They Aren't Talking About Me . . .' Crunk Feminist Collective, 14 March 2010, http://www.crunkfeministcollective.com/2010/03/14/they-arent-talking-about-me [accessed 9 December 2020].

38. Megan Slack, 'Tammy Bruce Calls the Obamas "Trash in the White House"', *HuffPost UK*, 23 April 2009, https://www.huffpost.com/entry/tammy-bruce-calls-the-oba_n_178109 [accessed 30 December 2020].

39. Spielberg admits playing down the sexual relationship between two women for fear of the film losing its more universal rating. However, it's worth noting that he wasn't concerned about the effect of portraying domestic violence. It is also telling that same-sex sexual content is deemed to be inappropriate for younger people, but gender-based violence is not.

40. E. R. Shipp, 'Blacks in Heated Debate Over "The Color Purple"', *New York Times*, 27 January 1986, https://www.nytimes.com/1986/01/27/us/blacks-in-heated-debate-over-the-color-purple.html [accessed 8 December 2020].

41. Kimberlé Crenshaw, 'Mapping the Margins: Intersectionality, Identity Politics, and Violence Against Women of Color', *Stanford Law Review* 43 (1990): 1241.

42. Hadley Freeman, 'The "Karen" Meme Is Everywhere – and It Has Become Mired in Sexism', *Guardian*, 13 April 2020, http://www.theguardian.com/fashion/2020/apr/13/the-karen-meme-is-everywhere-and-it-has-become-mired-in-sexism [accessed 29 December 2020].

43. Michael Hughes and Steven A. Tuch, 'Gender Differences in Whites' Racial Attitudes: Are Women's Attitudes Really More Favorable?', *Social Psychology Quarterly* 66, 4 (2003): 384–401.

44. Charles M. Blow, 'How White Women Use Themselves as Instruments of

Terror', *New York Times*, 27 May 2020, https://www.nytimes.com/2020/05/27/opinion/racism-white-women.html [accessed 29 December 2020].

45. Salma Yaqoob, 'Muslim Women and War on Terror', *Feminist Review* 88, 1 (2008): 150–61.

46. Karen Attiah, 'So Much for the West "Saving" Muslim Women from Terrorism', *Washington Post*, 18 November 2015, https://www.washingtonpost.com/blogs/post-partisan/wp/2015/11/18/so-much-for-the-west-saving-muslim-women-from-terrorism/ [accessed 29 December 2020].

## Chapter 2: Has 'Political Correctness' Gone Too Far?

1. Kayla Epstein, 'Trump Responds to Megyn Kelly's Questions on Misogyny – With More Misogyny', *Guardian*, 6 August 2015, http://www.theguardian.com/us-news/2015/aug/06/donald-trump-misogyny-republican-debate-megyn-kelly [accessed 31 August 2021].

2. Ibid.

3. Simon Kuper, 'Political Correctness: The UK v the US', *Financial Times*, 6 February 2020, https://www.ft.com/content/31ed22f8-47a6-11ea-aee2-9ddbdc86190d [accessed 21 January 2021].

4. Tom Clark, 'Free Speech? New Polling Suggests Britain Is "Less PC" Than Trump's America', *Prospect Magazine*, 16 February 2018, https://www.prospectmagazine.co.uk/magazine/free-speech-new-polling-suggests-britain-is-less-pc-than-trumps-america [accessed 12 February 2021].

5. Peter Walker, 'Use Gareth Southgate's Tactics for Culture War, Pollster Tells MPs', *Guardian*, 6 July 2021, http://www.theguardian.com/society/2021/jul/06/use-gareth-southgates-tactics-for-culture-war-pollster-tells-mps [accessed 6 July 2021].

6. Edwin L. Battistella, 'The Not-so Ironic Evolution of the Term "Politically Correct"', OUPblog, 7 July 2019, https://blog.oup.com/2019/07/politically-correct-evolution [accessed 31 August 2021].

7. Debra L. Schultz, 'To Reclaim a Legacy of Diversity: Analyzing the "Political Correctness" Debates in Higher Education' (National Council for Research on Women, 1993).

8. Martha Nussbaum, 'Undemocratic Vistas', *Prometheus* 6, 2 (1988): 382–400.

9. Noam Chomsky, *Understanding Power: The Indispensable Chomsky* (New Press, 2002).

10. Richard Bernstein, 'The Rising Hegemony of the Politically Correct', *New York Times*, 28 October 1990, https://www.nytimes.com/1990/10/28/weekinreview/ideas-trends-the-rising-hegemony-of-the-politically-correct.html [accessed 6 July 2021].

11. Ibid.

12. Robert Booth, 'Grenfell Inquiry: Ex-ministers and Serving Secretary of State to Be Cross-examined', *Guardian*, 4 January 2022, https://www.theguardian.com/uk-news/2022/jan/04/grenfell-inquiry-ex-ministers-and-serving-secretary-of-state-to-be-cross-examined [accessed 19 January 2022].

13. Paul Karp, 'Senate Blocks Government Attempt to Restore Compulsory Plebiscite for Marriage Equality', *Guardian*, 9 August 2017, http://www.theguardian.com/australia-news/2017/aug/09/abbott-says-vote-no-to-marriage-equality-and-stop-political-correctness-in-its-tracks [accessed 8 February 2021].

14. Afua Hirsch, 'The Government Does Have a Strategy on Racism After All. It's called "War on Woke" ', *Guardian*, 17 June 2020, http://www.theguardian.com/commentisfree/2020/jun/17/boris-johnson-racism-woke-tories [accessed 6 September 2021].

15. 'Freedom of Speech – Joint Committee on Human Rights – House of Commons', 2018, https://publications.parliament.uk/pa/jt201719/jtselect/jtrights/589/58909.htm#_idTextAnchor058 [accessed 31 August 2021].

16. Kwame Asamoah Kwarteng et al., *Taking the Debate Forward: A New Code to Secure and Champion Freedom of Speech and Political Diversity on Campus*, Wonkhe, February 2021, https://wonkhe.com/wp-content/wonkhe-uploads/2021/01/Taking-the-debate-forward-Feb-2021.pdf

17. Sarah Schwartz, 'Map: Where Critical Race Theory Is Under Attack', *Education Week*, 11 June 2021, https://www.edweek.org/policy-politics/map-where-critical-race-theory-is-under-attack/2021/06 [accessed 6 September 2021].

18. Christopher F. Rufo, @realchrisrufo and @ConceptualJames, Twitter, 15 March 2021, https://twitter.com/realchrisrufo/status/1371541044592996352 [accessed 12 September 2021].

19. Paraphrased from Stanley Cohen, *Folk Devils and Moral Panics* (Routledge, 2011), p. 1.

20. Kevin Arscott, 'Winterval: The Unpalatable Making of a Modern Myth', *Guardian*, 8 November 2011, http://www.theguardian.com/commentisfree/2011/nov/08/winterval-modern-myth-christmas [accessed 12 February 2021].

21. Jessica Elgot, '"We Really Don't Want to Ban Christmas," Muslims Insist', *HuffPost UK*, 17 December 2013, https://www.huffingtonpost.co.uk/2013/12/17/ban-christmas-muslims_n_4460151.html [accessed 12 February 2021].

22. David Emery, 'FALSE: Sweden Bans Christmas Lights to Avoid Angering Muslim Refugees', Snopes.com, 26 October 2016, https://www.snopes.com/fact-check/sweden-bans-christmas-lights [accessed 12 February 2021].

23. Dominic Ponsford, '*Express* Corrects Story Suggesting Muslims Wanted to Ban New Fivers, But IPSO Rules No Breach of Code', *Press Gazette*, 7 April 2017, https://www.pressgazette.co.uk/express-corrects-story-suggesting-muslims-wanted-to-ban-new-fivers-but-ipso-rules-no-breach-of-code [accessed 6 July 2021].

24. Naomi I. Eisenberger, Matthew D. Lieberman and Kipling D. Williams, 'Does Rejection Hurt? An fMRI Study of Social Exclusion', *Science* 302, 5643 (2003): 290–2.

25. Catharine A. MacKinnon, *Only Words* (Harvard University Press, 1993).

26. John Langshaw Austin, *How to Do Things with Words* (Oxford University Press, 1975).

27. Quoted in: Rae Langton, 'Speech Acts and Unspeakable Acts', *Philosophy & Public Affairs* 22, 4 (1993): 293–330.

28. Srinivasan, *Right to Sex*, p. 46.

29. Amy Guttman, 'Set to Take Over Tech: 70% of Iran's Science and Engineering Students Are Women', *Forbes*, 9 December 2015, https://www.forbes.com/sites/amyguttman/2015/12/09/set-to-take-over-tech-70-of-irans-science-and-engineering-students-are-women [accessed 14 December 2021].

30. Pascal Huguet, Sophie Brunot and Jean Marc Monteil, 'Geometry Versus Drawing: Changing the Meaning of the Task as a Means to Change Performance', *Social Psychology of Education* 4, 3 (2001): 219–34.

31. Lionel Shriver, 'Great Writers Are Found with an Open Mind', *The Spectator*, 27 December 2018, https://www.spectator.co.uk/article/great-writers-are-found-with-an-open-mind/ [accessed 2 February 2023].

32. Shelly Romero and Adriana M. Martínez Figueroa, ' "The Unbearable Whiteness of Publishing" Revisited', PublishersWeekly.com, 29 January 2021, https://www.publishersweekly.com/pw/by-topic/industry-news/publisher-news/article/85450-the-unbearable-whiteness-of-publishing-revisited.html [accessed 22 December 2021].

33. Richard Jean So and Gus Wezerek, 'Just How White Is the Book Industry?', *New York Times*, 11 December 2020, https://www.nytimes.com/interactive/2020/12/11/opinion/culture/diversity-publishing-industry.html [accessed 22 December 2021].

34. Helena Vieira, 'Gender Quotas and the Crisis of the Mediocre Man', *LSE Business Review*, 13 March 2017, https://blogs.lse.ac.uk/businessreview/2017/03/13/gender-quotas-and-the-crisis-of-the-mediocre-man [accessed 8 September 2021].

35. McKinsey & Co., 'Why Diversity Matters', https://www.mckinsey.com/business-functions/organization/our-insights/why-diversity-matters [accessed 8 September 2021]; Cristina Díaz-García, Angela González-Moreno and Francisco Jose Sáez-Martínez, 'Gender Diversity Within R&D Teams: Its Impact on Radicalness of Innovation', *Innovation* 15, 2 (2013): 149–60; Max Nathan and Neil Lee, 'Cultural Diversity, Innovation, and Entrepreneurship: Firm-level Evidence from London', *Economic Geography* 89, 4 (2013): 367–94.

36. Samuel R. Sommers, 'On Racial Diversity and Group Decision Making: Identifying Multiple Effects of Racial Composition on Jury Deliberations', *Journal of Personality and Social Psychology* 90, 4 (2006): 597.

37. Reni Eddo-Lodge, *Why I'm No Longer Talking to White People About Race* (Bloomsbury, 2017).

38. Douglas Murray, 'The Consequence of This New Sexual Counter-revolution? No Sex at All', *The Spectator*, 25 December 2017, https://www.spectator.co.uk/article/the-consequence-of-this-new-sexual-counter-revolution-no-sex-at-all [accessed 31 August 2021].

39. Sarah Young, 'Argos Defends Advert Featuring All-black Family Amid Online Criticism', *Independent*, 30 August 2020, https://www.independent.co.uk/life-style/argos-advert-defend-tweet-black-family-complaints-gay-couple-racist-reaction-a9695996.html [accessed 23 December 2020].

40. 'Trump: NFL Kneelers "Maybe Shouldn't Be in Country" ', BBC News, 24 May 2018, https://www.bbc.com/news/world-us-canada-44232979 [accessed 22 December 2021].

41. Susan Christian, 'Seal Beach School Principal Draws Fire for Facebook Post Over Controversial Nike Ad', *Orange County Register*, 5/6 September 2018, https://www.ocregister.com/seal-beach-school-principal-draws-fire-for-facebook-post-over-controversial-nike-ad [accessed 22 December 2021].

42. Lucy Pasha-Robinson, 'Teenager "Thrown Out of US School" for Sitting During Pledge of Allegiance', *Independent*, 8 October 2017, https://www.independent.co.uk/news/world/americas/teenager-17-year-old-india-landry-suspended-windfern-high-school-houston-texas-sitting-pledge-of-allegiance-us-a7988856.html [accessed 22 December 2021].

43. Angelique Chrisafis, 'Pork or Nothing: How School Dinners Are Dividing France', *Guardian*, 13 October 2015, http://www.theguardian.com/world/2015/oct/13/pork-school-dinners-france-secularism-children-religious-intolerance [accessed 30 August 2021].

44. 'Newsreader Jon Snow Rails Against "Poppy Fascism"', *Evening Standard*, 13 April 2012, https://www.standard.co.uk/hp/front/newsreader-jon-snow-rails-against-poppy-fascism-7263001.html [accessed 31 August 2021].

45. John K. Wilson, *The Myth of Political Correctness* (Duke University Press, 1995).

46. Alex Nowrasteh, 'The Right Has Its Own Version of Political Correctness. It's Just as Stifling', *Washington Post*, 7 December 2016, https://www.washingtonpost.com/posteverything/wp/2016/12/07/the-right-has-its-own-version-of-political-correctness-its-just-as-stifling [accessed 22 December 2021].

47. Many of these manners are fine if taken in isolation: offering to help somebody and not taking too big a helping are reasonable aims for anybody. Yet men do not, as a rule, offer to carry each other's bags or remove a spider from the house of a frightened friend. They generally do not sacrifice their jackets for one another or walk each other home. And while men in the street will often smile as a form of greeting at women they do not know, they do not smile at each other; to do so might be seen as a provocation. Women often smile at other women, but rarely initiate smiling as a greeting towards unknown men, who are liable to take women's niceness as a sign that they should make sexual advances.

48. Frye, *Politics of Reality*, pp. 5–6.

49. Though note that the survey was carried out by an upmarket grocery

chain whose core demographic is white, middle-class people from older age categories, which may overlap with those most likely to be mourning older forms of etiquette.

50. 'Schools "Should Help Pupils Mind Their Manners"', BBC News, 15 October 2012, https://www.bbc.com/news/education-19946480 [accessed 8 August 2021].

51. Natalie Morris, 'Young Adults Say Traditional Manners – Like Saying Please – Are "Outdated"', Metro, 12 May 2019, https://metro.co.uk/2019/12/05/young-adults-think-traditional-manners-like-saying-please-thank-outdated-11277824 [accessed 8 August 2021].

52. André Spicer, 'Toughen Up, Senior Snowflakes, Swearing at Work Is Good for Us', Guardian, 15 January 2018, http://www.theguardian.com/commentisfree/2018/jan/15/toughen-up-senior-snowflakes-swearing-at-work-is-good-for-us [accessed 26 August 2021]; Ellie Abraham, 'People More Likely to Use Strong Swearing in Everyday Life Compared to Five Years Ago, Research Finds', Independent, 10 June 2021, https://www.independent.co.uk/life-style/swear-words-everyday-life-swearing-b1863451.html [accessed 26 August 2021].

53. Mark Brown, 'Swearing on Rise but Parents Still Don't Want Kids Hearing It, Report Finds', Guardian, 10 June 2021, http://www.theguardian.com/science/2021/jun/10/swearing-on-rise-but-parents-still-dont-want-kids-hearing-it-report-finds [accessed 26 August 2021].

54. Roxane Gay, Not That Bad: Dispatches from Rape Culture (Atlantic Books, 2018).

55. Rae Langton, 'Beyond Belief: Pragmatics in Hate Speech and Pornography', in I. Maitra and M. K. McGowan (eds), Speech and Harm: Controversies Over Free Speech (Oxford University Press, 2012): 72–93.

56. Those interested in learning more may wish to read: Robin Jeshion, 'Slurs and Stereotypes', Analytic Philosophy 54, 3 (2013): 314–29; Elisabeth Camp, 'A Dual Act Analysis of Slurs', in David Sosa (ed.), Bad Words: Philosophical Perspectives on Slurs (Oxford University Press, 2018): 29–59; Chang Liu, 'Slurs as Illocutionary Force Indicators', Philosophia (2020): 1–15.

57. Judith Butler, Excitable Speech (Routledge, 1997), p. 80, original emphasis.

58. Alexander Pollatsek, 'The Role of Sound in Silent Reading', in The Oxford Handbook of Reading (Oxford University Press, 2015): 185–201.

59. German Lopez, 'Ta-Nehisi Coates Has an Incredibly Clear Explanation for Why White People Shouldn't Use the N-word', *Vox*, 9 November 2017, https://www.vox.com/identities/2017/11/9/16627900/ta-nehisi -coates-n-word [accessed 4 July 2021].

60. Roxane Gay, *Bad Feminist: Essays* (Corsair, 2014), p. 221.

61. Renée Jorgensen Bolinger, 'The Pragmatics of Slurs', *Noûs* 51, 3 (2017): 439–62, at p. 452.

62. Cassie Herbert, 'Talking About Slurs', unpublished paper (2018), p. 21.

63. '*Daily Mail* Opts to Use "Niggling" on the Cover of Meghan Markle, Prince Harry Engagement Photos', TheGrio, 22 December 2017, https://thegrio.com/2017/12/22/daily-mail-niggling-meghan-markle [accessed 26 August 2021].

64. Liam Bright, @lastpositivist, Twitter, 13 March 2021, https://twitter.com /lastpositivist/status/1370738955612786693 [accessed 13 March 2021].

65. Thanks to Bob Brecher for pushing me on this point.

66. Hannah Arendt, *Essays in Understanding, 1930–1954: Formation, Exile, and Totalitarianism* (Schocken, 2011).

67. James Baldwin, 'On Being White . . . and Other Lies', *Essence* 14, 12 (1984): 90–2.

## Chapter 3: What's Wrong with Dog Whistles?

1. More detailed guidance on identifying symbols of neo-Nazi hate (often seen as tattoos, patches on clothing or stickers and posters in public spaces) are available here, for the US: https://www.splcenter. org/fighting-hate/intelligence-report/2006/look-racist-skinhead- symbols-and-tattoos and here, for the UK: https://www.trafford.gov. uk/residents/community/community-safety/docs/extreme-right- wing-symbols.pdf.

2. Dawn Foster, 'Who's Watching?', LRB Blog, *London Review of Books*, 22 October 2020, https://www.lrb.co.uk/blog/2020/october/who-s- watching [accessed 23 October 2020].

3. This phrase, which is now commonly seen on social media, seems to originate in a 1995 episode of *The Simpsons* ('A Star Is Burns') in which Krusty the Clown admonishes himself for blurting out that he was bribed by evil magnate Mr Burns. When asked how he could bring himself to vote for Burns' movie in a local film competition, he responds,

'Let's just say it moved me . . . TO A BIGGER HOUSE. Oops, I said the quiet part loud and the loud part quiet.'

4. A reference to the famous 'Schrödinger's cat' thought experiment in quantum mechanics, in which the decay of radioactive material in a sealed room (which is probabilistically determined) triggers the release of poison, killing the unfortunate cat who is enclosed in the room. Before we open the door of the room to check what's happened, the cat is neither alive nor dead, but is in a mixed probabilistic state of both outcomes at once. This result follows from the strange way in which probability operates in quantum mechanics.

5. Sarah Prager, 'Four Flowering Plants That Have Been Decidedly Queered', JSTOR Daily, 29 January 2020, https://daily.jstor.org/four-flowering-plants-decidedly-queered [accessed 6 February 2022].

6. Chris Thomas, 'Untucking the Queer History of the Colorful Hanky Code', 19 June 2017, Out, https://www.out.com/out-exclusives/2017/6/19/untucking-queer-history-colorful-hanky-code [accessed 6 February 2022].

7. This deserves further analysis. Claiming to have a boyfriend (whether or not it's true) is one of the most effective ways for a woman to bring an end to unwanted sexual attention from a man. Rejecting his advances on the grounds of not being interested is not nearly as effective, which is testament to the fact that another man's claim on a woman is stronger grounds to back off than her own claims upon herself in choosing to refuse a sexual advance. Many men are liable to interpret another man's relationship to a woman as a proprietary claim which activates a code among men, the violation of which could lead to violence. If a woman makes reference to her girlfriend, or to her lack of interest in men, this can have the effect of inflaming the unwanted advances, which is a result of the ways in which sex between women has been sexualised by men.

8. Gary Younge, 'How the Far Right Has Perfected the Art of Deniable Racism', Guardian, 26 January 2018, http://www.theguardian.com/commentisfree/2018/jan/26/far-right-racism-electoral-successes-europe-us-bigotry [accessed 11 September 2021].

9. I owe this line of thought to Tali Mendelberg's discussion of the 'Norm of Racial Equality' in Tali Mendelberg, *The Race Card: Campaign Strategy, Implicit Messages, and the Norm of Equality* (Princeton University Press, 2017).

10. Gay, *Bad Feminist*, p. 292.

11. 'Racial Prejudice in Britain Today', NATCEN Social Research, September 2017, http://natcen.ac.uk/our-research/research/racial-prejudice-in-britain-today [accessed 31 December 2020].

12. 'Pupils Perform "Alarming" Feat', *Metro*, 24 May 2006, https://metro.co.uk/2006/05/24/pupils-perform-alarming-feat-155361 [accessed 19 November 2020].

13. As quoted in William Safire, *Safire's Political Dictionary* (Oxford University Press, 2008), p. 190.

14. Katherine Runswick-Cole, Rebecca Lawthom and Dan Goodley, 'The Trouble with "Hard Working Families"', *Community, Work & Family* 19, 2 (2016): 257–60.

15. 'Hardworking families' is what's known as a 'glittering generality': a phrase that is so obviously positive and morally pleasing that it is frequently used to bring about a particular emotional response even when it's vague and contentless. Other examples include 'democracy' and 'freedom', which are also bandied around by politicians to create an atmosphere of positivity and virtue without their having to say anything more specificc.

16. Wesley Lowery, 'Paul Ryan, Poverty, Dog Whistles, and Electoral Politics', *Washington Post*, 18 March 2014, https://www.washingtonpost.com/news/the-fix/wp/2014/03/18/paul-ryan-poverty-dog-whistles-and-racism [accessed 3 November 2022].

17. Jonathan Martin, 'Trump, Trailing in Pennsylvania, Launches Familiar Attacks on Biden', *New York Times*, 13 October 2020, https://www.nytimes.com/2020/10/13/us/politics/trump-rally-pennsylvania.html [accessed 31 December 2020].

18. Ian Olasov, 'Offensive Political Dog Whistles: You Know Them When You Hear Them. Or Do You?', Vox, 7 November 2016, https://www.vox.com/the-big-idea/2016/11/7/13549154/dog-whistles-campaign-racism [accessed 31 December 2020].

19. Images can also function as dog whistles. See: Ray Drainville and Jennifer Saul, 'Visual and Linguistic Dogwhistles' in Luvell Anderson and Ernie Lepore (ed.), *The Oxford Handbook of Applied Philosophy of Language* (Oxford University Press, forthcoming), published online 2020, https://www.researchgate.net/publication/344441861_Visual_and_Linguistic_Dogwhistles.

20. Mendelberg, *Race Card*.

21. Vincent L. Hutchings and Ashley E. Jardina, 'Experiments on Racial

Priming in Political Campaigns', *Annual Review of Political Science* 12 (2009): 397–402; Tatishe M. Nteta, Rebecca Lisi and Melinda R. Tarsi, 'Rendering the Implicit Explicit: Political Advertisements, Partisan Cues, Race, and White Public Opinion in the 2012 Presidential Election', *Politics, Groups, and Identities* 4, 1 (2016): 1–29.

22. Jennifer M. Saul, 'Racial Figleaves, the Shifting Boundaries of the Permissible, and the Rise of Donald Trump', *Philosophical Topics* 45, 2 (2017): 97–116.

23. John Eligon, 'The "Some of My Best Friends Are Black" Defense', *New York Times*, 16 February 2019, https://www.nytimes.com/2019 /02/16/sunday-review/ralph-northam-blackface-friends.html [accessed 12 November 2020].

24. Jessica Elgot and Peter Walker, 'Javid Under Fire Over "Illegal" Cross-Channel Asylum Seekers Claim', *Guardian*, 2 January 2019, https://www.theguardian.com/politics/2019/jan/02/people-crossing-channel-not-genuine-asylum-seekers-javid [accessed 3 November 2022].

25. Rachel Hall, 'Suella Braverman: Five Controversial Statements from UK Home Secretary', *Guardian*, 26 October 2022, https://www. theguardian.com/politics/2022/oct/26/suella-braverman-five-contro-versial-statements-home-secretary [accessed 3 November 2022].

26. Jessica Murray, 'Teaching White Privilege as Uncontested Fact Is Illegal, Minister Says', *Guardian*, 20 October 2020, http://www.theguardian. com/world/2020/oct/20/teaching-white-privilege-is-a-fact-breaks-the-law-minister-says [accessed 31 December 2020].

27. Kurt Andersen, 'How to Talk Like Trump', *Atlantic*, 15 March 2018, https://www.theatlantic.com/magazine/archive/2018/03/how-to-talk -trump/550934 [accessed 31 December 2020].

28. Saul, 'Racial Figleaves', p. 109.

29. Mary Kate McGowan, 'On "Whites Only" Signs and Racist Hate Speech: Verbal Acts of Racial Discrimination', in Maitra and McGowan, *Speech and Harm*, pp. 222–50.

30. Ian Haney-López, *Dog Whistle Politics: How Coded Racial Appeals Have Reinvented Racism and Wrecked the Middle Class* (Oxford University Press, 2015).

31. Anand Giridharadas, 'How America's Elites Lost Their Grip', *Time*, 21 November 2019, https://time.com/5735384/capitalism-reckoning-elit-ism-in-america-2019 [accessed 31 December 2020].

32. thereisnospoon, 'Why the Right-Wing Gets It – and Why Dems Don't [UPDATED]', *Daily Kos*, 10 May 2006, https://www.dailykos.com/story/2006/5/9/208784 [accessed 31 December 2020].

## Chapter 4: Is It Sexist to Say 'Men Are Trash'?

1. Sarah Young, 'Gabriela Cattuzzo Dropped by Sponsor for Tweeting "Men Are Trash" After Being Sexually Harassed', *Independent*, 27 June 2019, https://www.independent.co.uk/life-style/gabriela-cattuzzo-razer-gaming-influencer-twitter-sexual-harassment-reaction-a8976871.html [accessed 15 July 2020].
2. Samuel Gibbs, 'Facebook Bans Women for Posting "Men Are Scum" After Harassment Scandals', *Guardian*, 5 December 2017, https://www.theguardian.com/technology/2017/dec/05/facebook-bans-women-posting-men-are-scum-harassment-scandals-comedian-marcia-belsky-abuse [accessed 15 July 2020].
3. Casey Newton, 'Why You Can't Say "Men Are Trash" on Facebook', The Verge, 3 October 2019, https://www.theverge.com/interface/2019/10/3/20895119/facebook-men-are-trash-hate-speech-zuckerberg-leaked-audio [accessed 10 September 2021].
4. Jeanette Chabalala, ' "I Put Petrol on Her and Walked Away" - Court Hears in Karabo Mokoena Murder Trial', News24, 25 April 2018, https://www.news24.com/news24/southafrica/news/i-put-petrol-on-her-and-walked-away-court-hears-in-karabo-mokoena-murder-trial-20180425 [accessed 13 July 2020].
5. Lou-Anne Daniels, '#CourtneyPieters: Timeline of a Child Murder', IOL, 6 November 2018, https://www.iol.co.za/news/south-africa/western-cape/courtneypieters-timeline-of-a-child-murder-17782970 [accessed 13 July 2020].
6. 'South Africa's Sandile Mantsoe Guilty of Karabo Mokoena Murder', BBC News, 2 May 2018, https://www.bbc.com/news/world-africa-43979207 [accessed 13 July 2020].
7. Nic Andersen, '#MenAreTrash - The Important Phrase Sending South Africa into a Divided Frenzy', *South African*, 16 May 2017, https://www.thesouthafrican.com/opinion/menaretrash-the-important-phrase-sending-south-africa-into-a-divided-frenzy [accessed 13 July 2020].
8. The eleventh of October is the United Nations' International Day of

the Girl Child, which highlights the human rights' violations that girls face. In 2016, as articles and social media posts circulated, citing statistics about inadequate educational opportunities, child marriage and sexual abuse, #WomenAreTrash also started trending, as men took to social media to post misogynistic comments.

9. 'U.S. Mass Shootings by Shooters' Gender', Statista, 2020, https://www.statista.com/statistics/476445/mass-shootings-in-the-us-by-shooter-s-gender [accessed 13 July 2020].

10. Mark Follman, 'Armed and Misogynist: A Mother Jones Investigation Uncovers How Toxic Masculinity Fuels Mass Shootings', *Mother Jones*, May/June 2019, https://www.motherjones.com/crime-justice/2019/06/domestic-violence-misogyny-incels-mass-shootings [accessed 13 July 2020].

11. Uma Narayan, *Dislocating Cultures: Identities, Traditions, and Third World Feminism* (Routledge, 1997), pp. 81–117.

12. Lois Beckett, 'The Gun Numbers: Just 3% of American Adults Own a Collective 133m Firearms', *Guardian*, 15 November 2017, https://www.theguardian.com/us-news/2017/nov/15/the-gun-numbers-just-3-of-american-adults-own-a-collective-133m-firearms [accessed 13 July 2020].

13. Office for National Statistics, 'Homicide in England and Wales: Year Ending March 2017', 2017, https://www.ons.gov.uk/peoplepopulationandcommunity/crimeandjustice/articles/homicideinenglandandwales/yearendingmarch2017 [accessed 13 July 2020]; Liam Kelly, 'Domestic abuse: "You're most at Risk of Being Killed When You Try to Leave"', *Guardian*, 10 December 2014, http://www.theguardian.com/society-professionals/2014/dec/10/domestic-abuse-risk-trying-leave-housing-community [accessed 13 July 2020].

14. Jana Kasperkevic, 'Private Violence: Up to 75% of Abused Women Who Are Murdered Are Killed After They Leave Their Partners', *Guardian*, 20 October 2014, https://www.theguardian.com/money/us-money-blog/2014/oct/20/domestic-private-violence-women-men-abuse-hbo-ray-rice [accessed 14 July 2020].

15. Sonke CHANGE Trial, 'Men's Use of Violence Against Women: Urgent Change Is Needed in Diepsloot', 2016, https://bhekisisa.org/wp-content/uploads/documents/sonkechangeresearchbrief30nov-16compressed1.pdf.

16. Anita Harris et al., 'Young Australians' Attitudes to Violence against

Women', VicHealth, 2015, https://www.vichealth.vic.gov.au/-/media/ResourceCentre/PublicationsandResources/PVAW/SurveyReport_YoungPeople-attitudes-violence-against-women.pdf

17. Future Men 2018 Survey, *Future Men*, 2018, https://futuremen.org/future-men-2018-survey [accessed 14 July 2020].

18. Joanna Neary, @MsJoNeary, Twitter, 13 October 2021, https://twitter.com/MsJoNeary/status/1448217101425168386 [accessed 22 October 2021].

19. Daphna Motro and Aleksander P. J. Ellis, 'Boys, Don't Cry: Gender and Reactions to Negative Performance Feedback', *Journal of Applied Psychology* 102, 2 (2017): 227–35.

20. Siobhan Fenton, 'Modern Men Cry Twice as Much as Their Fathers, Report Suggests', *Independent*, 17 March 2016, http://www.independent.co.uk/life-style/health-and-families/health-news/modern-men-cry-twice-as-much-as-their-fathers-research-suggests-a6936321.html [accessed 15 July 2020].

21. Yasemin Besen-Cassino and Dan Cassino, 'Division of House Chores and the Curious Case of Cooking: The Effects of Earning Inequality on House Chores Among Dual-earner Couples', *AG About Gender* 3, 6 (2014); George Lowery, 'Men Who Earn Less Than Their Women Are More Likely to Cheat', *Cornell Chronicle*, 26 August 2010, https://news.cornell.edu/stories/2010/08/men-more-likely-cheat-higher-earning-women [accessed 13 July 2020]; Michael Bittman et al., 'When Does Gender Trump Money? Bargaining and Time in Household Work', *American Journal of Sociology* 109, 1 (2003): 186–214.

22. D. N. Kyriacou et al., 'Risk Factors for Injury to Women from Domestic Violence', *New England Journal of Medicine* 341, 25 (1999): 1892–8.

23. Robb Willer et al., 'Overdoing Gender: A Test of the Masculine Overcompensation Thesis', *American Journal of Sociology* 118, 4 (2013): 980–1022.

24. 'Bank Crimes Drove Iowa Man to Slay Family', CBS News, 27 March 2008, https://www.cbsnews.com/news/bank-crimes-drove-iowa-man-to-slay-family/ [accessed 9 July 2020].

25. Jon Ronson, 'I've Thought About Doing Myself in Loads of Times . . .', *Guardian*, 22 November 2008, https://www.theguardian.com/uk/2008/nov/22/christopher-foster-news-crime [accessed 9 July 2020].

26. Catharine Skipp, 'Inside the Mind of Family Annihilators', *Newsweek*, 10 February 2010, https://www.newsweek.com/inside-mind-family-annihilators-75225 [accessed 9 July 2020].

27. Katie Collins, 'Study: Family Killers Are Usually Men and Fit One of Four Distinct Profiles', *Wired UK*, 16 August 2013, https://www.wired.co.uk/article/family-killers [accessed 9 July 2020].

28. Neil Websdale, *Familicidal Hearts: The Emotional Styles of 211 Killers* (Oxford University Press, 2010).

29. Kate Manne, *Down Girl: The Logic of Misogyny* (Oxford University Press, 2017).

30. Janet K. Swim, Ashley J. Gillis and Kaitlynn J. Hamaty, 'Gender Bending and Gender Conformity: The Social Consequences of Engaging in Feminine and Masculine Pro-Environmental Behaviors', *Sex Roles* 82, 5 (2020): 363–85.

31. Kristin Musulin, 'Study: Men Litter More, Recycle Less to "Safeguard Their Gender Identity"', Waste Dive, 31 August 2016, https://www.wastedive.com/news/study-men-litter-more-recycle-less-to-safeguard-their-gender-identity/425506 [accessed 14 July 2020].

32. Attila Pohlmann, 'Threatened at the Table: Meat Consumption, Maleness and Men's Gender Identities', unpublished PhD thesis (University of Hawai'i at Manoa, 2014).

33. Paul Rozin et al., 'Is Meat Male? A Quantitative Multimethod Framework to Establish Metaphoric Relationships', *Journal of Consumer Research* 39, 3 (2012): 629–43.

34. bell hooks, *The Will to Change: Men, Masculinity, and Love* (Beyond Words/Atria Books, 2004).

35. United Nations Office on Drugs and Crime, *Global Study on Homicide 2013: Trends, Contexts, Data* (UNODC, 2013).

36. World Health Organization, *Fact-Sheet on Self-Directed Violence* (WHO, 2002), https://www.who.int/violence_injury_prevention/violence/world_report/factsheets/en/selfdirectedviolfacts.pdf.

37. See: Cordelia Fine, *Delusions of Gender: The Real Science behind Sex Differences* (Icon, 2005); Gina Rippon, *The Gendered Brain: The New Neuroscience That Shatters the Myth of the Female Brain* (Bodley Head, 2019).

38. Andrea Waling, 'Problematising "Toxic" and "Healthy" Masculinity for Addressing Gender Inequalities', *Australian Feminist Studies* 34, 101 (2019): 362–75.

39. Kieran Snyder, 'Women Should Watch Out for This One Word in Their Reviews', *Fortune*, 26 August 2014, https://fortune.com/2014/08/26/performance-review-gender-bias/ [accessed 15 July 2020].

40. Kate Zasowski @katezasowski, Twitter, 15 March 2019, https://twitter.com/katezasowski/status/1106625316326260736 [accessed 21 July 2020].

41. You might wonder how we can know it's so disproportionately gendered if some people aren't reporting. The firmest evidence for the gender discrepancy comes from rates of hospitalisation and murder. While not all violence leaves marks, we can infer quite a lot about the unreported cases from those that are reported because the victim is dead or critically hurt.

42. Frederick Douglass, 'If There Is No Struggle, There Is No Progress', 1857, https://www.blackpast.org/african-american-history/1857-frederick-douglass-if-there-no-struggle-there-no-progress [accessed 12 August 2020].

43. Lonnae O'Neal, 'The 53 Percent Issue', The Undefeated, 20 December 2016, https://theundefeated.com/features/black-women-say-white-feminists-have-a-trump-problem [accessed 21 July 2020].

44. Lorna Finlayson, *An Introduction to Feminism* (Cambridge University Press, 2016), p. 8.

45. Sandeep Prasada et al., 'Conceptual Distinctions Amongst Generics', *Cognition* 126, 3 (2013): 405–22.

46. Joe Wells, @joewellscomic, Twitter, 11 March 2021, https://twitter.com/joewellscomic/status/1370059804975194116 [accessed 10 September 2021].

47. Susan A. Graham, Samantha L. Nayer and Susan A. Gelman, 'Two-year-olds Use the Generic/Nongeneric Distinction to Guide Their Inferences About Novel Kinds', *Child Development* 82, 2 (2011): 493–507.

48. Sarah-Jane Leslie and Adam Lerner, 'Generic Generalizations', *Stanford Encyclopedia of Philosophy*, 2016.

49. Katherine Ritchie, 'Should We Use Racial and Gender Generics?', *Thought: A Journal of Philosophy* 8, 1 (2019): 33–41, at p. 37.

50. Elizabeth Dwoskin, Nitasha Tiku and Heather Kelly, 'Facebook to Start Policing Anti-Black Hate Speech More Aggressively Than Anti-White Comments, Documents Show', *Washington Post*, 3 December 2020, https://www.washingtonpost.com/technology/2020/12/03/facebook-hate-speech [accessed 12 September 2021].

51. Andrea Dworkin, 'I Want a Twenty-Four-Hour Truce During Which

There Is No Rape', in Johanna Fateman and Amy Scholder (ed.), *Last Days at Hot Slit: The Radical Feminism of Andrea Dworkin* (Semiotext(e), 1983), pp. 199–210, https://mitpress.mit.edu/blog/i-want-twenty-four -hour-truce-during-which-there-no-rape-excerpt-last-days-hot-slit-radical [accessed 14 July 2020].

52. For example, Daniella Emanuel, 'People Are Sharing the Things That Men Would Rather Do Than Go to Therapy and It's Scarily Accurate', BuzzFeed, 5 January 2021, https://www.buzzfeed.com/daniellaemanuel/men-rather-do-than-therapy [accessed 8 February 2022].

53. Mirel Zaman, 'Why Will Men Do Literally Anything to Avoid Going to Therapy?', Refinery29, 24 May 2021, https://www.refinery29.com/en-us/2021/05/10442178/why-do-men-avoid-therapy-memes [accessed 8 February 2022].

54. hooks, *Will to Change*.

## Chapter 5: Do All Lives Matter?

1. Portland State Library Special Collections, 'Black Studies Center Public Dialogue, Pt. 2', 30 May 1975, https://soundcloud.com/portland-state -library/portland-state-black-studies-1 [accessed 11 August 2021].

2. Chelsea Ritschel, 'Wedding Photographer Donates Bride's Deposit to Black Lives Matter After She Demands Refund', *Independent*, 18 June 2020, https://www.independent.co.uk/life-style/wedding-photographer-black-lives-matter-refund-shakira-rochelle-photography-bride-a9571701.html [accessed 13 September 2021].

3. Kevin Liptak and Kristen Holmes, 'Trump Calls Black Lives Matter a "Symbol of Hate" as He Digs in on Race', CNN, 1 July 2020, https://www.cnn.com/2020/07/01/politics/donald-trump-black-lives-matter -confederate-race/index.html [accessed 1 July 2021].

4. Lizzy Buchan, 'Conservative MP Says Black Lives Matter Movement Is "Divisive"', *Independent*, 24 June 2020, https://www.independent.co.uk /news/uk/politics/black-lives-matter-tory-mp-ben-bradley-george-floyd-premier-league-a9582901.html [accessed 11 August 2021].

5. Kim Parker, Juliana Menasce Horowitz and Monica Anderson, 'Majorities Across Racial, Ethnic Groups Express Support for the Black Lives Matter Movement', Pew Research Center Social & Demographic Trends Project, 12 June 2020, https://www.pewresearch.org/social

-trends/2020/06/12/amid-protests-majorities-across-racial-and-ethnic
-groups-express-support-for-the-black-lives-matter-movement
[accessed 28 June 2021].

6. 'Disinformation: #AllWhitesAreNazis and #AWAN', Anti-Defamation League, 21 June 2020, https://www.adl.org/disinformation-allwhite-sarenazis-and-awan [accessed 11 August 2021].

7. Daniel Funke, @dpfunke, 'Conservative Pundits Share False Claim About Black Lives Matter, ActBlue', PolitiFact, 12 June 2020, https://www.politifact.com/factchecks/2020/jun/12/ryan-fournier/conserva-tive-pundits-share-false-claim-about-black [accessed 11 August 2021].

8. Naomi Oreskes and Erik M. Conway, 'Defeating the Merchants of Doubt', *Nature* 465, 7299 (2010): 686–7.

9. Deja Thomas and Juliana Menasce Horowitz, 'Support for Black Lives Matter Movement Down Since June', Pew Research Center, 16 September 2020, https://www.pewresearch.org/wp-content/uploads/2020/09/ft_2020.09.16_BLM_01.png [accessed 28 June 2021].

10. bell hooks, *Teaching Community: A Pedagogy of Hope* (Routledge, 2003), pp. 25–6.

11. Chanda Prescod-Weinstein, *The Disordered Cosmos* (Bold Type Books, 2021), p. 111.

12. Michelle Alexander, *The New Jim Crow: Mass Incarceration in the Age of Colorblindness* (New Press, 2010).

13. MBRRACE-UK, 'Perinatal Mortality Surveillance Report: UK Perinatal Deaths for Births from January to December 2020', https://www.npeu.ox.ac.uk/mbrrace-uk/reports [accessed 6 November 2022].

14. Office for National Statistics, 'Births and Infant Mortality by Ethnicity in England and Wales: 2007 to 2019', https://www.ons.gov.uk/people-populationandcommunity/healthandsocialcare/childhealth/articles/birthsandinfantmortalitybyethnicityinenglandandwales/2007to2019#trends-in-ethnicity [accessed 6 November 2022].

15. Stephen Colegrave, '12 Facts That Prove Black Lives Don't Matter in Britain', Byline Times, 6 August 2020, https://bylinetimes.com/2020/06/08/black-lives-dont-matter-in-britain/ [accessed 28 June 2021].

16. Patrick Butler, 'Nearly Half of BAME UK Households are Living in Poverty', *Guardian*, 1 July 2020, http://www.theguardian.com/society/2020/jul/01/nearly-half-of-bame-uk-households-are-living-in-poverty [accessed 28 June 2021].

17. 'Black Caribbean Ethnic Group: Facts and Figures', GOV.UK, 27 June

2019,https://www.ethnicity-facts-figures.service.gov.uk/summaries/black-caribbean-ethnic-group#stop-and-search [accessed 28 June 2021].

18. Ibid.

19. 'Black People Dying in Police Custody Should Surprise No One', *Guardian*, 11 June 2020, http://www.theguardian.com/uk-news/2020/jun/11/black-deaths-in-police-custody-the-tip-of-an-iceberg-of-racist -treatment [accessed 28 June 2021].

20. 'Criminal Justice Fact Sheet', NAACP, 2021, https://naacp.org/resources/criminal-justice-fact-sheet [accessed 23 July 2021].

21. J. Correll et al., 'The Influence of Stereotypes on Decisions to Shoot', *European Journal of Social Psychology* 37, 6 (2007): 1102-17, https://onlinelibrary.wiley.com/doi/abs/10.1002/ejsp.450 [accessed 24 June 2021].

22. Justin Nix et al., 'A Bird's Eye View of Civilians Killed by Police in 2015', *Criminology & Public Policy* 16, 1 (2017): 309–40.

23. Lynne Peeples, 'What the Data Say About Police Brutality and Racial Bias – and Which Reforms Might Work', *Nature* 583, 7814 (2020): 22–4.

24. This number would be greater still if the more justifiable 'ethical poverty line' was instead used in these calculations. The ethical poverty line stands at \$7.40 per person per day, which is what is needed to ensure basic nutrition, average human life expectancy and low infant mortality. 4.2 billion people now live below this line, the highest number ever. See: Peter Edward, 'The Ethical Poverty Line: A Moral Quantification of Absolute Poverty', *Third World Quarterly* 27, 2 (2006): 377–93.

25. Max Roser and Esteban Ortiz-Ospina, 'Global Extreme Poverty', *Our World in Data*, 2013, https://ourworldindata.org/extreme-poverty [accessed 8 July 2021].

26. International Organization for Migration, 'Missing Migrants Project', https://missingmigrants.iom.int/ [accessed 9 July 2021].

27. 'Asylum and Resettlement Datasets', GOV.UK, 22 August 2019, https://www.gov.uk/government/statistical-data-sets/asylum-and-resettle-ment-datasets [accessed 9 July 2021].

28. Judith Butler and George Yancy, 'What's Wrong with "All Lives Matter"?', *New York Times*, 12 January 2015, http://mobile.nytimes.com/blogs/opinionator/2015/01/12/whats-wrong-with-all-lives-matter/?_r=3&referrer [accessed 9 July 2021].

29. 'Read Martin Luther King Jr's "I Have a Dream" Speech, in Its Entirety',

NPR, https://www.npr.org/2010/01/18/122701268/i-have-a-dream-speech-in-its-entirety [accessed 28 June 2021].

30. Joan Biskupic, 'Where John Roberts Is Unlikely to Compromise', CNN, 26 March 2019, https://www.cnn.com/2019/03/26/politics/john-roberts-race-the-chief/index.html [accessed 10 July 2021].

31. Gary Younge, 'What Black America Means to Europe', *Guardian*, 11 June 2020, https://www.theguardian.com/world/2020/jun/11/what-black-america-means-to-europe-protests-racism-george-floyd [accessed 13 February 2022].

32. Dan Balz and Scott Clement, 'On Racial Issues, Americans Are Divided Both Black and White and Red and Blue', *Washington Post*, 27 December 2014, https://www.washingtonpost.com/politics/on-racial-issues-america-is-divided-both-black-and-white-and-red-and-blue/2014/12/26/3d2964c8-8d12-11e4-a085-34e9b9f09a58_story.html [accessed 10 July 2021].

33. 'On Views of Race and Inequality, Blacks and Whites Are Worlds Apart', Pew Research Center Social & Demographic Trends Project, 2016, https://www.pewresearch.org/social-trends/2016/06/27/on-views-of-race-and-inequality-blacks-and-whites-are-worlds-apart/ [accessed 10 July 2021].

34. Anushka Asthana, 'Racism in the UK Still Rife, Say Majority of Britons', *Guardian*, 16 July 2020, https://www.theguardian.com/world/2020/jul/16/racism-in-the-uk-still-rife-say-majority-of-britons [accessed 13 February 2022].

35. Richard Allen Greene, 'Britain's Big Race Divide', CNN, 22 June 2020, https://www.cnn.com/interactive/2020/06/europe/britain-racism-cnn-poll-gbr-intl [accessed 13 February 2022].

36. Lois Beckett, 'Nearly All Black Lives Matter Protests Are Peaceful Despite Trump Narrative, Report Finds', *Guardian*, 5 September 2020, http://www.theguardian.com/world/2020/sep/05/nearly-all-black-lives-matter-protests-are-peaceful-despite-trump-narrative-report-finds [accessed 12 August 2021].

37. Frantz Fanon, *The Wretched of the Earth* (Grove Press, 1963).

38. Andreas Malm, *How to Blow Up a Pipeline: Learning to Fight in a World on Fire* (Verso, 2021).

39. Martin Luther King, Jr, 'Letter from a Birmingham Jail [King, Jr]', 1963, https://www.africa.upenn.edu/Articles_Gen/Letter_Birmingham.html [accessed 13 November 2018].

40. Arianne Shahvisi, 'The Backlash', LRB Blog, *London Review of Books*,

27 June 2020, https://www.lrb.co.uk/blog/2020/june/the-backlash [accessed 22 June 2021].

41. Valentina Romei, 'Ethnic Minority Pay Gap in UK Still Stubbornly Wide', *Financial Times*, 9 July 2019, https://www.ft.com/content/fd47bc10-a238-11e9-974c-ad1c6ab5efd1 [accessed 22 June 2021].

42. Pamela Duncan and Matty Edwards, 'Huge Effect of Ethnicity on Life Chances Revealed in Official UK Figures', *Guardian*, 10 October 2017, http://www.theguardian.com/world/2017/oct/10/huge-effect-of-ethnicity-on-life-chances-revealed-in-official-uk-figures [accessed 22 June 2021].

43. 'Arrests', GOV.UK, 17 September 2020, https://www.ethnicity-facts-figures.service.gov.uk/crime-justice-and-the-law/policing/number-of-arrests/latest [accessed 13 September 2021].

44. Rianna Croxford, 'Why Your Name Matters in the Search for a Job', BBC News, 18 January 2019, https://www.bbc.com/news/uk-46927417 [accessed 22 June 2021].

45. 'All the Ways White People Are Privileged in the UK', *Al Jazeera*, 11 October 2017, https://www.aljazeera.com/news/2017/10/11/all-the-ways-white-people-are-privileged-in-the-uk [accessed 22 June 2021].

46. Michael I. Norton and Samuel R. Sommers, 'Whites See Racism as a Zero-sum Game That They Are Now Losing', *Perspectives on Psychological Science* 6, 3 (2011): 215–18.

47. 'Opening Statement: Sen. Jeff Sessions', NPR, 13 July 2009, https://www.npr.org/templates/story/story.php?storyId=106540813 [accessed 10 July 2021].

48. David R. Francis, 'Employers' Replies to Racial Names', National Bureau of Economic Research, *The Digest* 9 (September 2003), https://www.nber.org/digest/sep03/employers-replies-racial-names [accessed 13 September 2021].

49. Holly Rubenstein, 'Can Anonymous CVs Help Beat Recruitment Discrimination?', *Guardian*, 11 April 2013, http://www.theguardian.com/money/work-blog/2013/apr/11/can-anonymous-cvs-help-beat-job-discrimination [accessed 10 July 2021].

50. Ibram X. Kendi, *How to Be an Antiracist* (One World, 2019).

51. Keon West, Katy Greenland and Colette van Laar, 'Implicit Racism, Colour Blindness, and Narrow Definitions of Discrimination: Why Some White People Prefer "All Lives Matter" to "Black Lives Matter"', *British Journal of Social Psychology* 60, 4 (2021): 1136–53, https://

bpspsychub.onlinelibrary.wiley.com/doi/abs/10.1111/bjso.12458 [accessed 24 June 2021].

52. Butler and Yancy, 'What's Wrong?'

53. I thank Eugenia Cheng for pointing this out in her excellent book on logic: Eugenia Cheng, *The Art of Logic: How to Make Sense in a World That Doesn't* (Profile, 2018), p. 250.

54. Jessica Keiser, 'The "All Lives Matter" Response: QUD-shifting as Epistemic Injustice', *Synthese* 199, 3–4 (2021): 8465–83, https://doi.org /10.1007/s11229-021-03171-y [accessed 24 June 2021].

55. See, e.g., Craige Roberts, 'Information Structure: Towards an Integrated Formal Theory of Pragmatics', *Semantics and Pragmatics* 5 (2012): 6–1.

56. Ashley Atkins, 'Black Lives Matter or All Lives Matter? Color-blindness and Epistemic Injustice', *Social Epistemology* 33, 1 (2019): 1–22, at p. 5.

57. James Baldwin, *Conversations with James Baldwin* (University Press of Mississippi, 1989), p. 8.

58. Stokely Carmichael, 'What We Want', *New York Review of Books* 7 (22 September 1966), https://www.nybooks.com/articles/1966/09/22 /what-we-want [accessed 23 July 2021].

59. '(1966) Stokely Carmichael, "Black Power"', 13 July 2010, https://www. blackpast.org/african-american-history/speeches-african-american-history/1966-stokely-carmichael-black-power [accessed 15 November 2022].

60. Cedric J. Robinson, *Black Marxism, Revised and Updated Third Edition: The Making of the Black Radical Tradition* (University of North Carolina Press, 2020), drawing on the earlier work of W. E. B. Du Bois, C. L. R. James and Eric Williams, among others.

61. 'A Statement from Brighton and Sussex Medical School (BSMS)', 5 June 2020, https://www.bsms.ac.uk/about/news/2020/06-05-a-statement-on -racism-from-brighton-and-sussex-medical-school.aspx [accessed 8 July 2021].

62. See, e.g., 'Home | Decolonize Palestine', 2021, https://decolonize-palestine.com [accessed 1 December 2022].

63. Gabrielle Gurley, 'For the Mayor of Washington, Black Lives Matter; Defunding the Police Does Not', The American Prospect, 18 June 2020, https://prospect.org/api/content/a6320c54-b106-11ea-97b3-1244d5f7c7c6 [accessed 15 November 2022].

## Chapter 6: Who Should We Believe?

1. Theophilus Painter was also president of the University of Texas, and in that role he refused to admit Black student Herman Marion Sweatt to the law programme. The ensuing case, *Sweatt v. Painter*, led to the university being required by law to admit qualified Black applicants. This was a serious challenge to the 'separate but equal' legal doctrine, and paved the way for desegregation in universities.

   Note also that Painter was counting chromosomes in testicular cells taken from three men who were inmates of the Texas State Asylum: two Black men and one white man. Their testicles had been removed in response to what was considered to be excessive masturbation. Painter claimed in his paper that they didn't feel any pain while being castrated. The idea that Black people feel less pain is a well-worn and convenient myth. Much of our modern medical knowledge is built on experiments that exploited people of colour, incarcerated people, the mentally ill and disabled people. Paul A. Lombardo, 'Tracking Chromosomes, Castrating Dwarves: Uninformed Consent and Eugenic Research', 2009, https:// papers.ssrn.com/abstract=1495134 [accessed 27 November 2022].

2. Rita R. Colwell, 'Alice C. Evans: Breaking Barriers', *Yale Journal of Biology and Medicine* 72, 5 (1999): 349.

3. Virginia Law Burns, *Gentle Hunter: A Biography of Alice Catherine Evans, Bacteriologist* (Enterprise Press, 1993).

4. Colwell, 'Alice C. Evans'.

5. Ibid.

6. Amy B. Wang, 'Gwyneth Paltrow's Goop Touted the "Benefits" of Putting a Jade Egg in Your Vagina. Now It Must Pay', *Washington Post*, 5 September 2018, https://www.washingtonpost.com/health/2018/09/ 05/gwyneth-paltrows-goop-touted-benefits-putting-jade-egg-your-vagina-now-it-must-pay [accessed 9 September 2021].

7. Herton Escobar, 'Brazil's New President Has Scientists Worried: Here's Why', *Science*, 20 January 2019, https://www.science.org/content/arti-cle/brazil-s-new-president-has-scientists-worried-here-s-why [accessed 27 November 2022].

8. John Cook et al., 'Consensus on Consensus: A Synthesis of Consensus Estimates on Human-caused Global Warming', *Environmental Research Letters* 11, 4 (2016): 048002.

9. Hilaire Belloc, 'Matilda: Who Told Lies, and Was Burned to Death', *Cautionary Tales for Children* (Eveleigh Nash, 1907).

10. Paul Lewis and Rob Evans, *Undercover: The True Story of Britain's Secret Police* (Faber & Faber, 2013), pp. 150–67.

11. 'The Stephen Lawrence Inquiry', GOV.UK, 24 February 1999, https://www.gov.uk/government/publications/the-stephen-lawrence-inquiry [accessed 18 March 2021].

12. Miranda Fricker, 'Epistemic Justice as a Condition of Political Freedom?', *Synthese* 190, 7 (2013): 1317–32; Miranda Fricker, *Epistemic Injustice: Power and the Ethics of Knowing* (Oxford University Press, 2007).

13. Tom Traill, 'What Can We Learn from Diane Abbott's Journey to Success?', Runnymede, 7 January 2017, https://www.runnymedetrust.org/blog/what-can-we-learn-from-diane-abbotts-journey-to-success [accessed 5 August 2021].

14. Abbott cut back that 'If Mr Smith believes that having black people in parliament for the first time is in some sense a backward step, thousands of people that voted for me in Hackney North would disagree.' Robin Bunce and Samara Linton, 'How Diane Abbott Fought Racism – And Her Own Party – to Become Britain's First Black Female MP', *Guardian*, 29 September 2020, http://www.theguardian.com/politics/2020/sep/29/how-diane-abbott-fought-racism-and-her-own-party-to-become-britains-first-black-female-mp [accessed 5 August 2021].

15. Bailey, 'They Aren't Talking'.

16. Bunce and Linton, 'Diane Abott'.

17. Diane Abbott, 'I Fought Racism and Misogyny to Become an MP: The Fight Is Getting Harder', *Guardian*, 14 February 2017, http://www.theguardian.com/commentisfree/2017/feb/14/racism-misogyny-politics-online-abuse-minorities [accessed 5 August 2021].

18. 'Suspended Tory Admits Inappropriate Diane Abbott Tweet', BBC News, 10 February 2017, https://www.bbc.com/news/uk-england-lancashire-38930689 [accessed 5 August 2021].

19. Matt Dathan, 'Labour MP Jess Phillips Told Diane Abbott to "F*** Off" in Jeremy Corbyn Sexism Row', *Independent*, 17 September 2015, https://www.independent.co.uk/news/uk/politics/labour-mp-jess-phillips-told-diane-abbott-f-jeremy-corbyn-sexism-row-10505493.html [accessed 5 August 2021].

20. Michael Segalov, 'Diane Abbott: "The Abuse and the Attacks Have Never Made Me Falter"', *Guardian*, 27 January 2018, http://www.

theguardian.com/lifeandstyle/2018/jan/27/diane-abbott-the-abuse-never-made-me-falter [accessed 5 August 2021].

21. 'Black and Asian Women MPs Abused More Online', Amnesty International UK, https://www.amnesty.org.uk/online-violence-women-mps [accessed 5 August 2021].

22. Carl Linnaeus, *Systema Naturae*, 12th edn (Laurentius Salvius, 1768), p. 28.

23. In 2014, science writer Nicholas Wade emerged from his retirement to publish *A Troublesome Inheritance: Genes, Race and Human History*, in which he claimed that race is a biological category (it is not) and that the brains of people of different races evolved separately (they did not), resulting in race-based differences in intelligence. A group of around 140 biologists whose work Wade has cited condemned the book for its 'misappropriation of research from our field to support arguments about differences among human societies'. They wrote to the *New York Times Book Review* (8 August 2014): 'Wade juxtaposes an incomplete and inaccurate account of our research on human genetic differences with speculation that recent natural selection has led to worldwide differences in I.Q. test results, political institutions and economic development. We reject Wade's implication that our findings substantiate his guesswork. They do not.' 'Letters: "A Troublesome Inheritance"', Stanford Center for Computational, Evolutionary, and Human Genomics, https://cehg.stanford.edu/letter-from-population-geneticists [accessed 21 July 2021].

24. For an example of this trend, see Sean Coughlan, 'Poorer White Pupils Let Down and Neglected – MPs', BBC News, 22 June 2021, https://www.bbc.com/news/education-57558746 [accessed 9 February 2022].

25. Aristotle, 'History of Animals' IX, https://penelope.uchicago.edu/aristotle/histanimals9.html [accessed 17 March 2021].

26. Rippon, *Gendered Brain*.

27. Quoted ibid., p. 8.

28. Ibid., p. 6.

29. Rebecca Maksel, 'Flying White Female', *Air & Space Magazine*, 24 June 2010, https://www.airspacemag.com/daily-planet/flying-while-female-140369153 [accessed 20 July 2021].

30. Brigitte Leeners et al., 'Lack of Associations Between Female Hormone Levels and Visuospatial Working Memory, Divided Attention and Cognitive Bias Across Two Consecutive Menstrual Cycles', *Frontiers in Behavioral Neuroscience* 11 (2017): 120.

31. Brooke Magnanti, 'Could Women's "Squeaky Voices" Be the Reason

Many Brits Don't Trust Female Pilots?', *Daily Telegraph*, 5 November 2013, https://www.telegraph.co.uk/women/womens-life/10427208/Could-womens-squeaky-voices-be-the-reason-many-Brits-dont-trust-female-pilots.html [accessed 14 July 2021].

32. Olivia Pavco-Giaccia et al., 'Rationality Is Gendered, *Collabra: Psychology* 5 (1), 54 (2019), https://doi.org/10.1525/collabra.274 [accessed 17 March 2021].

33. Silvia Knobloch-Westerwick, Carroll J. Glynn and Michael Huge, 'The Matilda Effect in Science Communication: An Experiment on Gender Bias in Publication Quality Perceptions and Collaboration Interest', *Science Communication* 35, 5 (2013): 603–25.

34. Bridget A. Larson and Stanley L. Brodsky, 'When Cross-examination Offends: How Men and Women Assess Intrusive Questioning of Male and Female Expert Witnesses', *Journal of Applied Social Psychology* 40, 4 (2010): 811–30.

35. Jiang Yang et al., 'Microblog Credibility Perceptions: Comparing the USA and China', *Proceedings of the 2013 Conference on Computer Supported Cooperative Work* (Association for Computing Machinery, 2013): 575–86, https://doi.org/10.1145/2441776.2441841 [accessed 8 April 2021].

36. 'This Woman Changed Her Name to a Man's on Her CV. What Happened Next Won't Surprise You', indy100, 3 August 2017, https://www.indy100.com/discover/cv-name-male-female-man-woman-gender-wage-gap-job-applications-sexism-7874456 [accessed 12 August 2021]; Amy Sippitt, 'Job Applicants with Ethnic Minority Sounding Names Are Less Likely to Be Called for Interview', Full Fact, 26 October2015,https://fullfact.org/economy/job-applicants-ethnic-minority-sounding-names-are-less-likely-be-called-interview/ [accessed 9 February 2022].

37. Lillian MacNell, Adam Driscoll and Andrea N. Hunt, 'What's in a Name: Exposing Gender Bias in Student Ratings of Teaching', *Innovative Higher Education* 40, 4 (2015): 291–303.

38. Amee P. Shah, 'Why Are Certain Accents Judged the Way They Are? Decoding Qualitative Patterns of Accent Bias', *Advances in Language and Literary Studies* 10, 3 (2019): 128–39.

39. Yuko Hiraga, 'British Attitudes Towards Six Varieties of English in the USA and Britain', *World Englishes* 24, 3 (2005): 289–308.

40. Tamara Rakić, Melanie C. Steffens and Amélie Mummendey, 'When It Matters How You Pronounce It: The Influence of Regional Accents

on Job Interview Outcome', *British Journal of Psychology* 102, 4 (2011): 868–83.

41. Shiri Lev-Ari and Boaz Keysar, 'Why Don't We Believe Non-Native Speakers? The Influence of Accent on Credibility', *Journal of Experimental Social Psychology* 46, 6 (2010): 1093–6.

42. Rudolf Kalin and Donald S. Rayko, 'Discrimination in Evaluative Judgments Against Foreign-Accented Job Candidates', *Psychological Reports* 43, 3_suppl. (1978): 1203–9.

43. Cameron Anderson et al., 'A Status-Enhancement Account of Overconfidence', *Journal of Personality and Social Psychology*, 103, 4 (2012): 718-35, https://papers.ssrn.com/abstract=2532677 [accessed 14 July 2021].

44. This is worrying because those who overestimate their skills tend to be less competent, an observation that is known as the Dunning–Kruger effect. This effect is intuitive: less competent people are also likely to be less competent at judging their own competence.

45. Katty Kay and Claire Shipman, 'The Confidence Gap', *The Atlantic*, May 2014, https://www.theatlantic.com/magazine/archive/2014/05/the-confidence-gap/359815 [accessed 22 December 2020].

46. Armand Chatard, Serge Guimond and Leila Selimbegovic, '"How Good Are You in Math?" The Effect of Gender Stereotypes on Students' Recollection of Their School Marks', *Journal of Experimental Social Psychology* 43, 6 (2007): 1017–24; Andrew G. Karatjas and Jeffrey A. Webb, 'The Role of Gender in Grade Perception in Chemistry Courses', *Journal of College Science Teaching* 45, 2 (2015): 30–5.

47. Melissa J. Williams and Larissa Z. Tiedens, 'The Subtle Suspension of Backlash: A Meta-analysis of Penalties for Women's Implicit and Explicit Dominance Behavior', *Psychological Bulletin* 142, 2 (2016): 165–97.

48. Victoria L. Brescoll, 'Who Takes the Floor and Why: Gender, Power, and Volubility in Organizations', *Administrative Science Quarterly* 56, 4 (2011): 622–41.

49. Madeline E. Heilman et al., 'Penalties for Success: Reactions to Women Who Succeed at Male Gender-typed Tasks', *Journal of Applied Psychology* 89, 3 (2004): 416.

50. Kate Manne, *Entitled: How Male Privilege Hurts Women* (Allen Lane, 2020), p. 162.

51. Jennifer Rankin, 'Fewer Women Leading FTSE Firms than Men Called John', *Guardian*, 6 March 2015, https://www.theguardian.com/business

/2015/mar/06/johns-davids-and-ians-outnumber-female-chief-execu-
tives-in-ftse-100 [accessed 12 August 2021].

52. Soraya Chemaly, 'How Police Still Fail Rape Victims', *Rolling Stone*, 16
August 2016, https://www.rollingstone.com/culture/culture-features/
how-police-still-fail-rape-victims-97782/ [accessed 17 March 2021].

53. Owen Bowcott, 'Rape Investigations "Undermined by Belief That
False Accusations are Rife"', *Guardian*, 13 March 2013, http://www.
theguardian.com/society/2013/mar/13/rape-investigations-belief-false
-accusations [accessed 14 July 2021].

54. Alexandra Topping, 'Four-fifths of Young Women in the UK Have
Been Sexually Harassed, Survey Finds', *Guardian*, 10 March 2021, http:
//www.theguardian.com/world/2021/mar/10/almost-all-young-
women-in-the-uk-have-been-sexually-harassed-survey-finds [accessed
20 July 2021].

55. Manne, *Down Girl*, p. 197.

56. Sandra Newman, 'What Kind of Person Makes False Rape Accusations?',
*Quartz*, 11 March 2017, https://qz.com/980766/the-truth-about-false-
rape-accusations/ [accessed 20 July 2021].

57. While I was writing this chapter, Cosby's conviction was overturned
and he was released from prison.

58. It pays to think about the ages of Cosby and Weinstein at the time of
their convictions: eighty and sixty-seven, respectively. In *Entitled*, Kate
Manne describes the way in which older perpetrators of sexual abuse
are more readily cast as 'dirty old men'. They're therefore more disposable and convictable because they're less useful to a system that values
economic productivity, which means that people are less likely to
protect them on the basis of their career contributions, and also that
their actions are assumed not to reflect on men more generally but
rather to apply to a subset of men whose sexual identities are supposed
to disgust us. This is despite the fact that many of these abusers began
their long careers of wrongdoing when they were still young men.

59. Sarah Banet-Weiser, 'The Labor of Being Believed', *Los Angeles Review
of Books*, 19 April 2020, https://lareviewofbooks.org/article/the-labor-
of-being-believed [accessed 5 August 2021].

60. Esther H. Chen et al., 'Gender Disparity in Analgesic Treatment of
Emergency Department Patients with Acute Abdominal Pain', *Academic
Emergency Medicine* 15, 5 (2008): 414–18.

61. Katarina Hamberg, Gunilla Risberg and Eva E. Johansson, 'Male and

Female Physicians Show Different Patterns of Gender Bias: A Paper-case Study of Management of Irritable Bowel Syndrome', *Scandinavian Journal of Public Health* 32, 2 (2004): 144–52.

62. Anke Samulowitz et al., ' "Brave Men" and "Emotional Women": A Theory-guided Literature Review on Gender Bias in Health Care and Gendered Norms Towards Patients with Chronic Pain', *Pain Research and Management* 3 (2018): 1–14.

63. Brian D. Earp et al., 'Featured Article: Gender Bias in Pediatric Pain Assessment', *Journal of Pediatric Psychology* 44, 4 (2019): 403–14; Lindsey L. Cohen, Jean Cobb and Sarah R. Martin, 'Gender Biases in Adult Ratings of Pediatric Pain', *Children's Health Care* 43, 2 (2014): 87–95.

64. Goyal et al., 'Racial Disparities'.

65. Kevin M. Summers, Gina A. Paganini and E. Paige Lloyd, 'Poor Toddlers Feel Less Pain? Application of Class-Based Pain Stereotypes in Judgments of Children', *Social Psychological and Personality Science*, 2022: DOI: 19485506221094090.

66. In reality, doctors tend not to take the law so literally, but it informs and reflects the broader discourse, in which doctors are presented as being highly credible, whereas pregnant people are presented as lacking credibility (regarding their own pregnancies), besides being required to deprive themselves further of credibility by conforming to the narrow criteria of being mentally ill and/or an unfit parent (with all the associated stigma that these entail). This is despite the fact that doctors are health experts, not moral or social experts, and only have a fleeting sense of their patients' situations.

67. Miranda Fricker and Katharine Jenkins, 'Epistemic Injustice, Ignorance, and Trans Experiences', *The Routledge Companion to Feminist Philosophy* (Routledge, 2017), pp. 268–78.

68. Anouchka Grose, 'Why Do Women Lie More Than Men? Because We're "Nicer"', *Guardian*, 5 June 2015, http://www.theguardian.com/comment-isfree/2015/jun/05/women-lie-untruths-human [accessed 17 March 2021].

69. Emily J. Thomas, Monika Stelzl and Michelle N. Lafrance, 'Faking to Finish: Women's Accounts of Feigning Sexual Pleasure to End Unwanted Sex', *Sexualities* 20, 3 (2017): 281–301.

70. Lili Loofbourow, 'The Female Price of Male Pleasure', *The Week*, 25 January 2018, https://theweek.com/articles/749978/female-price-male-pleasure [accessed 8 April 2021].

71. Debby Herbenick et al., 'Pain Experienced During Vaginal and Anal Intercourse with Other-sex Partners: Findings from a Nationally Representative Probability Study in the United States', *Journal of Sexual Medicine* 12, 4 (2015): 1040–51.

72. Daniella Graham, '"Too Tired" Tops List of Excuses Women Give for Not Having Sex with Partner', *Metro*, 4 April 2012, https://metro.co.uk /2012/04/04/too-tired-tops-list-of-excuses-women-give-for-not-having-sex-with-partner-376771 [accessed 17 March 2021].

73. Katherine Angel, *Tomorrow Sex Will Be Good Again: Women and Desire in the Age of Consent* (Verso, 2021).

74. Koritha Mitchell, 'Identifying White Mediocrity and Know-your-place Aggression: A Form of Self-care', *African American Review* 51, 4 (2018): 253–62.

75. Maria do Mar Pereira, 'Girls Feel They Must "Play Dumb" to Please Boys', News & Events, University of Warwick, 5 August 2014, https:// warwick.ac.uk/newsandevents/pressreleases/girls_feel_they/ [accessed 5 August 2021].

76. Rebecca Flood, 'Study Confirms Men Are Turned Off by a Clever Woman – Unless She Is Beautiful', *Independent*, 6 August 2016, https://www.inde-pendent.co.uk/life-style/study-confirms-men-are-turned-off-by-a-clever-woman-unless-she-is-beautiful-a7176051.html [accessed 5 August 2021].

77. Lily Kuo, 'In China, Highly Educated Women Are Mocked as a Sexless "Third Gender"', *Quartz*, 29 January 2014, https://qz.com/312464/in -china-highly-educated-women-are-mocked-as-a-sexless-third-gender [accessed 5 August 2021].

78. Yael Bame, '63% of Men Think Women Mainly Wear Makeup to Trick People into Thinking They're Attractive', YouGovAmerica, 1 May 2017, https://today.yougov.com/topics/lifestyle/articles-reports/2017/ 05/01/makeup [accessed 8 April 2021].

79. Suketu Mehta, 'The Asylum Seeker', *New Yorker*, 1 August 2011, http:/ /www.newyorker.com/magazine/2011/08/01/the-asylum-seeker [accessed 24 August 2021].

80. Kristie Dotson, 'Tracking Epistemic Violence, Tracking Practices of Silencing', *Hypatia* 26, 2 (2011): 236–57.

81. Crenshaw, 'Mapping the Margins'.

82. Anita E. Kelly and Lijuan Wang, 'A Life Without Lies: Can Living More Honestly Improve Health?', presentation, American Psychological Association Annual Convention, 4 August 2012: 2–5.

83. Leanne ten Brinke, Jooa Julia Lee and Dana R. Carney, 'The Physiology of (Dis) honesty: Does It Impact Health?', *Current Opinion in Psychology* 6 (2015): 177–82.

84. Neil Garrett et al., 'The Brain Adapts to Dishonesty', *Nature Neuroscience* 19, 12 (2016): 1727–32.

85. Daniel D. Langleben et al., 'Brain Activity During Simulated Deception: An Event-related Functional Magnetic Resonance Study', *Neuroimage* 15, 3 (2002): 727–32.

86. Danielle Polage, 'The Effect of Telling Lies on Belief in the Truth', *Europe's Journal of Psychology* 13, 4 (2017): 633–44.

87. Areeq Chowdhury, 'Sarah Champion, I Think You're Racist. There. I Said It', The Blog, *HuffPost UK*, 14 August 2017, https://www.huffingtonpost.co.uk/areeq-chowdhury/sarah-champion_b_17750700.html [accessed 10 September 2021].

88. Jamie Grierson, 'Most Child Sexual Abuse Gangs Made Up of White Men, Home Office Report Says', *Guardian*, 15 December 2020, http://www.theguardian.com/politics/2020/dec/15/child-sexual-abuse-gangs-white-men-home-office-report [accessed 10 September 2021].

89. Angela Y. Davis, *Women, Race & Class* (Vintage, 2011).

90. He was described as having a speech impediment which he managed through whistling. Adeel Hassan, 'Emmett Till's Enduring Legacy', *New York Times*, 6 December 2021, https://www.nytimes.com/article/who-was-emmett-till.html [accessed 31 October 2022].

91. Rory Carroll, 'Woman at Center [*sic*] of Emmett Till Case Tells Author She Fabricated Testimony', *Guardian*, 27 January 2017, http://www.theguardian.com/us-news/2017/jan/27/emmett-till-book-carolyn-bryant-confession [accessed 10 September 2021].

92. Susan Faludi, ' "Believe All Women" Is a Right-Wing Trap', *New York Times*, 18 May 2020, https://www.nytimes.com/2020/05/18/opinion/tara-reade-believe-all-women.html [accessed 11 September 2021].

93. The key to suppression is to have carefully coordinated, patchy, low intensity fires early in the dry season to minimise the amount of grass that is burnt.

94. Jon Altman and Rohan Fisher, 'The World's Best Fire Management System Is in Northern Australia, and It's Led by Indigenous Land Managers', The Conversation, 10 March 2020, http://theconversation.com/the-worlds-best-fire-management-system-is-in-northern

-australia-and-its-led-by-indigenous-land-managers-133071 [accessed 5 August 2021].

95. Niki JP Alsford, '500 Whales Stranded in Tasmania – Indigenous Elders Are Best Guides to Understanding This Tragedy', The Conversation, 2 October 2020, http://theconversation.com/500-whales-stranded-in-tasmania-indigenous-elders-are-best-guides-to-understanding-this-tragedy-146962 [accessed 5 August 2021].

96. Laura Jones, 'Research Shows Four in Five Experts Cited in Online News Are Men', The Conversation, 19 July 2018, http://theconversation.com/research-shows-four-in-five-experts-cited-in-online-news-are-men-100207 [accessed 8 April 2021].

97. Ann Mari May, Mary G. McGarvey and David Kucera, 'Gender and European Economic Policy: A Survey of the Views of European Economists on Contemporary Economic Policy', Kyklos 71, 1 (2018): 162–83.

## Chapter 7: Where Does a Mansplainer Get His Water?

1. Aldous Huxley, Those Barren Leaves (Chatto & Windus, 1925).

2. R. Solnit, 'Men Explain Things to Me; Facts Didn't Get in Their Way', TomDispatch, 2008.

3. Kay and Shipman, 'Confidence Gap'.

4. Sarah Young, 'Man Tells Women to "Stop Whining" About Tampon Prices – Is Suitably Ridiculed', Independent, 7 March 2019, https://www.independent.co.uk/life-style/women/man-tampons-mansplaining-twitter-women-cost-reaction-a8812456.html [accessed 22 December 2020].

5. Jenn Selby, 'Ben Bradley Defends "Crack Den" Tweets as Another Tory MP Hits Out at Free School Meal Offers', inews.co.uk, 24 October 2020, https://inews.co.uk/news/politics/ben-bradley-selaine-saxby-free-school-meals-marcus-rashford-736757 [accessed 10 February 2022].

6. Annunziata Rees-Mogg, @zatzi, Twitter, 27 July 2020, https://twitter.com/zatzi/status/1287701202763943943 [accessed 10 February 2022].

7. Jack Monroe, '"Annunziata Rees-Mogg Assumes Poor People Don't Cook More Because They're Lazy or Stupid – Here's Why She's Wrong"', Grazia, 9 August 2020, https://graziadaily.co.uk/life/real-life/jack-monroe-annunziata-rees-mogg-food-poverty [accessed 10 February 2022].

8. See Jon Stone, 'Dominic Raab Says He Would Only Take the Knee for Queen or His Wife', *Independent*, 18 June 2020, https://www.independent.co.uk/news/uk/politics/dominic-raab-take-knee-queen-wife-black-lives-matter-a9572401.html [accessed 28 December 2020].

9. Casey Rebecca Johnson, 'Mansplaining and Illocutionary Force', *Feminist Philosophy Quarterly* 6, 4 (2020).

10. Stephanie Glen, 'Monty Hall Problem: Solution Explained Simply', Statistics How To, https://www.statisticshowto.com/probability-and-statistics/monty-hall-problem/ [accessed 28 December 2020].

11. Solnit, 'Men Explain Things', p. 4.

12. Robin Lakoff, 'Language and Woman's Place', *Language in Society* 2, 1 (1973): 45–79.

13. Shereen Marisol Meraji and Gene Demby, 'Care to Explain Yourself?' NPR, 11 August 2021, https://www.npr.org/2021/08/10/1026507758/care-to-explain-yourself [accessed 10 February 2022].

14. This is a form of 'hermeneutical injustice' which philosopher Miranda Fricker describes as 'the injustice of having some significant area of one's social experience obscured from collective understanding owing to hermeneutical marginalization' (Fricker, *Epistemic Injustice*, p. 158).

15. Martin Belam, 'Alan Sugar Under Fire Over "Racist" Senegal World Cup Team Tweet', *Guardian*, 20 June 2018, https://www.theguardian.com/uk-news/2018/jun/20/lord-sugar-under-fire-over-racist-senegal-world-cup-team-tweet [accessed 5 November 2022]; Sabrina Barr, 'Alan Sugar Sparks Outrage Over "Sexist" World Cup Tweet', *Independent*, 27 June 2018, https://www.independent.co.uk/life-style/alan-sugar-sexist-tweet-world-cup-outrage-backlash-social-media-a8417526.html [accessed 5 November 2022]; Rianne Houghton, 'Lord Sugar Is Under Fire Yet Again, This Time for a "Sexist" Tweet', *Digital Spy*, 31 July 2018, http://www.digitalspy.com/showbiz/a862872/the-apprentice-lord-alan-sugar-twitter-sexist-tweet [accessed 5 November 2022].

16. Scott Bryan, 'Karren Brady Shut Down a Sexist Comment on "The Apprentice" and It's Great', BuzzFeed, 5 October 2017, https://www.buzzfeed.com/scottybryan/none-of-you-strike-me-as-shy [accessed 3 April 2019].

17. I owe the consideration of this example in this context to the work of Gaile Pohlhaus. See: Gaile Pohlhaus, 'Wrongful Requests and Strategic Refusals to Understand', *Feminist Epistemology and Philosophy of Science* (Springer, 2011), pp. 223–40.

18. Patricia J. Williams, *The Alchemy of Race and Rights* (Harvard University Press, 1991), p. 129.

19. Julie Millican, Christine Schwen and Justin Berrier, 'What Does Brian Kilmeade Have to Say to Get Fired?', Media Matters for America, 15 October 2010, https://www.mediamatters.org/fox-friends/what-does-brian-kilmeade-have-say-get-fired [accessed 5 October 2017].

20. Gay, *Bad Feminist*, p. 293.

21. Arianne Shahvisi, 'Resisting Wrongful Explanations', *Journal of Ethics and Social Philosophy* 19, 2 (2021), 168–91.

22. There is a certain irony in it: disunderstanding often requires that a person who is seen as less knowledgeable performs ignorance in order to force the person who is seen as more knowledgeable to face up to their actual ignorance.

23. Further, due to widespread epistemic prejudices, they are also the most likely to be deemed to have actually misunderstood and require additional instruction from a person who believes himself to have greater expertise.

## Chapter 8: Who Is Cancelling Whom?

1. I don't have space here to get into the politics and ethics of relationships with large age gaps, but a famous man in his fifties sleeping with the teenage daughter of his girlfriend is not a difficult moral problem.

2. See e.g. Koshka Duff, 'Break the Long Lens of the Law! From Police Propaganda to Movement Media', in J. Saunders and C. Fox (eds), *Routledge Handbook of Philosophy and Media Ethics* (Routledge, forthcoming).

3. Eve Ng, 'No Grand Pronouncements Here . . . Reflections on Cancel Culture and Digital Media Participation', *Television & New Media* 21, 6 (2020): 621–7.

4. Moya Bailey and Trudy, 'On Misogynoir: Citation, Erasure, and Plagiarism', *Feminist Media Studies* 18, 4 (2018): 762–8.

5. Meredith D. Clark, 'DRAG THEM: A Brief Etymology of So-called "Cancel Culture"', *Communication and the Public* 5, 3–4 (2020): 88–92.

6. Ryan Lizza, 'Americans Tune In to "Cancel Culture" – and Don't Like What They See', Politico, 22 July 2021, https://www.politico.com/news/2020/07/22/americans-cancel-culture-377412 [accessed 3 August 2021].

7. 'National Tracking Poll 200766', Politico, 17–19 July 2020, p. 12, https://www.politico.com/f/?id=00000173-7326-d36e-abff-7ffe72dc0000 [accessed 22 July 2021].

8. Kate Clanchy, @KateClanchy1, 'Replying to @SharonEckman @goodreads "Flag the reviews? None of these terms are in my book" – it's all made up."', Twitter, 30 July 2021, https://twitter.com/KateClanchy1 /status/1421146790808670208 [accessed 7 February 2022].

9. Nesrine Malik, *We Need New Stories: Challenging the Toxic Myths Behind Our Age of Discontent* (Weidenfeld & Nicolson, 2019), p. 83.

10. 'Thom Yorke Breaks Silence on Israel Controversy', *Rolling Stone*, 2 June 2017, https://www.rollingstone.com/music/music-news/thom-yorke-breaks-silence-on-israel-controversy-126675 [accessed 8 January 2022].

11. Piers Morgan, 'A little note to all my followers . . . Hi everyone. To all my supporters, I just wanted to drop you a note of thanks. (To all my haters . . .', Instagram, 12 March 2021, https://www.instagram.com/p/CMUfgGSncQI/ [accessed 12 February 2022].

12. Tom Breihan, 'Kanye: "I'm Canceled Because I Didn't Cancel Trump"', *Stereogum*, 25 June 2018, https://www.stereogum.com/2003271/kanye-im-canceled-because-i-didnt-cancel-trump/news/ [accessed 23 August 2021].

13. Steve Salaita, 'No Flags, No Slogans', 10 August 2021 [25 August 2013], https://stevesalaita.com [accessed 6 June 2021].

14. Arianne Shahvisi, 'Epistemic Injustice in the Academy: An Analysis of the Saida Grundy Witch-hunt', Academe Blog, 20 May 2015, https://academeblog.org/2015/05/20/epistemic-injustice-in-the-academy-an-analysis-of-the-saida-grundy-witch-hunt [accessed 12 November 2018].

15. Saida Grundy, 'A History of White Violence Tells Us Attacks on Black Academics Are Not Ending (I Know Because It Happened to Me)', *Ethnic and Racial Studies* 40, 11 (2017): 1864–71.

16. Christina M. Xiao, 'The Case Against Mandatory Preferred Gender Pronouns', Harvard Crimson, 16 October 2020, https://www.thecrimson.com/article/2020/10/16/xiao-against-mandatory-preferred-gender-pronouns [accessed 6 May 2022]; Arwa Mahdawi, 'He, She, They . . . Should We Now Clarify Our Preferred Pronouns When We Say Hello?' *Guardian*, 13 September 2019, https://www.theguardian.com/lifeandstyle/2019/sep/13/pronouns-gender-he-she-they-natalie-wynn-contrapoints [accessed 6 May 2022]; Brian D. Earp, 'On Sharing Pronouns', *Philosopher* 109, 1 (2021): 107–15.

17. Ash Sarkar, 'The Slumflower Beef Has Exposed the Limits of Influencer Activism', Novara Media, 20 January 2021, https://novaramedia.com/2021/01/20/the-slumflower-beef-has-exposed-the-limits-of-influencer-activism [accessed 6 May 2022].

18. Natalie Wynn, 'Transcript of "Canceling"', ContraPoints, 2 January 2020, https://www.contrapoints.com/transcripts/canceling [accessed 6 May 2022].

19. Mauro Caselli and Paolo Falco, 'When the Mob Goes Silent: Uncovering the Effects of Racial Harassment Through a Natural Experiment', DEM Working Papers, 1 (2021), Department of Economics and Management, University of Trento, https://ideas.repec.org/p/trn/utwprg/2021-01.html [accessed 14 September 2021].

20. Lanre Bakare, 'Roseanne Barr Blames Racist Tweet on Sleeping Pills', Guardian, 30 May 2018, http://www.theguardian.com/culture/2018/may/30/roseanne-barr-blames-racist-tweet-on-sleeping-pills [accessed 4 August 2021].

21. Sarah Maslin Nir, 'The Bird Watcher, That Incident and His Feelings on the Woman's Fate', New York Times, 27 May 2020, https://www.nytimes.com/2020/05/27/nyregion/amy-cooper-christian-central-park-video.html [accessed 4 August 2021].

22. (((David Shor))), @davidshor, 'Post-MLK-assassination race riots reduced Democratic vote share in surrounding counties by 2%, which was enough to tip the 1968 election to Nixon. Non-violent protests *increase* Dem vote, mainly by encouraging warm elite discourse and media coverage', Twitter, 28 May 2020, https://t.co/S8VZSuaz3G https://t.co/VRUwnRFuVW, Twitter, https://twitter.com/davidshor/status/1265998625836019712 [accessed 23 August 2021].

23. Asher Perlman, @asherperlman, Twitter, 28 January 2022, https://twitter.com/asherperlman/status/1486865575158636548 [accessed 28 January 2022].

24. Josh Jackman, 'Stormzy Has Posted Homophobic Tweets Calling People "Faggots"', PinkNews, 21 November 2017, https://www.pinknews.co.uk/2017/11/21/stormzy-has-posted-homophobic-tweets-calling-people-faggots-and-proper-gay [accessed 29 May 2021].

25. Ben Beaumont-Thomas, 'Stormzy Apologises for Unearthed Homophobic Tweets', Guardian, 22 November 2017, http://www.theguardian.com/music/2017/nov/22/stormzy-apologises-for-unearthed-homophobic-tweets [accessed 29 May 2021].

26. Ikran Dahir, 'There Is an App That Scans All Your Tweets to See How Problematic They Are and I Tried It Out', BuzzFeed, 21 December 2018, https://www.buzzfeed.com/ikrd/vanilla-app-problematic-tweets [accessed 5 September 2021].

27. Alona Ferber, 'Judith Butler on the Culture Wars, JK Rowling and Living in "Anti-intellectual Times"', New Statesman, 22 September 2020, https://www.newstatesman.com/uncategorized/2020/09/judith-butler-culture-wars-jk-rowling-and-living-anti-intellectual-times [accessed 28 January 2022].

28. Roy J. Lewicki, Beth Polin and Robert B. Lount, 'An Exploration of the Structure of Effective Apologies', Negotiation and Conflict Management Research 9, 2 (2016): 177–96.

29. Olúfẹ́mi O. Táíwò, 'Being-in-the-Room Privilege: Elite Capture and Epistemic Deference', Philosopher, Autumn 2020, https://www.thephilosopher1923.org/essay-taiwo [accessed 1 September 2021].

30. Sandra Harding, Whose Science? Whose Knowledge? Thinking from Women's Lives (Cornell University Press, 1991), p. 127.

31. Claudia Card, The Unnatural Lottery: Character and Moral Luck (Temple University Press, 2010), p. 53.

32. C. Thi Nguyen, 'Echo Chambers and Epistemic Bubbles', Episteme 17, 2 (2020): 141–61.

33. Audre Lorde, 'The Uses of Anger', Women's Studies Quarterly 25, 1/2 (1997): 278–85.

34. Meredith D. Clark, 'DRAG THEM'.

35. Card, Unnatural Lottery, p. 41.

36. Sarah Lamble, 'Practicing Everyday Abolition', Abolitionist Futures, 19 August 2020 [also in K. Duff (ed.), Abolishing the Police (Dog Section Press, 2021)], https://abolitionistfutures.com/latest-news/practising-everyday-abolition [accessed 28 January 2022].

37. Opposition to carceral logics underwrite the prison abolition movement and the movement against 'carceral feminism', neither of which I have space to get into here. See, e.g., Ruth Wilson Gilmore, Golden Gulag (University of California Press, 2007); Elizabeth Bernstein, 'The Sexual Politics of the "New Abolitionism"', differences 18, 3 (2007): 128–51; Srinivasan, Right to Sex.

38. Melanie Brazzell, 'Theorizing Transformative Justice', in K. Duff (ed.), Abolishing the Police.

39. Manne, Down Girl, p. 66.

40. Waleed Aly and Robert Mark Simpson, 'Political Correctness Gone Viral', in C. Fox and J. Saunders (eds), *Media Ethics, Free Speech, and the Requirements of Democracy* (Routledge, 2018).
41. Jia Tolentino, *Trick Mirror: Reflections on Self-Delusion* (Fourth Estate, 2020).
42. Tyler Hersko, 'The Average American Is Streaming 8 Hours of Content Daily', IndieWire, 14 April 2020, https://www.indiewire.com/2020/04/average-american-streaming-eight-hours-daily-1202225085 [accessed 10 June 2021].
43. Michael Flood, 'Pornography Has Deeply Troubling Effects on Young People, But There Are Ways We Can Minimise the Harm', The Conversation, 5 January 2020, http://theconversation.com/pornography-has-deeply-troubling-effects-on-young-people-but-there-are-ways-we-can-minimise-the-harm-127319 [accessed 10 June 2021].
44. Hannah Ellis-Petersen, 'Gender Bias in the Film Industry: 75% of Blockbuster Crews Are Male', *Guardian*, 22 July 2014, http://www.theguardian.com/film/2014/jul/22/gender-bias-film-industry-75-percent-male [accessed 23 August 2021].
45. '2019 Statistics', Women and Hollywood, https://womenandhollywood.com/resources/statistics/2019-statistics [accessed 23 August 2021].
46. Sonia Elks, 'Women Are Four Times More Likely To Be Shown Undressed in Films Than Men', World Economic Forum, 11 October 2019, https://www.weforum.org/agenda/2019/10/harmful-female-gender-stereotypes-film-industry [accessed 23 August 2021].
47. Huimin Xu, Zhang Zhang, Lingfei Wu and Cheng-Jun Wang, 'The Cinderella Complex: Word Embeddings Reveal Gender Stereotypes in Movies and Books', *PLOS ONE* 14, 11 (2019): e0225385.
48. Which isn't to say that this is always unproblematic. See, e.g., Srinivasan, *Right to Sex*, Chapter 3.
49. Celeste Ng, @pronounced_ing, 'If someone's an asshole to you, it's your right to decide not to work w/them. Right? If someone's an asshole to your friend/mom/kid/neighbor, etc., it's still your right to decide not to work w/ them. Right? So . . .', Twitter, 12 February 2021, https://twitter.com/pronounced_ing/status/1360300089009459200 [accessed 26 August 2021].

# Chapter 9: Are We Responsible for Structural Injustice?

1. Peter Muiruri, 'Drought Puts 2.1 Million Kenyans at Risk of Starvation', *Guardian*, 15 September 2021, https://www.theguardian.com/global-development/2021/sep/15/drought-puts-21-million-kenyans-at-risk-of-starvation [accessed 18 February 2022].

2. Robert H. Beach et al., 'Combining the Effects of Increased Atmospheric Carbon Dioxide on Protein, Iron, and Zinc Availability and Projected Climate Change on Global Diets: A Modelling Study', *Lancet Planetary Health* 3, 7 (2019): e307–17.

3. Louise Tickle, 'Why Does So Much of the NHS's Surgical Equipment Start Life in the Sweatshops of Pakistan?', *Independent*, 19 January 2015, http://www.independent.co.uk/life-style/health-and-families/features/why-does-so-much-of-the-nhss-surgical-equipment-start-life-in-the-sweatshops-of-pakistan-9988885.html [accessed 30 January 2020].

4. James Randerson, 'Surgeon Warns NHS Over Sweatshop Instruments', *Guardian*, 28 July 2006, http://www.theguardian.com/society/2006/jul/28/health.uknews [accessed 30 July 2021].

5. I've worked with Mahmood and anthropologist Mei Trueba on the specific ethical challenges raised by producing medical equipment under these conditions: Mei L. Trueba, Mahmood F. Bhutta and Arianne Shahvisi, 'Instruments of Health and Harm: How the Procurement of Healthcare Goods Contributes to Global Health Inequality', *Journal of Medical Ethics* 47 (2021): 423–9.

6. Tansy Hoskins, 'Cotton Production Linked to Images of the Dried Up Aral Sea Basin', *Guardian*, 1 October 2014, http://www.theguardian.com/sustainable-business/sustainable-fashion-blog/2014/oct/01/cotton-production-linked-to-images-of-the-dried-up-aral-sea-basin [accessed 30 July 2021].

7. David Wallace-Wells, 'Time to Panic', *New York Times*, 16 February 2019, https://www.nytimes.com/2019/02/16/opinion/sunday/fear-panic-climate-change-warming.html [accessed 24 January 2022].

8. Mark Kaufman, 'The Devious Fossil Fuel Propaganda We All Use', Mashable, 2021, https://mashable.com/feature/carbon-footprint-pr-campaign-sham [accessed 15 April 2021].

9. Michelle Roberts, 'Asthma Carbon Footprint "as Big as Eating Meat"',

BBC News, 30 October 2019, https://www.bbc.com/news/health-50215011 [accessed 15 April 2021].

10. Furthermore, we must not forget that our complicity runs deep. Every time we buy products and services through Amazon, we bolster the wealth of a company that dodges tax despite relying on tax-funded infrastructure (such as the roads that are used to deliver their goods), and where those who work for it complain that they are compelled to work long hours for inadequate pay. Our money ends up in the pockets of Jeff Bezos, who, once in June 2020 during the Covid-19 pandemic made $10 billion in a single day, which is more than the GDP of Chad, Rwanda, Congo or Haiti. That's money that is piling up outside of any system of democratic accountability. What can we do? We can boycott the Amazon store, but that's less of an option for those on strict budgets. And besides, the Amazon shop is peanuts compared with the fact that Amazon owns an alarming amount of the infrastructure of the internet, including services on which Apple, Facebook and Netflix are reliant. Boycotting Amazon pretty much means shunning the internet. That's an enormous individual sacrifice that will make no difference to the primacy of Amazon and its morally troubling practices.

11. Sandra Laville, 'Dumped Fishing Gear Is Biggest Plastic Polluter in Ocean, Finds Report', *Guardian*, 6 November 2019, https://www.theguardian.com/environment/2019/nov/06/dumped-fishing-gear-is-biggest-plastic-polluter-in-ocean-finds-report [accessed 27 January 2022].

12. Arwa Mahdawi, 'Don't Blame Men for the Climate Crisis – We Should Point the Finger at Corporations', *Guardian*, 27 July 2021, http://www.theguardian.com/commentisfree/2021/jul/27/dont-blame-men-for-the-climate-crisis-we-should-point-the-finger-at-corporations [accessed 30 July 2021].

13. Richard Rorty, 'Religion as Conversation-stopper', *Common Knowledge* 3, 1 (1994).

14. I don't have space here to explore the many other compelling arguments which relate to the rights of animals not to be penned into cramped, filthy enclosures, pumped with growth hormones, torn from their kin, aggressively milked and then eventually slaughtered with scarce regard for their stress or pain.

Another important issue is methane production. Cattle chew on high-fibre vegetation which is broken down in their digestive systems through a process of bacteria-aided fermentation which produces methane, a gas that is then released as belches or flatulence. Once released, it floats up into the atmosphere (since it is less dense than air) and its unique chemical shape means that it captures more heat than carbon dioxide, contributing to the greenhouse effect. It is eighty times more damaging than carbon dioxide in the short term, and twenty-eight times more damaging in the long term.

15. Hannah Ritchie, 'How Much of the World's Land Would We Need in Order to Feed the Global Population with the Average Diet of a Given Country?', Our World in Data, 3 October 2017, https://ourworldin-data.org/agricultural-land-by-global-diets [accessed 13 April 2021].

16. World Wide Fund for Nature, 'Soy', February 2020, https://wwf.panda.org/discover/our_focus/food_practice/sustainable_production/soy/ [accessed 13 April 2021].

17. Immanuel Kant believed in a hierarchy of human groups and supported colonialism and slavery, so his attempts to be good had their imaginative limits. Pauline Kleingeld, 'On Dealing With Kant's Sexism and Racism', *SGIR Review* 2, 2 (2019).

18. A helpful map of these three categories can be found here: 'Share of Global Habitable Land Needed for Agriculture if Everyone Had the Diet of . . .', Our World in Data, https://ourworldindata.org/grapher/share-of-global-habitable-land-needed-for-agriculture-if-everyone-had-the-diet-of [accessed 24 January 2022].

19. Karen McVeigh, 'Over 30 Million People "One Step Away From Starvation", UN Warns', *Guardian*, 24 March 2021, http://www.theguardian.com/global-development/2021/mar/24/over-30-million-people-one-step-away-from-starvation-un-warns [accessed 1 August 2021].

20. 'World Consumption of Meat', TheWorldCounts, https://www.theworldcounts.com/challenges/consumption/foods-and-beverages/world-consumption-of-meat/story [accessed 15 September 2021].

21. 'The EAT-Lancet Commission on Food, Planet, Health', EAT, https://eatforum.org/eat-lancet-commission/ [accessed 1 August 2021].

22. Ruth Maclean, 'Chocolate Industry Drives Rainforest Disaster in Ivory Coast', *Guardian*, 13 September 2017, http://www.theguardian.com/environment/2017/sep/13/chocolate-industry-drives-rainforest-disaster-in-ivory-coast [accessed 15 April 2021].

23. Jason Hickel, 'Quantifying National Responsibility for Climate Breakdown: An Equality-Based Attribution Approach for Carbon

Dioxide Emissions in Excess of the Planetary Boundary', *Lancet Planetary Health* 4, 9 (2020): e399–404.

24. Fiona Harvey, 'Enormous Emissions Gap Between Top 1% and Poorest, Study Highlights', *Guardian*, 1 November 2022, https://www.theguardian.com/environment/2022/nov/01/polluting-elite-enormous-carbon-dioxide-emissions-gap-between-poorest-autonomy-study [accessed 8 November 2022].

25. Derek Parfit, *Reasons and Persons* (Oxford University Press, 1984), p. 79.

26. This is a moral version of the famous Sorites (Greek for 'heap') paradox, in which you remove successive grains of sand from a heap. Removing a single grain of sand still leaves you with a heap of sand. You wouldn't even notice the difference. But if you keep going, you'll eventually have a few specks of sand and then a single grain, and that is definitely not a heap. So clearly removing a single grain of sand does make a difference!

27. Parfit, *Reasons and Persons*, pp. 80–1.

28. Elizabeth Cripps, *Climate Change and the Moral Agent: Individual Duties in an Interdependent World* (Oxford University Press, 2013).

29. 'Housing First in Finland', Y-Säätiö, https://ysaatio.fi/en/housing-first-finland [accessed 11 August 2021].

30. Robin Zheng, 'What Is My Role in Changing the System? A New Model of Responsibility for Structural Injustice', *Ethical Theory and Moral Practice* 21, 4 (2018): 869–85; Robin Zheng, 'Attributability, Accountability, and Implicit Bias', in J. Saul and M. Brownstein (eds), *Implicit Bias and Philosophy, Volume 2: Moral Responsibility, Structural Injustice, and Ethics* (Oxford University Press, 2016), https://oxford.universitypressscholarship.com/10.1093/acprof:oso/9780198766179.001.0001/acprof-9780198766179-chapter-4 [accessed 1 August 2021].

31. James Randerson, 'Surgeon Warns NHS'.

32. 'Timeline: Smoking and Disease', BBC News, 30 June 2007, http://news.bbc.co.uk/1/hi/health/4377928.stm [accessed 15 April 2021].

33. Office for National Statistics, 'Adult Smoking Habits in the UK: 2019, 2020', https://www.ons.gov.uk/peoplepopulationandcommunity/healthandsocialcare/healthandlifeexpectancies/bulletins/adultsmokinghabitsingreatbritain/2019 [accessed 15 April 2021].

34. David Hammond, 'Health Warning Messages on Tobacco Products: A Review', *Tobacco Control* 20, 5 (2011): 327–37.

35. Edward L. Bernays, *Propaganda* (Horace Liveright, 1928).

36. Richard Gunderman, 'The Manipulation of the American Mind:

Edward Bernays and the Birth of Public Relations', The Conversation, 9 July 2015, http://theconversation.com/the-manipulation-of-the-american-mind-edward-bernays-and-the-birth-of-public-relations-44393 [accessed 25 February 2022].

37. A. M. O'Keefe and R. W. Pollay, 'Deadly Targeting of Women in Promoting Cigarettes', *Journal of the American Medical Women's Association (1972)* 51, 1–2 (1996): 67–9.

38. Like Kant, Mill's ideas about morality are marred by his views on race. Mill was a defender of colonialism, writing in 1859 that 'Despotism is a legitimate mode of government in dealing with barbarians, provided the end be their improvement.' John Stuart Mill, *J. S. Mill: 'On Liberty' and Other Writings* (Cambridge University Press, 1989), p. 13.

39. John Stuart Mill, 'Utilitarianism (1863)', *Utilitarianism, Liberty, Representative Government*, 1859: 7–9.

40. Andrew Jameton, *Nursing Practice: The Ethical Issues* (Prentice-Hall, 1984).

41. Jonathan Shay, *Odysseus in America: Combat Trauma and the Trials of Homecoming* (Simon & Schuster, 2003).

42. See, e.g., Robinson, *Black Marxism*, p. 3.

43. Gilmore, *Golden Gulag*, p. 28.

44. Theodor Adorno, *Minima Moralia: Reflections from Damaged Life* (Verso, 2005).

# Index

References to notes are indicated by n.